EDMONTON ON LOCATION

EDMONTON ON LOCATION
River City Chronicles

EDITED BY HEATHER ZWICKER

Library and Archives Canada Cataloguing in Publication
Edmonton on location : River City chronicles / edited
by Heather Zwicker.

Includes bibliographical references.
ISBN 1-897126-02-6

1. Canadian literature (English)—Alberta—Edmonton.
2. Canadian literature (English)—21st century.
3. Edmonton (Alta.)—
Literary collections. I. Zwicker, Heather Sharon

PS8295.7.E46E46 2005   C810.8'032712334   C2005-903529-3

Editors for the Press: Douglas Barbour and Michael Penny
Cover and interior design: Ruth Linka
Cover image: Dennis Pozniak, www.seeshare.com
Interior photos: Credit listed with each photo.

 Canada Council   Conseil des Arts   Canadian   Patrimoine   edmonton
for the Arts   du Canada   Heritage   canadien   arts
                                                                                     council

NeWest Press acknowledges the support of the Canada Council for the Arts and the
Alberta Foundation for the Arts for our publishing program. We also acknowledge the
financial support of the Government of Canada through the Book Publishing Industry
Development Program (BPIDP) for our publishing activities.

Every effort has been made to obtain permission for quoted material and photographs. If there is
an omission or error, the editor and publisher would be grateful to be so informed.

NeWest Press
201-8540-109 Street
Edmonton, Alberta T6G 1E6
t: (780) 432-9427 / f: (780) 433-3179
www.newestpress.com

NeWest Press is committed to protecting the environment and to the responsible use of
natural resources. This book is printed on 100% post-consumer recycled and ancient-forest-
friendly paper. For more information please visit www.oldgrowthfree.com.

1   2   3   4   5   08   07   06   05

PRINTED AND BOUND IN CANADA

For Brian and Carol Zwicker, inveterate travellers, westerners.

TABLE OF CONTENTS

FOREWORD

MICHAEL PHAIR

I have always thought a "foreword" to a book was just code for fore-play. So I do see this as a chance for me to titillate and excite you before the BIG event—reading *Edmonton on Location: River City Chronicles*. Sure enough, Lynne Van Luven's memoir "City of My Groin" verifies my suspicion: she writes how "Edmonton in the '80s always re-inhabits my memory as a city of sex and seduction." And here I have always assumed that Ms. Van Luven was an erudite academic who revelled in literary criticism in a very staid and proper Edmonton, not at all fascinated with my groin (or anyone else's)!

And that's only the beginning, as Heather Zwicker has gathered a fascinating array of writers who chronicle personal memoirs, stories, or glimpses into the life and history of this city. *Chronicles* uncovers little-known facts as well as personal memories of this multi-layered city called Edmonton. For example, although I have been told about the former Club 70, the first bar for "our kind" in Edmonton, Brenda Mann's "Places of Refuge" is a personal memoir that poignantly recalls how this refuge, the Club 70 bar, was for her both a place of safety that she savoured yet also a painful reminder of the necessity of living two lives in Edmonton thirty years ago.

Besides sex, these chronicles have those other ingredients that all popular and successful writing must have: namely, power and money. A mystery man from New York, awash in American dollars in late 1950s River City, is the historical figure in Ruth DyckFehderau's "The Magnificent 'Rogue' of the Miracle Mile." Read how L. Edgar Detwiler, a smooth-talking New York tycoon, promised to redevelop Edmonton's civic centre into a "Miracle Mile" at NO COST TO THE CITY! The three-hour debate in front of the city council of the day was "dominated by accusations of lies and misrepresentations." The Miracle Mile scheme finally went to a public referendum, where it was narrowly defeated. To a local politician like myself, this tale sounds almost too familiar: "Do I have a deal for you—and it will cost you nothing!"

Sex, money, and power: the only item left to get Edmonton into the big leagues is blood and guts. And Ms. Zwicker does not disappoint. As the editor, she has included Scott Davies' story with a dark side. It is a tale complete with decapitation—decapitation by a rotor of a helicopter in 1980, right here in a River City park!

The many voices in *Edmonton on Location* bring to life events and personalities that reflect our city. Some are familiar; many are new. In fact, as I read the chronicles I found myself thinking about my own River City stories: 1981 and a front-page picture in the *Edmonton Sun* of the Pisces II raft with a big pink triangular mast that I helped paint, sailing down the North Saskatchewan River in the Klondike Raft Races—now, that's my story for a future book.

Sex, money, power, blood and guts—*Edmonton on Location: River City Chronicles* is an exciting read. Don't settle for the mere titillation of the foreword—move on and fulfill your desires! Read Heather Zwicker's chronicle.

My Mother's House

MY EDMONTON HAUNTS,
OR A HAUNTOLOGY OF BELONGING
DIANNE CHISHOLM

Deadmonton

I grew up in Edmonton hating it. As far back as I can remember, Edmonton was "Deadmonton," where nothing of vital importance ever happened. Quintessence of *nowhere*, Edmonton was not north enough to be North, not rustic enough to be Country, not large and diverse enough to be Cosmopolitan, yet sufficiently provincial to despair of its own provincialism, or so felt my alienated '60s generation. I yearned for where it was happening: Vancouver, Toronto, New York. Even Calgary, a crude cowtown that territorial tradition taught us to disdain, was *somewhere* with its rowdy and swaggering Stampede.

My parents, like all parents in our brand-new suburb of Fulton Place, had roots *elsewhere*. Dad hailed from small-town Alberta, where Grandpa managed a lumberyard and coached the local hockey team, and Grandma gardened, pickled, and baked prize-winning pies. His was a heritage of homesteading. Hockey pucks made of horse shit, lessons in a one-room school, daily chores like hauling coal and water, wrestling your chum on the butcher's sawdust floor for a spiced sausage: now that was the stuff of real life! Mom descended from Manitoba farmers, a rogues' gallery of Orangemen and Scots whose fierce, titanic pride extended to their Percheron stallions, teams of Clydes, and turkey gobblers. Mom was born in Edmonton, where Grandad, lured by urban prosperity, became a travelling salesman for Ashdown's Hardware. But her prairie yarns left me spellbound. She'd play Nana's favourite cowboy ballads on the piano with heart enough to spur this impressionable, suburban soul into "the wild blue yonder"—wherever that was. But I doubted Mom's attachment to Edmonton, as if its boundaries would delimit my horizons. Didn't her mother pine for the open prairie? The story goes that Nana felt reined-in by the city, whereas on the range she had galloped bareback.

Nana died before I got to know her, but the image of her riding with abandon was the image I gave my own restlessness.

I learned that I was adopted. With a girl's imagination, I premised my self-consciousness on myths of displaced origin. I confused the nowhereness that Edmonton emanated with my missing genealogy. Retrieved from Beulah Home (a respite for unwed mothers) within days of my birth, I was too young to interpret this first dispossession. Yet, my growing up on the city's edge sowed a fantasy trajectory of vagabondage. Wasn't I a feral child, half-human half-wolf, raised by wild horses that left me for my kind on the city's outskirts? Or the foundling of secret agents who'd gone to the ends of the earth, where their maneuvers would not be traced? Drawn to the river's lure of danger and adventure, I spent many renegade afternoons exploring spruce-choked banks and willow-tangled ravines. Between Capilano's last walk-ups and the Imperial Oil refineries, I revelled in narratives of frontier and escape. I invented a cold-war comic strip about spies who, like Ali Baba's thieves, made their headquarters in sandstone caves. Once, I scouted tramps camping in the bush. Their vagrancy, if not their homelessness, excited a runaway craving some might call wanderlust, or a wild wish for notoriety to veil my obscurity.

Deadmonton. What failure of imagination blessed Edmonton with this epithet? Where were city storytellers when I was growing up? Why hadn't I heard of "River City," or "Redmonton?" Why did tales abound of elsewhere but not of historic Old Strathcona and story-rich Mill Creek, where Mom grew up?

The Great Depression

Nana died when I was three. Mom would take my little sister and me to visit Grandad in the old Mill Creek neighbourhood. He and Nana had lived there since the '20s, in several houses over the years. But Mom never showed us her girlhood haunts. Not until The Citadel Theater staged *The Aberhardt Summer* in 2000 did she recall to me girlhood memories of the events of 1935 that shook the community with their extreme politics, religion, and psychological drama, involving a mystery-hanging in a barn at the end of her alley. *That* is history. Did she and her generation think that Edmonton-past was unconnected to our future, to progress? Had the city changed so much that it was no longer hers to relay? After Grandad died when I was nine, we never visited the neighbourhood again.

As a girl, I was moved by Mom's stories of finding Nana crying inexplicably at home in the middle of the afternoon. It was the dirty thirties and the Great Depression. Grandad managed to keep his job, so the Steeles were relatively economically secure. While he was on the road, Nana was left with three kids to care for. She bravely gave lunch to down-and-out strangers who'd beg at her door. I could imagine her fear at hosting such desperate men. But the pervasive feeling was Mom's perplexed sadness in relating Nana's anxious solitariness, a solitariness I could only think came with housewifely confinement.

Solitaire was the game Mom resorted to when she couldn't sleep at night. I listened to the fraught slapping of cards on the kitchen table, where she'd play hour after woeful hour. For awhile I caught her insomnia, alarmed by her lostness in her own house. She performed household chores with a vengeance, vacuuming, washing, and ironing with ferocious fastidiousness. And wore herself out without exercising her creative energies. This was the great era of stay-at-home moms. We Chisholms, we thought, were fortunate to occupy an affordably new "Golden home" in Edmonton's golden age of suburbanization. Yet fortune depressed the collective memory and outgoingness of housebound women—as was the case for my mother. Staying-at-home in the suburbs, I sensed, made Mom remote, even to herself.

Except when she played the piano, Mom occupied the house with a heaviness. A great malaise seemed to pass through her from Nana to me. I was heir to a dis-ease that transferred over generations at a growing distance from home. If home was with the folk and their tales of belonging, then I grew up at its furthest remove. How else can I explain the "nostalgia" I felt for country where I'd never lived, or the melancholy that overcame me as I listened to Mom play those cowboy tunes less and less often? There, in the suburbs, something was dying without our attending. Something I'd chase for the next three decades.

Crypt(ic)s on the Mount

My sister and I helped Mom salvage the roots of her belonging on Mount Pleasant Cemetery. Nana and Grandad, "Vera (Cochrane) Steele" and "David Lyle Steele," lay buried at the foot of a grand, black marble headstone under heavy conifers partway up the slope. We came to water "the mums." Carol would wander off to linger over infants' graves and ponder the freak paradox of mortal birth. I wondered at the change that overcame Mom, her sternness softened by a sadness that she deflected onto caring for the grave. "Mount Pleasant" was the most intensely affecting landscape of my childhood.

There I felt the ghosts—not of my grandparents, whose memories I could put faces to, but of some strange mass, a strangeness greater than my familiar dead. Less a presence than a pressure, the feeling arose as I read the engravings of myriad names. As I stumbled up the small summit that overlooks the city, it accrued gravity and mystery. Anonymous hosts of ghosts whose stories were clamouring for the telling.

"Deadmonton:" a city haunted by its un-telling.

City Sorties

A short story I wrote in junior high began with the epigram: "A stranger gone away and alone knows better the changes than those left back home." As if yearning for a departure of return, I made it my refrain. Mom offered to type the story without questioning the sentiment. She participated vicariously in my pursuit of elsewhere and she accepted my Deadmonton disaffection with ironic detachment.

I *did* escape the suburbs. First to the mountains between university terms. Then I took my studies abroad, travelling and living in foreign world-cities: Johannesburg, Athens, Jerusalem, Oxford, Rome, and Montréal. I made pilgrimages to bohemian New York. I revelled in Sydney's thriving gay scene. I cycled across the Rockies and down the coast to Mexico, stretching Highway 16 out of town to the Baja. I drove a 4 x 4 to and around Alaska, stretching the road up to where it ends in rugged Wrangall-St. Elias. Off-road, I trekked trackless valleys and moraines. I got far away, but despite my aspirations, I always came back. Beat boho Brion Gyson left Edmonton at sixteen *forever*. Unlike Gyson,

I returned, again and again, even in time for the EAG's retrospective of his visionary art. Why couldn't I see my way out with finality?

After I re-returned to take a post at the University of Alberta, my colleague Janice Williamson wryly suggested that my nomadic self-image was self-deceiving. Own your roots, she challenged. Still taunted by nowhere, I sought to establish my career elsewhere. Before I moved anywhere, Janice localized me in caricature in her picaresque adventures of *Alberta Borges*.

I tried living elsewhere and nowhere simultaneously, commuting between Montréal and Edmonton. The world split into two. I resided with a Montréal novelist, an Anglo-outsider who adopted the Plateau as her artistic reserve. My distance from myself lent a mirror to her projections of "the West," reflecting a sovereignty more hick than historic. "Edmonton," we'd joke, was "the middle of nowhere," from where I came and went as if into and out of oblivion. I was a (city-) lover's fiction, who entered Montréal's scene of writing as a novel entity, or at least as material for another caricature.

Yet how could I say "My Edmonton" with the symbolic meaning that "My Montréal" implies? Edmonton was too unworldly and insufficiently unique to express the particular with global irony. To apply "my" to "Edmonton" would but personalize the obscure. Still, it shocked me to hear my Montréalaise say so definitively that she had no time for Edmonton "since there was nothing there." Our affair was to be a one-way street, with Montréal as destiny and Edmonton the departed.

I retreated.

I started to think of Edmonton as base camp; if not binding, then a base from which to launch out. Jackie Dumas agrees. Writer, world traveller, bookstore owner, community builder, and Whyte Avenue personality, Jackie regards Edmonton as a place people love to leave—repeatedly. She sees an outward-bound city, whose restless and rootless self-image propels serial adventure.

"Helen's Ghosts"

So what makes a space a place? Place is alive with ghosts. It is an architecture capable of housing deceased loves, for and beyond living memory. All cities are necropoli. First cities were both palaces and tombs. They were made to last—like Knossos, whose walls survived the tsunami that destroyed Atlantis. Or like Athens, whose still-standing pillars bear witness to democracy's ancient trajectory. Walking with friend Athena around Greece, I felt the ground shift underfoot with the strata of world history: an earth-quaking self-awakening to the geopolitical. Hellas, a place name, derived from Helen, my mother's name.

Mom died in the Royal Alexandra Hospital where she was born. My father, sister, and I were with her when she died. During our seven-day vigil in Intensive Care, there was no elsewhere. Place at her side was absolute, overwhelmingly here and now. She left us in mid-November. The city was poised for winter, but a bright, crisp fall persisted. Next day it rained. The day after it snowed. Her passing located me.

In the wake of Mom's death, a crypt of memory broke open. Out came this *other* city. This was not the suburb where I grew up and where she grew estranged from her self. This was the city that she took in her stride and travelled with confidence, in love, in community, on skates, theatre-going, square-dancing, bridge-playing, working downtown, and flushed with the prospects of belonging. The city became spirited with the presence of her absence.

Uncanny city! Unfamiliarly familiar. Spectral faces of Mom's past regard me from shop windows and building façades. No one memory possesses me, but many memories jump out at once, animating city sites. At first, they are near and recent. Then time cracks into a constellation of localities from all stages of maternal history. Her spectre appears everywhere, from when she was a little girl, a middle-aged woman, a young woman, an older woman, and an old woman. The city bursts out of its time capsule and re-presents itself at multiple moments of a lifetime. My mother, too, is *out there,* all over the city, not stifling in a hospital room or incarcerated in a failing, arthritic body. This phantom mother is superbly mobile: speed skating on Scona rink, where she pursues my hockey-star father, or shifting gears into acute reverse as she backs out of her snowed-up parking stall at the General Hospital. Here at the General, she transcribes complex case histories at 100 WPM. Here again, she waltzes across the ballroom of her wedding party at the Hotel Macdonald. And here she cruises The Bay's bargain basement with a melting malted in her hand. As a girl, I could barely keep apace of her. Now, she's pacing my memory. Here appears the high-trotting sulky she so loved to watch and the Exhibition Grounds where I saw my first horse race.

Edmonton surges with haunts of her memory. They are cosmic haunts: for here she is in the hoot and stare of the hawk owl on Riverside Golf Course, the night after she died. (She took the owl as her totem; the hawk owl is one of many owl species that hunt the river valley.) Here she spirits meteorites (the Leonids) that shower over city environs the night after. We witness the spectacle from our perch in Elk Island Park, where she picnicked on Sunday outings. She flies in space above the city, having requested that donations in her memory be sent to STARS—the air ambulance that brings emergency patients from remote Alberta to the Royal Alex and University Hospitals. If her memory is "in the air," so are my senses alert to it. I will be working, concentrating, a million miles away, when a slight tapping of wind on window focuses my ears and eyes on the city outside. Do I hear her whisper, "Di"? I look around from where I am and here she is connecting my research to the world at hand.

They are haunts of collective memory. Here's Mom dancing in the aura of her own memorial. Strange, she didn't want a memorial for fear that few would remember her well enough to come. Isolated by illnesses that invalided her social energies, she despaired of keeping, let alone making, friends. We hold one anyway, expecting a loyal few. Hundreds arrive, and from so many eras they rattle my understanding of my age. The Old Timers Cabin fills with spirits past, present, and becoming. My friends and colleagues mingle with her pals from primary school. Old man Fraser, friend of Dad's father and father of our current university president, is here. A city genealogy weaves knots.

Wake becomes party, an Edmonton happening. Four generations of extended family arrive, from babies to octogenarians, from as far away as New York City and the bush near Fort St. John. Queer as folk: we are a host of disparate communities (Lions' Club, Ottewell Curling

Club, several long-standing bridge clubs, Red Barn Dance Club, Walterdale Theatre society, Edmonton All Girl Drum and Bugle Band, and Booby Orr intramural women's hockey team) that meet, mix, laugh and cry, feast and reminisce together. From an assemblage of old photos, Ted Bishop spots a commercial snapshot of my mother in full stride, arm in arm with girlfriend Max. It's Jasper Avenue in the late '40s. To Ted, another third-generation Edmontonian and metropolitan modernist, she looks so chic and cosmopolitan as to be misplaced on Fifth Avenue. Here's the city mother/mother city I want to know. Not elsewhere but earlier! Downtown before the exodus to suburbs and super malls.

Here is a city primed for excavation.

Haunted Houses

That first Christmas without Mom found me searching for digs that housed her memory *before* I could remember her. Two mother houses were still standing in Mill Creek: her childhood home on 88th Avenue just west of 99th Street, and a house on 84th Avenue just east of 99th Street, where she lived as a young woman, working downtown and waiting for news of Dad overseas in the war. It was at this latter house that I found myself suspended in the Now-time of history that New Year's Eve.

Hovering out front, I raise a query or two from the present owner-occupant before she welcomes me in. Tricia Smith is more than equal to the marvel of Mom's haunts, for she houses local spirits of her own. "Feel free to look around," she says, as she proceeds to make New Year's dinner for a family party of four generations. I do, overcome with the sense of being "inside" what has so long been exterior: namely, Mom's memory of home. "Here"—actually her mother's home—is uncannily close to where Mom had been sheltered, nurtured, and cultured en route to setting out into the world. The living room has been little altered since Nana's day. Here is a piano, and on all the walls, paintings of mountains and horses. Local mountains and local horses. My mother's mother's house is presenced by a kindred soul.

Tricia Smith grew up on a homestead near Grand Cache. She first earned her living by outfitting and guiding pack trains through the Rockies' front ranges. She acquired a historical curiosity from books she found in abandoned trappers' cabins and warden outposts— battered leather-bound volumes of early explorers and pioneers of the Canadian west. She renovated the back of the house for a studio that is lined floor to ceiling with learned tomes. Tricia Smith is, of all things, a classical archeologist.

With each passage through this house, I am moved—we are mutually moved—by a discovery of primary correspondences. I know these mountains in the paintings from my days of roughing it at Black Cat Ranch near Brûle, where I roomed and boarded while teaching in Hinton. As we share stories of the backcountry, I feel as if I am coming from *somewhere*. A strange genealogy winds its way along the hallways. Upstairs, she cautions, her severely disabled son lies in bed in one of the bedrooms—the room where, as a young man, Uncle Bruce spent months convalescing after a botched surgery that left him paralyzed and never fully to recover. A prime reason for Tricia Smith's return to Edmonton, after living elsewhere across North America, is the unusually strong caregiving community she has been able to raise here.

The phone rings. It's her youngest daughter. When Tricia tells her about me, her daughter tells of having attended a party of mostly university students the night before where my name came up. Here in my mother's mother's house, I'm receiving relays of unfathomable connection. I've an ear like that of Stephen Daedalus when he hears his mother in the Irish sea. Omphalos sounding. Calling him in natal waves and rifts to a nativity he never reckoned on, after wild goose escapades in Europe. My place begins making sense to me. City of maternal *pre*-history. Living on. Not Deadmonton, but Delphi.

My Edmonton

My homecoming has been multi-staged. Staggered. Just when Edmonton was resurrecting itself, a position at the Université de Montréal opened in my field with precisely my qualifications. I applied and got it. An administrative technicality forced my hiring to be deferred a year. How uncannily timely. The delay in going there afforded more rediscovery here. When Montréal was finally ready, I declined the move.

Sometime last year, the compulsion to live elsewhere died.

I now live with my partner in "Westmount," a neighbourhood linked to Montréal in name only. Walking here amidst the multi-storied (and much-ghosted) Victorian houses, I'm reminded of Mill Creek, though we're a half-block from 124th Street—downtown. Edmonton's Westmount is the only residential area in the city to retain its century-old architecture with care. Our house was built in 1913, the same year as the High Level Bridge. The High Level, one of the country's most elevated and enduring bridges, and the city's most prominent industrial icon, spans times that beg telling. Another "haunted house." I could begin that history with stories Mom would tell of her hair-raising trolley rides atop the platform of rails, rides that became truly terrifying in high winds. I'd pursue the living memories of bridge riders, walkers, builders, climbers, and perhaps jumpers; but that's another story. I'm amazed to be so absorbed by the "realm" of Edmonton, so at home in my adopted native city.

Not settled down. Not rooted, rested, resigned. But immersed in the becoming of belonging.

WHAT IS A RIVER FOR?

MYRNA KOSTASH

"The Saskatchewan, they say, drains the Rocky Mountains into the Atlantic Ocean." So begins Marjorie Wilkins Campbell's 1950 epic *The Saskatchewan,* about the river I look at from my living room window. It rises on the eastern slope of the Rockies—dribbling out of the Saskatchewan glacier in the Columbia Icefield—then, shooting out of clefts in the scree of Mount Saskatchewan, it sucks in the waters of tributary rivers for some three hundred kilometres until, swift and broad and still cutting its channel in cretaceous bedrock, it finally emerges, cradled in dramatically perpendicular banks (as here, in Edmonton), onto the great plains. It rolls another nineteen hundred kilometres, having been joined by the South Saskatchewan, to the great Manitoba lakes from which it drains, at last, northward into the Atlantic salt of Hudson Bay.

I have spent most of my life a stone's throw from the north branch of this majestic river. I have never given it much more thought than idly to note its seasonal changes—"Oh, look, the ice is breaking"— and to curse the havoc its twists and turns make of the grid system of Edmonton's streets.

I have been aware, however, of the *hype* about my river. "River City," we Edmontonians call ourselves, meaning our identity is tied up with the number of times we fling ourselves across a river spanned by numerous bridges that soar over golf courses, municipal parks, cross-country ski trails, an athletic facility, and the sloping grounds of the Folk Festival site, just to go about our urban business. Along Victoria Promenade where I live, on the heights over the river as it streams downtown, historical markers tell strollers that Judge Lucien Dubuc (1877-1956) was an enthusiastic tree-planter in the valley and that Nellie McClung, formidable feminist, lobbied for playgrounds and recreation facilities in the 155-acre property ceded to the city of Edmonton as parkland in perpetuity by the Hudson's Bay Company in 1911.

River City

The Bay. In October 1795 the Company of Adventurers Trading into Hudson Bay built Edmonton House—open for fur-trading business with seven great Indian nations, the Assiniboine and Cree who lived nearby all the time, and the Blackfoot, Sarcee, Gros Ventres, Peigans, and Blood, who came twice a year—and Edmonton has been a place name on maps ever since. But the Hudson's Bay Company post lives on now only in replica at Fort Edmonton Park, miles upstream from its original site. And, by the time I was growing up, "The Bay" denoted the big department store at Jasper Avenue and 103rd Street. Now it's an emptied shell and The Bay is a stop on the LRT subway route, ghostly signage flashing past our incurious gaze.

But some Edmontonians have longer memories. As drivers dash off the 105th Street bridge and zip past the EPCOR power plant, they see an unofficial cluster of simple wooden crosses implanted in the grass alongside the flow of traffic. The power plant sits on one of Fort Edmonton's early sites—"the flats," as it was consistently described in the HBC journals—and nearby lie remnants of a river landing and cemetery. (Some two hundred Indians, Métis, and European men, women, and children were buried here from 1800 to 1870, taken off by scarlet fever, murder, suicide, and lucklessly, in 1828, by a New Year's Day cannon explosion.) And underneath these lie the artifacts of six thousand years' worth of First Nations' gatherings and trading assemblies.

The same water—the current, the tow, the shoals—that had once confounded the hide bumboats of the Indians, the crude scows and ferries of the homesteaders, and the heavy mass of loaded York boats whose boatmen laboured fiercely to pull them along the shore, now flows along rarely disturbed by anything more than the occasional canoe paddling effortlessly downstream. (There is a whole literature of the earlier drama of river crossing, hair-raising narratives of voyageurs on a portage, surveyors hoisting their precious instruments, missionaries soaked to the skin.) Every Canada Day, by means of pipes and hydraulics, it flows up and over the upper deck of the High Level bridge, to tumble 150 feet back down to its bed, in a display known as The Great Divide Waterfall by artist Peter Lewis. And we all line up on the river banks to ooh and aah as though only an artificial extravaganza can make us pay attention. The rest of the year, or at least while the river is free of ice, we stand on the Dawson Bridge or on the clayey banks or alongside the shallows, and dump things into it: shopping carts, road signs, picnic tables, and computers.

It's the twenty-first century: what is a river for?

◆◆◆◆

Beams of empire spanning a river.
A canoe could become jammed in the ghosts beneath the bridges.
—Wade Bell, *The North Saskatchewan River Book* (1976)

According to the Blackfoot *Genesis*, all of creation heard and knew its creator, Old Man: "All things that he had made understood him, when he spoke to them—the birds, the animals, and the people." Old Man came from the south, travelling north, making the mountains, prairies, timber, and brush as he passed along. "So he went along, travelling northward, making things as he went, putting rivers here and there and falls on them, putting red paint here and there in the ground—fixing up the world as we see it today."

Of the creation of rivers in the Rocky Mountains, the Piikani (Peigan) tell much the same story, an account of the Creator walking northwards in what Calgarian archaeologist Brian Reeves calls "a deep time memory" of the ice and lakes receding from the headwaters of the Saskatchewan. In its melt 12,500 years ago, the ice front created a spillway along its watery edges, which became the Battle River, the main tributary of the future bed of the North Saskatchewan, which still lay trapped in ice. "And *Waka Taga*, who is Life-Maker, then sings into existence these medicine spirits: *Mu* the spirit of Thunder, *Waheambah*, Sun . . . *Owsni Ti*, the Cold Air Spirit, and the Water Spirits."

Through generations of narration, before and even after the invention of a written language, the First Nations reproduced the memory of those primordial events and later historical ones with a vivid concreteness akin to the data of professional historians. Those who heard them—at least those with narrative genius—in turn passed the stories on in a process of listening and telling that was a kind of "writing," or *orature*. And when the first Europeans arrived in their midst, they told them again these "sacred geographies" of the lakes, rivers, and streams, of origins and first causes.

If a river is an artifact of aboriginal deep time memory, then no matter how many dams plug it up or how many trestle bridges span it bearing locomotives, if you get in a canoe and ride it, it is still an elemental current. Wherever it's going, you're going with it. Those who, within living memory, rode the river, working it, like the *coureurs de bois* and their Métis descendents, still think about it as a basic force. At least, that's how people talk in the documentary film *Saskatchewan*, by Wayne Schmalz (1993). "I start thinking about those things," we hear in voice-over, "and about history when I'm on the river, much more than when I'm on a road, for instance. Because the river *was* a road but a road that wasn't man-made."

Saskatchewan means "swift flowing," sometimes spelled by English-speakers trying to catch the Cree sounds as Kisiscatchewan, Kisiscachiwin, Sisiscachiwin, Saskawjawun, Saskutchawin, even Kejeechewon. The French explorers, La Vérendryes, had already in 1750 named the river the Poskaiao, which means "narrows between wooded banks," presumably a good description of where their post, Fort Paskoyac, stood, near today's The Pas. But it was the Englishman Henry Kelsey in 1691 who was the first white man to canoe the Saskatchewan, six hundred miles upstream, from Cumberland House, a feat he committed to verse ("I set forth as plainly may appear, / Through God's assistance for to understand / The natives language & to see their land"). In all languages, the river was named for what it was—a swift-running watery course that bore Indians and Europeans and Métis alike up and down its current between traplines and trading posts for more than a hundred years.

◆◆◆◆

The site itself was imposing, that of "old" Fort Edmonton, high on the river's 200-foot ramparts, on one of the numberless curves so that the river flowed halfway around it. Behind stretched the prairie to its far horizon. . . . Leather tepees, bright with tribal insignia, dotted the benches below the hexagonal palisade.
—Marjorie Wilkins Campbell, *The Saskatchewan*

Moving Fort Edmonton in 1832 to its fourth and final location on the "ramparts" described by Campbell, Chief Factor John Rowand then built the grandest fur post ever built in the northwest, known as "Rowand's Folly." But he had a point. Edmonton was now the strategic centre for the vast Saskatchewan District reaching from Cumberland House, on the Saskatchewan near the Manitoba border, to the Rockies.

The English artist Paul Kane visited on his way to and from the Pacific coast, 1845-47, and, like almost every visitor before and since, kept a journal, *Wanderings of an Artist Among the Indians of North*

America (1859). Journals, or at least field notes, were the first prose written in Alberta, according to literary historian George Melnyk, and displaced the aboriginal voice. Stopping en route toward Edmonton to paint at river's edge one dusky late summer evening, Kane rhapsodized a scene that had become pastoral, as though anticipating the shifting fortunes in Saskatchewan River country from fur trading to farming: "The sleepy buffaloes grazing upon the undulating hills, here and there relieved by clumps of small trees, the unbroken stillness, and the approaching evening, rendered it altogether a scene of most enchanting repose."

In 1845 Kane wrote of buffalo herds so vast that it took them three days to pass over the trail Kane was riding to Edmonton House. By 1879—a mere generation later—this once great herd of sixty million beasts across the North American plains had dwindled to the near point of extinction. "Traders came to our encampments too, and it was always buffalo hides and pemmican they wanted. Hides. Hides. Shoot. Shoot. See who can shoot most. A curse upon man's greed and on the Crees for that inordinate slaughter," lamented Thunderchild, old Plains Cree Chief, in 1923, to his interviewer Edward Ahenakew in *Voices of the Plains Cree*. Starving, their land claims forfeited, the Indians were told to learn to plough, while Edmonton House operated until 1914. Then the brash new Edmonton Board of Trade, decreeing there were no historic buildings worth preserving, tore it down to clear the skyline for the provincial capitol.

◆◆◆◆

And on the prairie
the ghosts who own it continue to walk in clans,
searching for food and for what they once knew.
—John Newlove, "Like a River"

The Oblate missionary Father Albert Lacombe saw Edmonton House in 1852; he arrived, a passenger on a York boat manned by eighty boatmen who reminded him of "slaves in darkest Africa" as they pulled the heavy boat up against the current, "walking in the mud, the rocks, the swamps, along cliffs and sometimes in water up to their armpits," like beasts of burden. The population of the post that winter was about 150: boatmen, Rowand and his family, the interpreter, boat-builders, coopers, carpenters, hunters, and blacksmiths.

Thirty years later on a return visit to Edmonton, Lacombe "blinked incredulously at a new Edmonton," reports his biographer, Kathleen Hughes. "Stockades, bastions and sentinel's gallery [of the old fort] had all ingloriously given way to a low plank fence. Up on the hill log-shacks were set down in clearings. There was even the semblance of a village street at an elbow in the trail as it wound eastward up the valley from the Fort. A telegraph wire ran into the village bringing messages from the great Outside. . . . Where was his wilderness gone?"

Gone to creeping urbanization. In 1905 the Australian travel writer John Foster Fraser, who had already tackled *America at Work, The Real Siberia*, and *Round the World on a Wheel*, landed on the banks of the broad and whirling Saskatchewan River where not so long ago there had once been only the log cabins. "The place is lit with electric light," he marvelled. "There are six grain elevators . . . [T]here are flour mills, saw mills, brickyards, tanneries . . . all proof of a pushful western town." Fraser caught the city on the cusp of one of its spells of boosterism. The first threshing machine had been delivered by steamboat in 1880, and by 1894 coal mined out of the riverbanks and some three thousand bushels of oats were shipped out.

No longer in danger from "wild, red Indians," settlers had streamed across the river and out to their homestead claims. "They seek a lonely country / a place empty & smooth / as an unwritten page," in the words of poet T. D. MacLulich in 1981, as though nothing had happened here until their arrival. It is the beginning of a new kind of heroic yarn, about the homesteader who can handle anything the country throws at him. These people own land and they're not going anywhere.

One cold winter, eighteen Ukrainians were forced by their poverty to live in a cave in the riverbank of the North Saskatchewan, but my great-uncle Peter Svarich, writing his memoirs in 1953 for the

Ukrainian Voice newspaper, was luckier. In exchange for forty dollars and lodging with a family in Edmonton, he agreed to build them another house: "I had to cut the logs myself and float them on a raft as far as the bridge. This work took me a week, and I barely escaped drowning in the river." This was the river in one of its last acts as a force to be reckoned with, still capable of running in swift currents up- and downstream, powerful enough to bear men away to a grave in Hudson Bay.

But at some point in the new century, Edmontonians stopped going up and down the river. Thanks to the new bridges flung across it, we *crossed* it. Three men died constructing the High Level Bridge, that bravura of steel girders that nails together the yawning jaws of the river banks just upstream from Fort Edmonton, which still stood there, in 1913, when the first train rumbled across. Writer Wade Bell in *The North Saskatchewan River Book* imagines the view of a working man in 1912, who has helped build this bridge, "the skeleton bridge thrust from the riverbank, partly made, already immense and to my mind ugly, already looking cold and ancient as if the winds of the North Saskatchewan had layered it with a century's grime and the northern clouds had bathed it in sour rain." As if it had always been there.

Soon the whistle of the Canadian Northern locomotives bearing down from Saskatoon and Battleford and out onto Edmonton's trestle bridges across the Saskatchewan became *the* emblematic sound of the prairie: "No sound was ever more welcome to mortal ears," writes the romantic historian of Edmonton, James G. MacGregor, thinking of the homesteader in the back of beyond, even as the new miles of rail track on to Jasper in the Rocky Mountains lay themselves down flat on top of the old fur-trade routes.

A couple of generations later, with the farming hinterland itself tamed and industrialized, the city, transmogrified by metaphor into a surrogate Nature, has become a beloved object of the writer's gaze. Here is poet and novelist Robert Kroetsch in his own travelogue, *Alberta*, looking at the river valley: "It is a valley that on a January morning might shelter ten thousand buffalo. Edmonton with its high towers illumined at six o'clock on a winter's night is a blue-green vision of a city, hung from the stars above a black chasm." And a generation after him comes Calgarian Aritha van Herk, novelist and essayist, with her new history of the province, *Mavericks: An Incorrigible History of Alberta*, to reaffirm what every Edmontonian is exquisitely aware of: the city "belongs to its river," or at least to its valley, "the sudden leap of the natural world close and intimate," its 160-foot-deep chasm cut by the North Saskatchewan, a drama of stereoscopic breadth as the broad, sinuous band of water slides along under entire architectures of cumulus cloud bearing down on the western horizon.

◆◆◆◆

What is a river for? In historic times, it has been primarily an economic instrument of human interests, whether among First Nations before contact, or after, between them and the Euro-Canadian bosses of the fur trade. For those who actually laboured on the river, the water represented the full spectrum of energies from mind-numbing tedium to deadly maelstrom that swallowed them whole. The river was besides the only means of efficient transportation and communication along the east-west grid of the continent. In those days, the river always flowed two ways, upstream to the furs, downstream to the fort. (Even today there are Métis communities along the North Saskatchewan who say they are "going east" when they go out shopping.) In the literature associated with this period, the river is still a force of Nature independent of human will upon it; humans adapted to it, and shared the rhythms of its dramatic cycle. It could be awesome in its primal forcefulness: Reverend Robert Rundle, laboriously making his way upstream to Fort Edmonton in 1840, whipped out his Bible on entering the muscular main channel of the Saskatchewan and read *Isaiah 60*: "Arise, Jerusalem, rise, clothed in light; Your light is come and the glory of the Lord shines over you."

All this changes with the coming of the telegraph and railway when, quite suddenly, the rivers are deserted of their traffic except for a brief period of steamboats and recreational paddlewheelers. Bridges become extensions of the railway tracks, and a whole literature of the drama of the perilous river crossing disappears (it will reappear in the age of tourism). In fact, the river all but disappears from human interest in the new age of agriculture and then urban-ization—"the river steams / a touch of hell / but it's only the power station / pouring waste energy into the water," sardonically writes Peter Stevens in "On The Edge" (1976)—and the literature produced by the first generation of non-Indian settlers is mainly concerned with the land (the figure-on-the-horizon school of poetics), not the river. The Australian John Foster Fraser, standing in downtown Edmonton in 1905, fancies he stands at a portentous border between a city growing up behind his back—"There are six thousand people in Edmonton; they have electric cars along their main streets"—and a journey north "to grim death," or at least to those gaunt men lin-gering at the end of the fur trade, "stalk[ing] the wild and frozen lands searching for skins." It has come to this.

◆◆◆◆

The river flows both ways
where it reverses, unexplorably shifts

. . . .

Until still points of spinning
nothing
nothing turn and wheel away
Time vanishes, in the flow of metaphor.
—Jon Whyte, "Homage, Henry Kelsey"

Perhaps in unconscious revenge against the industrial exploitation of the waterways, our poets have reimagined our relationship with an ideal "untamed" river as adventure, nostalgia, romance of the rugged, a process that began with the first urban canoeist or hiker who had no "reason" to be there. By the 1940s, Marjorie Wilkins Campbell tells us, the North Saskatchewan had spawned a brand new sport "that demands the utmost in skill, knowledge, and tact," namely, canoeing downstream on the lookout for old fur traders' sites at all the likely places—confluences of streams and the river, promontories, protected river bottom. Florence Page Jaques, who went overnight camping near the source of the Saskatchewan in the solidly massed "gloom" of mountain glaciers, wrote in *Canadian Spring* (1947) that she *liked* the feeling of "implacable hostility surrounding us." Metaphors of transportation and passage produce mystic currents that link us along its shores or "will take you where all things at last must come together," in Glen Sorestad's "Rivers" (2005) or, like the River Styx of Greek mythology, to your death, as in the celebrated short story "The Rivers Run to the Sea" (1980), by the late Prince Albert writer John V. Hicks, whose narrator stands on the bridge, staring down into the streaming current of the North Saskatchewan, "watching the dark water racing endlessly east." These are linear trajectories, carrying memory from its source in our wounded psyches to some scarcely apprehended outcome.

But there is another consistent metaphor—river as communique, linking us up—that is also, in this digital age, as literal as it is metaphoric. Harold Innis, the preeminent historian of the fur trade, began with his observation in 1956 that "a system of communication" was established among the trading posts and supply depots of the fur companies, citing David Thompson's *Narrative*: "There is always a Canoe with three steady men and a native woman waiting the arrival of the annual Ship from England to carry the Letters and Instructions of the company to the interior trading houses." The "distinctive economy" of the fur trade, then, laid down the communications grid that incorporated as a single, coherent unit the east-west orientation of the British and French colonies distinct from the colonies to the south (i.e., the future United States).

But other writers see the challenge differently. The era of national dreams held in common, of metaphors of shared revelation, yields to a time of fractious difference. Not even the ambition of conservationists contains everything we want, for the ceremonial and sacred places of the First Nations, for instance, their mountains and rivers, have become destinations of eco-tourism, "protected" even from the indigenous celebrants themselves. No, the best we can hope for is to talk it over. The writer and philosopher B. W. Powe boldly asserts in *A Canada of Light* (1997): "The old Canada is ending. . . . In the rampage of what seem to be terminal disagreements and divisions, rising confusions and intolerance, we can be certain only of this: our time and place have been electrified. . . . I perceive communication to be the value of Canada." For this to be true, no one needs a real river.

Yet the river is still a force of Nature independent of human will upon it. Even dammed and polluted and prettified, it acts out its own dramatic cycles of the primal and natural: floods, maelstroms, or, conversely, drying up on its own beds as glaciers shrink at its source. Of course, we still think we are in control. In 2002 Alberta's Environment Minister, Lorne Taylor, refloated the controversial 1960s idea of "hop-scotching" North Saskatchewan River water over a series of dams and canals into the Red Deer River and then moving it east to parched prairie. Against such hubris, the author of an Environment Canada website muses that, "just as the smallest trickle of water eventually flows and expands into a lake, perhaps our minds will follow a similar path in our own progression toward tolerance and stewardship."

But these ideas are not what's on my mind when I stand at the condo window and rejoice, at Spring breakup, about the liberated surge of water that has gushed out of the mountains and into this embrace of the loamy, bushy banks at Edmonton. I am with writer Hugh Maclennan in 1961 at the Columbia Icefield: . . . "and when you stand on the little bridge over the North Fork and look at that lithe, frigid stream, not glacial-green but milky from limestone, so narrow in August that a broad-jumper could clear it, you can have a strange sensation when you think how far this water has to go."

It has got to me, and then it rushes on.

We stop on its bridges and banks, staring down into the streaming current of murky water racing east, mesmerized by that quality a river has if we stand looking at it in one spot: a thing that is passing us, going somewhere else, leaving us and not coming back. Wherever it's going, we're not going with it. We may be lost in contemplation, but it does not stop its run to the sea. That's what rivers do. That's what this river is for.

A BENIGN SKYLINE

EUNICE SCARFE

We could go by boat, I said to my husband in November of 1970, sitting on the floor of our cold Yorkshire flat. He had just accepted a position at the University of Alberta. We were searching for the city of Edmonton in his Philips' School Atlas, left over from his grammar school days. Canada was given one page; the counties of England were given ten. Canada looked small. We had to squint to read the names in small print: Cypress Hills, Drumheller, Dunvegan, Peace River, Saskatoon, Medicine Hat, and a city called Edmonton, slung on the same latitude as the city of Leeds where we sat.

Edmonton, Alberta—equidistant, if we squinted, between his Norfolk family home and my family home in Seattle. Edmonton, Alberta—the most northern Canadian city of significant population, though not the most northern city in Canada. Edmonton, Alberta—with its back to the mountains and its face to the prairie. Edmonton, Alberta—named after a suburb of London and the royal family of England. Edmonton, Alberta—where he would recognize its British origins (or so we thought) and I would be at home, once again, in a North American mosaic made by immigration and relocation.

On a map, all things are possible. Why not go by sea? Why not sail as my ancestors had done from Norway to North America so long ago? It was twenty-six hundred miles from Liverpool to Quebec City and only twenty-nine hundred miles from Liverpool to Churchill, Manitoba on an inlet called Hudson's Bay. Why not sail to Churchill and arrive closer to Edmonton than if we landed in Quebec?

I called shipping companies. I said we were leaving England in January and asked what was going to Churchill. They laughed. I didn't know then what was so funny. I soon did. We flew (needless to say we flew), landing in Edmonton on a clear January night in 1971 with a temperature of minus forty. We didn't need to ask whether it was Celsius or Fahrenheit.

The cab driver drove us north down Calgary Trail to Saskatchewan Drive and stopped, not far from the Strathcona apartment where we were to stay: "That's our skyline, over there. Just like Manhattan, don't you think?"

We hadn't expected Manhattan. We had just come through New York. Edmonton's skyline in 1971 didn't look like Manhattan's skyline and today it still doesn't. We hadn't expected a river zipping two halves of a city together. We hadn't expected land as flat as the sea. (Hadn't the map shown mountains nearby?) We hadn't expected a thriving theatre and opera and symphony and university. We hadn't expected the extravagant expanse of sky.

We thanked him for the tour, not expecting that our entire life in Edmonton would be spent in sight of that skyline, along a drive named after the North Saskatchewan River, which was frozen and silent in the darkness below us. A year later we bought a home in Mill Creek at the east end of Saskatchewan Drive, one built in 1912 on land deeded to "Jenny Skinner, Widow." My husband began his professional life at the University of Alberta at the west end of Saskatchewan Drive, just before the Drive turns south with the River. We made friends with a couple in Skunk Hollow. We shopped in Old Strathcona and Garneau, communities attached to the Drive, and we celebrated children's birthday parties in Queen Elizabeth Park, which provided an outdoor swimming pool along one shoulder of the Drive. We swam at Kinsmen Pool, watched fireworks from the top of Scona Hill, and we cycled in the Saskatchewan River valley communities of Cloverdale and Riverdale and Rossdale. The names, run together, were, and still are, like music to me. We went nowhere without crossing Saskatchewan Drive, or travelling along it.

Both of us had visited Canada once. We were entirely ignorant of this place and its people. My husband had been to Montréal for the Expo in 1967. I had once sailed to Victoria on the Princess from Seattle. He knew that Canadians spoke French; I knew that Canadians had British backgrounds. We knew nothing of Alberta.

We didn't know that Head-Smashed-In Buffalo Jump was older than the Egyptian pyramids, that the markings at Writing-On-

Stone made up the largest body of native petrographs on the North American continent, that the highway between Montana and Calgary followed the oldest Indian trail in the Americas. We had never seen a prairie church with an onion dome. We didn't know the colour of canola or the devastation of the Frank slide, the location of Leduc oil or that homesteading was still possible in the Peace River country. We hadn't yet seen sun dogs or prairie dogs or heard that there were no rats in Alberta. We hadn't awakened to a chinook or rushed outside to embrace the sight of northern lights or view the slow symphony of a midsummer sunset. We'd never celebrated a holiday for a woman called Victoria, or heard the legacy of social credit.

And we didn't know that Alberta in 1971 was less than seventy-five years old.

Nor had we seen the map of Canadian literature. We didn't know what to expect. I had read *Anne of Green Gables*, but in my American girlhood I had inexcusably assumed she lived in New England. My husband and I went to a used bookstore. We bought the cheapest New Canadian Library paperbacks we could find, texts with the most utilitarian covers and smallest print ever designed by a publishing company that expected to sell books. We crossed Canada by text. We watched the 1917 Halifax explosion in *Barometer Rising*, saw the beautiful losers in Montréal, and entered Ontario with Alice Munro. In Manitoba we saw the stone angel above the town, on the hill brow. In Saskatchewan we saw the wind in Mitchell's classic, and lived the depression, and dust, in *As for Me and My House*. We entered, and escaped, the enclosure and arrogance of rigid religious community in *Peace Shall Destroy Many*. We travelled with the Barr Colony to the Saskatchewan border in Mary Heimstra's *Gully Farm*. And then at the border of Alberta we met the mythmakers: Robert Kroetsch and a blue stud stallion, Howard O'Hagan and the legend of Tay John, and, written in Alberta but set further west in the folds of the hills under Coyote's eye, we explored Sheila Watson's remarkable *The Double Hook*, a text which changed Canadian writing, and reading, forever.

Thirty years later and Alberta continues to be mapped and imagined and mythologized through Kroetsch and van Herk, Kogawa and Wiebe, Mandel and Dumas, Wharton and Huston, Riis and Miseck. In 1971 we couldn't read Liebhaber "remembering the future" or see Judith raising pigs; we didn't know Naomi would be "stabbed alive" by the mountain air, and we hadn't yet seen Wiebe's High Black Bridge spanning the text, and the river, in *My Lovely Enemy*. We weren't aware Miriam Mandel's prairies "should / be seen / only / on your knees" and couldn't hear Jacqueline Dumas asking what does the mother do in such a story? We couldn't see Wharton's elegant evocation of ancient ice and couldn't hear Huston composing a plain song of southern Alberta on a faraway Paris page or follow Miseck's naming of northern Alberta where land buckles into hills.

In 1971 this literary map was only in the making.

Pausing that cold clear night at the end-of-steel marker that intersects Calgary Trail and Saskatchewan Drive, we didn't expect a map of imaginative text to be written for us in the next decade, nor did we expect the map of our memory to be lived along this stretch of the Saskatchewan River. We didn't know that at one extremity of this Saskatchewan Drive our children would be born in University Hospital, and at the other end of this Saskatchewan Drive, just blocks away from where we viewed the skyline, one of us would die eighteen years later, hit by an impaired driver as he ran into a new day. Birth and death. Beginnings and endings. Joy and sorrow. From one extreme to another, a mere mile and two decades marking the two.

We made a map to the scale of our life, and in making the map, we invented our life. For absent relatives, we substituted families who like us had no living—or dead—relatives in this country of Canada, families who, also far away from Alberta, had pored over inadequate maps which had revealed as much as they concealed of this place Alberta, maps that had never—no, not ever—revealed the text of Alberta or the lives of Albertans.

We lived in a ghetto of relocation, with friends from New South Wales and Dublin, Montana and Connecticut, Northumberland and Grenoble, Saratoga Springs and St. Louis, London and Washington, DC.

None of us had relatives on the farm or small towns in Canada to which we might return. We filled in each other's names for the in-case-of-emergency line at schools and doctors' offices and summer camps. Having had no tradition of October Thanksgiving or Victoria Day or the first of July, we made tradition from scratch, little realizing that many others up and down the neighborhood streets in this city were doing the same: inventing tradition, mapping and memorizing the text of their lives.

We were immigrants, though not always seen as such, either by others or by ourselves. "Immigrant," we discovered, meant coming empty-handed, speaking a language other than English, fleeing from persecution or distress. We hadn't come empty-handed. We spoke English. We hadn't fled. We were, however, experiencing the ambiguity and ignorance and anxiety of relocation. If immigrant also meant a person who comes to a country to take up permanent residence, we were immigrants.

The first morning in Edmonton we walked from 100th Street, where our apartment faced King Edward School, to Whyte Avenue. We called our parents from a phone box at the A & W to say we had arrived. We saw a sign for Bee Bell Bakery and had breakfast at Albert's Pancake House. We marked out Army & Navy, where we were told we could find all the necessities we needed to set up house. We passed several car lots, a health food store, and a music store. We kept looking for the university until, cold and tired, we saw Corbett Hall ahead of us. We headed north to Saskatchewan Drive and saw again the Manhattan skyline of Edmonton, this time from the Earth Sciences Department, where my husband began making another map marking our lives: a vertical record of the earth's origin and history. Our walk that day defined a postage stamp of Canada we travelled thousands of time in the next eighteen years: west from Mill Creek to the University, east from the University to the Creek.

Some years I tell my people south of the border about Alberta, and some years I don't. Do I really want to tell them about the eugenics movement? About a man called Keegstra who taught years of schoolchildren that the Holocaust didn't exist? About a province that would prefer to invoke the notwithstanding clause rather than ensure tolerance for all of its citizens?

Some years I try to tell people outside Canada about the geography of this country, some years I don't. A professor of political science at the University of Denver went to a convention in Vancouver and called to ask if we could meet for lunch. An aunt visiting Calgary asked if I could meet her for supper. An English friend, coming by train from Kingston, got off at Winnipeg because she thought Edmonton was a one-day's journey, not two. "If you went by train for two days in England, you would no longer be in England," she said when she finally arrived.

No, you wouldn't.

I have written letters of our life here to the children's grandmother in England and to their grandparents in the United States: letters that told how our children were born on health care, without costing us an additional penny. That we received family allowances for each of them, as did all other parents of children in Canada. That our children went to neighborhood schools, without being bussed or assigned a far-flung destination. That immersion language programs taught them to read in French before they read in English. That a manmade waterfall flows off the High Level Bridge on holidays, a waterfall which one writer claimed could make Edmonton the second most popular honeymoon destination in Canada. That Edmonton has more parkland within the city limits than any other city in North America.

The skyline we saw across the North Saskatchewan River so many years ago became familiar and known and ours, a "cloud of witnesses" watching our life here on the south side of the Saskatchewan River, a mural of storefronts not unlike the false and true storefronts of Sinclair Ross's town of Horizon. I wouldn't trade the benign proximity of this skyline for all the Manhattans in the world.

Alberta is not a hinterland, and never was, though some have said as much. Alberta is where you live near land and in land, where you can't escape land, and where summer and winter, sunrise and sunset, you are held by land. A plain landscape, a landplace. The poet Theodore Roethke could have been speaking of this place when he wrote:

> I learned not to fear infinity,
> The far field, the windy cliffs of forever.
>
> . . . .
>
> What I love is near at hand,
> Always, in earth and air.

What we learned to love is here; what is here is now home.

TEN DEGREES OF SEPARATION
(43/53 COUSINS ACROSS LATITUDES)

LESLEA KROLL

The cabin of an Air Canada jet. The flight has been oversold and last-minute negotiations are underway to assign seats immediately prior to takeoff.

Flight Attendant
Right this way, please; this is your seat.

ToRonna
Well, now it is.

Flight Attendant
We sincerely appreciate your cooperation.

ToRonna
In the face of extortion, I don't really have a choice, do I? Here, take this.

Flight Attendant
(Accepting abrupt hand-off of designer carry-on bag.)
I'll put it in the storage compartment up here. Unless you'd like it at your feet.

ToRonna
At my feet? What, like . . . an ottoman?

Flight Attendant
I'll put it up here for now. You should take your seat. We'll be departing any minute. Is there anything I could get you just now?

ToRonna

I could sure use a drink. Could you get me a Cosmopolitan?

Flight Attendant

The bar will open once we've reached cruising altitude. Thanks again for agreeing to switch your ticket.

The flight attendant proceeds to the front of the cabin to demonstrate the in-flight safety procedures. ToRonna agitatedly takes her seat; at least the aisle provides her a glimpse into business class. She closes her eyes and reassures herself that soon she will be home, her painful ordeal behind her. Her oasis of calm is trespassed by the passenger immediately to her left.

D'Edmontonia

Wanna switch?

ToRonna

Sorry?

D'Edmontonia

Do you want the window? We can switch if you wanna.

ToRonna

No. That's . . . not necessary. But thank you.

The plane begins to taxi in preparation for takeoff.

D'Edmontonia

Packed out.

ToRonna

(Pretending not to hear and fantasizing that she is seated in business class—as she had been before the airline oversold the flight.)

D'Edmontonia

Biz-zee. You didn't get bumped, did you?

ToRonna

Bumped?

D'Edmontonia

Thought I was gonna get bumped. Want some gum?

ToRonna

No. No thank you.

D'Edmontonia

If I don't have gum—look out! I'm in trouble. They say, "Move your jaws," almost the same. And, "Pretend you're yawning."

ToRonna

Who has to pretend?

D'Edmontonia

But it doesn't work for me. Not like gum.

ToRonna

(Silently mortified by the prospect of several hours of captive companionship.)

D'Edmontonia

So. Were you bumped?

ToRonna

I agreed to alter my arrangements so that I could arrive home sooner. It was this or nothing. I've never been back here before.

D'Edmontonia

Whaddya mean?

ToRonna

It doesn't matter. I'm sorry, but . . . do you mind if we don't talk so much? I'm starting to get a headache.

D'Edmontonia

I have some pills . . . (Grabs her purse and begins rummaging through it.)

ToRonna

NO! I mean . . . thank you very much.

D'Edmontonia

Oh. Okay.

ToRonna

I'm very tired and I need my rest.

D'Edmontonia

Sure. Do you want me to wake you up when they serve dinner?

ToRonna

No. But be sure to let me know when they come around with drinks.

D'Edmontonia

Do we know each other somehow? You seem very familiar.

ToRonna

No. We definitely don't know each other.

ToRonna closes her eyes, attempting to block out her newfound friend, unbearable seating arrangement, and the duration of her trip.

◆◆◆◆

ToRonna's Dream
In stiletto heels and slinky slip dress, ToRonna vamps down the illuminated

strip of an airport runway, lined by thousands of her closest friends and admirers. She strides toward two strapping young men in tight, zippered jumpsuits positioned at either end of the runway, beckoning her arrival by waving white flashlights with wide, circling arm gestures. As she approaches her star turn, her gait becomes unsteady, and she nearly stumbles. Something has a hold on her! ToRonna looks down to see her ankles becoming ensnared in . . . what is that? God, it's ugly! Like the unspeakable horror of a macrame plant holder, eww! But no, it's something weirder and worse . . . like a giant umbilical cord! It continues to snake around her ankles, up her calves. No!!! She is powerless to move as thousands of her closest friends and admirers scream in horror and the two jumpsuited boy toys fruitlessly wave their wands. ToRonna collapses in the collective constriction of anonymous entwinement and public shame. In her final moments of consciousness, she looks down to see what has ensnared her: a mammoth pair of taupe reinforced-toe pantyhose.

ToRonna
(Waking from her dream in terror.) OMYGOD!!!

D'Edmontonia
(Taking off her headphones and munching pretzels.) Hey, you alright?

ToRonna
OMYGOD! I just had the worst dream of my life!

D'Edmontonia
Cool! What happened?

ToRonna
I don't know . . . it was really weird.

D'Edmontonia
Here, drink this. I know you said to wake you when they wheeled around the drinks, but you were sleeping, so . . .

ToRonna

They do cocktails back here?

D'Edmontonia

It's what I'm having. A Red-Eye.

ToRonna

A "Red-Eye."

D'Edmontonia

Beer and tomato juice.

ToRonna

OMYGOD.

D'Edmontonia

I made yours spicy like mine. Some people add an egg.

ToRonna

I'm living my dream.

D'Edmontonia

I really think I've met you before. You seem very familiar.

ToRonna

Maybe I can get a Cosmopolitan.

D'Edmontonia

(Reaches into her purse. Pulls out the latest issue.) I don't subscribe anymore, but I found this in the bathroom at the airport. Just be sure to give it back to me.

ToRonna

This doesn't have any egg in it, does it?

D'Edmontonia

No.

ToRonna

(Takes a hearty swig and begins coughing.)

D'Edmontonia

That's it! You're Ronnie! You're cousin Ronnie!

ToRonna

(Coughs harder and louder.)

D'Edmontonia

I knew I knew you from somewhere! OMYGOD! It's been years. You don't remember me, do you? I'm little cousin Tony!

ToRonna

(Regaining her composure.) Tony . . . Tony . . . I don't think I know any . . . Oh, yes! D'Edmontonia.

D'Edmontonia

Yeah, well, I don't really go by that anymore. You can call me Tony, or Dee. Most of my friends call me Dee. How are you, Ronnie?

ToRonna

I'm fine, thanks. Just fine. But please, call me ToRonna.

D'Edmontonia

ToRoNah?

ToRonna

ToRonna. Yes.

D'Edmontonia

Is that what your friends call you?

ToRonna

Yes.

D'Edmontonia

Okay. TO-RON-NAH. TO-RON-NAH?

ToRonna

That's it.

D'Edmontonia

It's . . . pretty.

The two newly reunited cousins sip their Red-Eyes. ToRonna imbibes with surprising relish and wonders if in addition to egg, some add relish. Maybe for the next round.

D'Edmontonia

It's been a long, long time since we last saw each other. That was years ago.

ToRonna

I honestly don't remember.

D'Edmontonia

Sure you do! It was so great to have everyone together, all of the cousins: Peggy, Gary, Couvie, Saskia, Reggie, Monty, Hallie, and Charlotte. Granny Na Da's one hundredth birthday! Remember?

ToRonna

No, not really. Not specific details anyway.

D'Edmontonia

And when we were leaving, remember what happened? It was so funny.

ToRonna

Hilarious.

D'Edmontonia

Granny Na Da got us mixed up! She thought I was you. I guess she was a hundred. Imagine mixing us up!

ToRonna

Imagine!

D'Edmontonia

Mistaking me for you!

D'Edmontonia finds this very, very funny and is nearly killing herself laughing. ToRonna is eager to lend a hand.

ToRonna

Well, you did always want to be like me.

D'Edmontonia

What?

ToRonna

You know . . . you were always a little . . . jealous. Oh, I didn't mind. I knew you admired my sophistication. I'm a little—

D'Edmontonia

A lot older.

ToRonna

More mature. I was flattered.

D'Edmontonia

I always admired you, ToRonNah.

ToRonna

I always knew you wanted to be me.

D'Edmontonia doesn't know what to say. She always admired ToRonna, but never wanted to be her. She decides to politely shut up and stare down her Red-Eye.

ToRonna

I'm not very good at keeping in touch.

D'Edmontonia

Well, everyone's busy.

ToRonna

But I'm really busy.

D'Edmontonia

Everyone's busy.

ToRonna

But I'm really, really busy!

D'Edmontonia

Are things okay with you?

ToRonna

Yes. Sure. What do you mean?

D'Edmontonia

Oh. I just wondered.

ToRonna

(Finishing off her Red-Eye.) I think I want another one of these.

D'Edmontonia

Are you coming from . . . from . . .

ToRonna

From what?

D'Edmontonia

Are you coming from a funeral?

ToRonna

No! Why would you ask that?

D'Edmontonia

I dunno. All that black I guess.

ToRonna

No. No funeral. Just my style. And you? Were you out delivering the mail? Your shirt, your collar . . . it's so . . . blue. (She tries desperately to get the attention of the flight attendant.)

D'Edmontonia

No. Just my style. But I am working.

ToRonna

(To flight attendant.) Could we have a couple more of these?

D'Edmontonia

On my way to do a little business. And you?

ToRonna

I'm headed home. I can't wait.

The flight attendant arrives with a fresh pair of Red-Eyes.

D'Edmontonia

It's so good to see you, Ronnie. I mean, TO-RON-NAH. You probably get around more than I do.

ToRonna

What do you mean by that?

D'Edmontonia

Maybe you'd like to come and visit the next time you're out. Come and stay for a long, long while.

ToRonna

No! I mean, I don't know when that will be. I'm really, really, really busy.

D'Emontonia

Oh . . . sure. I understand.

ToRonna

D'Edmontonia—

D'Edmontonia

Dee. Please, Dee or Tony.

ToRonna

Okay, DeeOrTony—uh. Okay: the next time I'm out your way, I'll call ahead and we'll get reacquainted. Catch up on all that's been happening. Shouldn't take too long.

D'Edmontonia

That would be great!

ToRonna

(Refreshened by her Red-Eye.) These are good. DT, what kind of business are you in, anyway?

D'Edmontonia

Accessories.

ToRonna

Fashion!

D'Edmontonia

Fashionable ladies' accessories.

ToRonna

I'm impressed!

D'Edmontonia

We're really, really, really busy. Booming. Especially with our signature product.

ToRonna

Which is?

D'Edmontonia

Style and practicality: taupe reinforced-toe pantyhose.

ToRonna

OMYGOD.

The jet cruises along, the cousins cruise into the heavens, and one lucky, busy lady gets to live her dreams.

ELEGANT EYESORE:
THE VIEW FROM THE MAC

TED BISHOP

I was here to sip single-malt Scotch. I held up a glass of pale Oban to the light as instructed, sniffed, and then rolled it back on my tongue. Where else would you go for a Scotch tasting but the Hotel Macdonald? Genteel, elegant, aloof from the raw development of downtown. Edmontonians refer to her as the "queen" of the city's buildings, and point out that the real Queen has visited her, twice. She sits serene on the side of the bluff, surveying the river and the valley below.

What I had before me was a "flight" of Scotch—three small tasting glasses with three very different Scotches, the smooth Oban, the darker Balvenie, and a slightly menacing-looking Laphroig. The low autumn sun came in under the terrace awning and made the liquor glow from within. We were on our second flight and beginning to glow a little from within ourselves. Our server told us the hotel was modelled on a sixteenth-century French chateau and we immediately felt more aristocratic.

••••

The Latest Word

"The Macdonald, New Grand Trunk Pacific Hotel, Has No Superior in Any City on the Continent"—so said the *Edmonton Bulletin* on 25 September 1914. Though the hotel would not open officially for another year, the writer had just been given a tour and been dazzled. There was the magnificent fireplace of the Confederation Lounge, the ballroom with a spring floor, the café that opened onto the terrace. Up above, five bedroom floors held 191 bedrooms in all: twenty-two rooms on each floor had their own bathrooms, with four public baths and a shower bath for men on each floor. And what bathrooms— porcelain tubs and ceramic tile floors, "the latest word in style and appointment." Not only that, "There are telephones in every room and the vacuum cleaning system connects with each room. There are

Rough Road to the Mac

watchman's clocks, fire alarms, and fire hoses on every floor." The sixth floor had bigger rooms intended as "sample rooms," where salesmen could lay out their wares; the smaller floors in the slope of the roof housed a printing office and space for valet work (on the seventh), and an area for plumbing work on the eighth. The whole structure rose to an amazing 175 feet at its highest point.

What really excited the *Bulletin* writer, though, was the basement. There the real work took place. He unleashed his verbs: "Heat is generated, power created, air circulated, ice made, water pumped, fire pressure exerted, clothes washed and ironed, floors swept and goodness knows what else is done." Edmonton had never seen anything like it: two ten-ton compressors; a three-ton ice-making plant; four two-hundred-horsepower boilers; a ten-thousand gallon water-filtering plant. Here was the laundry, the kitchen, the pantry (pantries!—a glass pantry, a silver pantry, a serving pantry, an oyster pantry), along with a billiard room and a barber shop. Amazing.

But hardly frivolous. This hotel meant business: speculation and land values were as much a part of the Macdonald as the oak panelling and the tile bathrooms. "Its completion will mark a very definite stage in the advance of the city. The world and his wife may very well stop off in Edmonton for a day or two to enjoy the comforts of this modern palace, while studying the resources, possibilities, and opportunities of the district." In 1910, when the plans for the hotel were first announced, Edmonton was still the end of the line: the Grand Trunk Pacific (which would become the CNR) was just thirty-six miles west of Edson, laying down track at two miles per day. Once the railway was finished, the Macdonald, city fathers hoped, would make Edmonton a player.

The war was going badly in Europe, and the front page of the *Bulletin* carried daily casualty lists. Edmontonians needed a celebration, and when the Hotel Macdonald opened on 5 July 1915, they got one: "It was perhaps the most brilliant social event in the city's history. . . . Myriads of lights diffused their soft rays over women garbed in fashion's latest dictates, over men in conventional evening dress, officers in active service khaki and retired officers in uniforms of brilliant red and gold."

Guests danced to an orchestra or watched "an exposition of the modern dances." The table decorations were "very simple and beautiful. Tall crystal vases held delicate bouquets of old fashioned garden blowers, Iceland poppies, white sweet william, oxalis, ribbon grass, and June grass." The *Bulletin* reporter seems to have been so busy taking it all in that he did not notice what he was eating (or maybe reporters did not get the deluxe meal): "Of the dinner itself little more can be said than that it created a new standard of cuisine, delighting the happy epicures who partook of it." But the first resident manager, Louis Low, recorded the menu for the 1915 opening in his diary:

Celery and Olives

Consomme Double

Filet of Sole Joinville

Chicken en casserole,

with string beans

and Parisiennes potatoes

Lettuce and tomato salad

Ice cream and petit fours

Demi-tasse

The latest word in sophistication.

◆◆◆◆

Our Scotch-master, Chris Gordon-Craig, was instructing an elegant young man in a three-piece suit who looked like he had wandered in out of 1925. "No no no, you don't sip Scotch. That's for wine tasters. You want more than the tip of your tongue to get it. Now look, grab your glass," he wrapped his hand around the delicate glass like he was going to crush it and hefted it like a tankard of ale. "Then take a big glug, one that fills your mouth. Got that? Good." The young man sat with his mouth full, looking slightly startled. "Now then, swish it all around in your mouth like mouthwash, really get it up there." The young man swished. "Now blow out through your nose. This forces the scotch up into the far upper regions of the palate. Then—and only then!—" Gordon-Craig held up an admonitory finger. He took a mouthful himself, sloshed it back and forth like Dizzie Gillespie doing warm-up exercises for his trumpet. His Adam's apple bobbed, he smiled, and said,

"Swallow." The young man swallowed and looked astonished. "There," said Gordon-Craig. "Admit you've never tasted Scotch till now."

••••

A Room with a View

By 1930 the Macdonald was the centre of a civic eyesore so hideous it moved a body to verse—a certain "N. O'Body" in the letters column of the *Edmonton Bulletin* wrote:

> I can see this noble edifice in all its strength and beauty
> From the sidewalks of Strathcona and the braes of Bonnie Doon,
> And as I gaze upon it I oft wonder whose the duty
> To blast the shacks that hide it as a black cloud hides the moon.
> From the Campus I can contemplate each window on the wall.
> But when I stroll down Jasper I can't see a light at all.

When King George VI and Queen Elizabeth visited in 1939, the *Journal* ran a photo of the "hideous line of shacks, garbage cans and washing" that the royal couple were forced to gaze over as they posed on the balcony. The editorial writers railed: "Disgraceful eyesore . . . evidence of indifference and lack of civic pride . . . no businessman was ever inspired to invest in Edmonton by such squalor, and many must have been deterred by it from doing so." They quoted the president of Royal Trust, R. P. Jellet, who found the view to the south beautiful, but to the north "not only inadequate but almost mean." The Mac was the window on the city, and it did not matter how many pantries it had if it was surrounded by slums.

••••

A man who looked like a general had taken my car keys as I pulled up. I had surrendered them without thinking, and now as I swirled the Balvenie around in my mouth I realized he had approached me just outside the direct view of the door. What if he wasn't a real valet, just a guy in a rented suit? He could be halfway to Montana by now.

••••

Company Men and Working Stiffs

While the editorials railed against the slovenly surroundings, the business pages celebrated promotions and retirements within the Macdonald system. In the 1930s we learn of H. H. Tillman moving up to Fort Garry in Winnipeg, of H. W. Aslin coming in from the Nova Scotian in Halifax, previously of the CNR hotel in Port Arthur. Chefs were always big news. In 1935 the Macdonald acquired Anedeo Franchi, who had cooked at the Waldorf-Astoria and the Savoy in New York.

Less high-profile workers were celebrated as well. In 1946 we hear of Harry Child, waiter since 1930, an Australian who worked for the Orient Steam Navigation Company for twenty years as a steward before finding himself in Edmonton. He liked it and stayed. Or Donald Ross, who retired in 1948 after thirty-one years as an electrician. Even in 1963, when John Krayco, the head doorman, retired, it was worthy of news: he had opened the door for Premier Manning, lieutenant governor Percy Page, and the Archbishop of Canterbury (who said "God Bless you"). Alf, a hotel employee for twenty-six years, said of the doormen, "Sometimes they almost look like generals, standing there in their official looking uniforms."

A job at the Mac brought stature, but also sometimes disaster. In 1919 one Elmer Smith was killed working with the big iron laundry machine: "While looking into the opening Smith's head was caught by the revolving drum and the upper portion was completely torn off," the *Bulletin* reported. Elmer had six sons serving with the American army, two at the front and four in camp, and his wife lived in Oregon. He had been in living in Edmonton for two years in rented rooms and had filed on a homestead in the Peace River country. Working at the Macdonald was to be his entry to a better life.

But industrial accidents were not the main problem. By the 1960s the hotel was described as a "city within a city;" the laundry that killed Elmer Smith now employed twenty-six workers who wrestled with fifty-six hundred pounds of laundry a day ("the equivalent of several years washing for the average housewife"). Staff were unhappy. The hotel had been criticized for hiring non-union labour, and in 1963 painters had been pulled off a job because they were not being paid union rates.

In September of 1965 the Macdonald staff were considering whether or not to strike because of CNR's refusal to adopt the $1.25 minimum hourly wage set out in the new Canada Labour Code. CN even defied a directive by federal labour minister Allan MacEachen, arguing that the Macdonald came under provincial rather than federal jurisdiction. CN claimed that such high wages would make it impossible to maintain competitive prices and ultimately force the railway out of the hotel business. Prime Minister Lester Pearson went so far as to organize a special cabinet meeting to look into the issue, and a wildcat strike was planned for the Chateau Laurier to correspond with Labour Day, but in the week before, CN suddenly caved in and granted the minimum wage.

◆◆◆◆

I was dubious about swirling single malt like mouthwash, but what the heck, Laphroig was the Listerine of Scotches.

◆◆◆◆

Offers They Couldn't Refuse

This was not the first time the grande dame had played hardball. The arguments—and the threats—were old. In 1918 the Grand Trunk Development Company appealed the fees being charged by the city, moaned that the Macdonald was being run at a loss, indeed less as a hotel than as a "philanthropic institution." And, they warned, the city would lose a quarter of a million dollars if the hotel were closed. This "not held out as a threat," their spokesman said, "but the action taken by the city council in regard to the licence fee might prove the last straw. . . . They did not want to close the hotel and deprive the public of the service which was being given, nor to lose for the city the money spent in the pay-roll and the purchase of supplies."

In 1946, when the proposal to add an extension with another three hundred rooms was placed before city council, they happily approved it. Edmonton's population had been booming and the city needed hotel space. Then in 1948, when Mayor Harry Ainlay refused tax and land concessions, the CNR coolly replied that they had no immediate plans to develop the project. City council was outraged; the deal had been signed. Ainlay travelled to Ottawa to negotiate with the CNR. Early in 1949 he struck a deal. But in March the project stalled again as CN refused to pay the tax of one hundred dollars per room. They would not go above seventy-five dollars. Ainlay had to quash rumours that the extension would not be built at all, and finally in June of 1949 the city gave in, with much bitterness on council, and settled for seventy-five dollars. This was to be the pattern. Edmonton needed the hotel and the developers knew it, and were prepared to let negotiations drag on for months, even years, until they got what they wanted.

So the city had a deal, but the disappointments were not over. No one had seen the architect's drawings yet, and when they did they were startled: the Chateau style had been abandoned and the sixteen-story addition looked like a box, one that would overshadow the present Macdonald and make it look like the adjunct to the new modern rectangular mass. Its arrival in 1953 was as brusque as its shape; there was no opening ceremony. CNR President Donald Gordon explained that "the urgent need for hotel space resulted in the decision," and as for the old Chateau section, he observed, "I believe that in time it will prove better to pull down the original structure and replace it with something modern."

There were more changes: a microwave tower was placed on top of the box, and red neon signs were designed with seven-foot-high letters to be visible for fifteen to twenty miles. Things changed inside too. They had the first heated underground parking garage in the city and the fastest elevators in western Canada, and, by 1966, even air conditioning. But trade was languishing. There was a general feeling in town that the Mac was stuffy, that it was only for special occasions like wedding receptions and graduations.

What to do?

◆◆◆◆

I took a glug, swirled it around. I could feel it whirlpooling around that jagged back molar that I need to get crowned, pinballing back and forth from cheek to cheek, under my tongue.

♦♦♦♦

Oh, Behave!

"That's right, it's topless—at Macdonald Hotel!—The last remnant of the Victorian era has fallen. The veil has dropped from the bosom of the crusty old Mac," cried the *Journal* one evening in April 1971. Topless dancing in the Hearth and Hound (the lounge that had opened in 1966 and was decorated to look like a baronial hall, with purple drapes and black leather chairs). This was the brainchild of manager Keith Murray, and the newspaper photo shows a winking Murray, looking like the precursor of Austin Powers, with a long-haired brunette in a polka-dot minidress. At forty-three he was the oldest hotel manager in Canada (food and beverage manager Jean Leblanc was twenty-seven, assistant manager Michael Shaw twenty-three), and whatever finger he had his pulse on, it was not the youth of Edmonton. Eight months later Murray had given up his job to run the thirty-unit Sawridge Motel in Slave Lake. Asked for comment, he said, "It was time for a change—basically that's it."

Things had worked out better for Leonard Cohen. When he arrived in the city on a bitterly cold night in 1967, he met two young women (either at the airport or in the doorway of a shop on Jasper Avenue—he has different versions of the event), who claimed to have brought the miniskirt to Edmonton. They went back to his room and although his erotic fantasies never materialized (or maybe because they didn't), he got up and wrote a poem about the two women by the light of the moon reflected off the ice of the Saskatchewan River. The words and the melody came together and by morning he had the song: "Sisters of Mercy."

If Cohen's sisters of mercy were waiting for him when he thought he could not go on, the Macdonald had no such luck. They flipped the name from Macdonald Hotel to Hotel Macdonald in the late '70s but it made no difference, and in 1983, after the Universiade World

Student Games, CN closed the hotel. Three years later they demolished the detested box (though Alderman Ed Ledger thought that they should keep it, and opposed the historical designation of the Macdonald, calling it a windfall for the owners). For several years CN toyed with the idea of renovating, of doing an addition, of adding office towers, and in the end walked away, selling off to Canadian Pacific Railways in 1988. They too had no definite plans. There was talk of demolishing it and putting office towers on the land.

Peter Pocklington proposed gutting the Mac and turning it into Edmonton's City Hall (vigorously denying that his plan had anything to do with repairing his own image after selling off Gretzky). Mayor Terry Cavanagh wanted it restored as a hotel. CP wanted a $1.5 million concession package and to change the name to Chateau Macdonald. The Westin complained that they got no concessions for their facelift and that the project could sink the Chateau Lacombe as CP's flagship Edmonton hotel. Everyone felt everyone else was behaving badly. Eventually the wrangles were resolved, and in May 1991 a new mayor, Jan Reimer, presided over the key-toss ceremony, a tradition in the hospitality industry that signifies that the hotel's front doors will never be closed again.

♦♦♦♦

Then I exhaled hard through my nose and felt the medicinal Laphroig forced back into the far upper reaches of my mouth.

♦♦♦♦

Plus ça Change

This time, unlike the furtive opening of the box, there was a celebration. Chefs reproduced the menu from the 1915 banquet, and the first official guest was Margery Clausen, ninety-five, who had joined the Mac staff in 1944 as a chambermaid. She remembered how US Air Force flyers stayed at the hotel in 1944, working on the DEW line (the Distant Early Warning system in the Arctic): "Female staff were often offered a drink when they went into a room and so many become pregnant that I think I was the only woman who worked for any length of time on my floor."

Three years after the reopening, the Rolling Stones came to town and booked all forty-five rooms on the seventh and eighth floors. The staff were sworn to secrecy and denied that the Stones were staying there, though fans swamped the phone lines. Mick Jagger took the two-storey Royal Suite (fifteen-hundred dollars per night); Charlie Watts took the Premier Suite, with a pantry stocked with salads and fresh fruit; Ron Wood and his wife stayed in a smaller room, stocked with Guinness; Keith Richards settled into the three-room Grandview Suite (there is no record of his pantry). The manager, Cary-Barnard, said that rumours that the Stones flooded the room service with demands for booze were false. But you could hardly have blamed them. The Confederation Lounge has a magnificent array of single-malt Scotches, a smaller but still fine list of bourbons, excellent beers. The Prince of Brunei and Luciano Pavarotti have also stayed in the Royal Suite (not at the same time) and I bet they liked it. The MacDonald is the smallest chateau-style hotel in the Fairmont chain, which it joined in 1999. With only 198 rooms, almost the same number as in 1915, the Macdonald now seems intimate instead of huge.

◆◆◆◆

Amazing. I didn't taste notes of sherry or detect an iodine finish, but this was new. It felt like someone had lit peat fires in my Eustachian tube and shot seaweed up my sinuses. But I liked it. Complex, rough, even a bit dodgy.

◆◆◆◆

Like the hotel itself. Jill, our server, told us about the horse that fell into the foundations and was buried there, and whose ghost still gallops around the basement. And about how in 1948, when Edmonton's first CBC radio station opened on the seventh and eighth floors, bats sheltering under the roof would fly down the hallways and through offices. Drunks would sometimes take a wrong turn and wander into the studio as well. The Macdonald was never as prim as she looked from the river. The dowager has always had her dark side.

Hub Hotel

MY DANCE WITH THE DOWAGERS

LISA GREGOIRE

Sliding into the thin, nubby sheets was always the hardest part. I didn't mind approaching strange men in windowless bars—the teasing, the flirting, the suspicion, the beery aggression. I could charm doubting hoteliers bent on discovering my "angle." I could abide brown towels, no hot water, sharing a toilet, even sleeping in the room over the stage where a cowboy band had the gall to play Kenny Rogers and Billy Idol—back to back. But the bed? Well, that was different.

I went on a trip last year to celebrate Edmonton's impending centennial. With grant money in my wallet, courtesy of the Alberta Foundation for the Arts, I took my toothbrush and pajamas to four old hotels in various Edmonton neighbourhoods. After spending a night at the Strathcona Hotel for another story three years ago, I had developed an unnatural fascination with dingy hotel rooms and working-class men. These fading grottos were depositories for decades of local toil and sweat between the Klondike and karaoke. They held secrets about this city and the ghosts who whispered them.

So it wouldn't be authentic if I slept on *top* of the faded pastel polyester bedspreads, which came in two motifs: paisley patterns from the 1970s and peach-and-tan tropical scenes. No way, Jack. Pull back the blankets to have a look—a quick one, coax an errant hair from the loose weave, feel slightly reassured that the stain you see is actually on the mattress, not the sheet, shake the stiff pillows, turn off the light, and bend yourself in. As I succumbed to the usual sloppy sleep of the slightly inebriated, I'd repeat to myself: Nothing in this bed can actually *kill* me. That was based on no facts whatsoever.

As with most stories I've followed during a dozen years of journalism, it's the people I find most intriguing. Old folks and storytellers: these hotels were full of them. They guarded memories of events and long-dead companions like archivists, describing how streets were once chockablock with barber shops and hardware stores, not overrun by the pawn shop and neon cheque-cashing brigade. They were once safe for single women and the elderly, not strips for spindly street toughs. Their nostalgia for an adolescent city in the 1950s, rapidly outgrowing dirt streets and shoeshiners, was matched only by scorn for an unsettled present that no longer obliged their blue-collar values.

So they gathered here: men with thick hands, coal miners, pipefitters, welders and riggers, carpenters and roofers, insulators, electricians, and sheet metal workers. Union men. This is where they've always gathered, in simple sanctuaries where minimum wage and workplace accidents coalesce those of disparate languages, religions, and ages. There is an old-fashioned camaraderie here where people protect each other from shiftless strangers; a roughly hewn kindness and ferocious sense of fairness which underpins sensible debates about politics and economic policy. They argue and tangle their limbs sometimes, all the while knowing they are family.

Like most newcomers, I had discovered Edmonton through the politicians and entrepreneurs who lent their names to parks, hills, roads, and neighbourhoods. Last year I met the people who paved the roads, dug for coal, laid the railroad ties, and built the neighbourhoods so waves of newcomers like me could make Edmonton home. And as the city changes—gets faster, busier, wealthier—they retreat to old hotels and taverns with their ball hats and pony jugs of draft beer. And their stories of easier times.

At the nearly hundred-year-old Transit Hotel on Fort Road, the receptionist initially refused to rent me a room because I'm a woman. I'm a working girl, sure, but not the kind she suspected. The manager, Santa Claus look-alike Bob Ruzycki, relented once I told him my stay was for posterity. Then he gave me the room above the live stage on a Friday night. I'll never forgive him for that.

At the even older Hub Hotel on Jasper Avenue, near the upscale Hardware Grill, which used to be a hardware store, owner Natalie Jerwak responded to my request for a room reservation by repeating, "You know, it is a *men's* hotel." She too acquiesced, thinking me mad, naïve, or both. Like a protective mother, she tried to make me comfortable in withering digs with a clean, bright room and fruity toiletries on the bedside table.

I had allowed myself one luxury during this journey through River City's transient underbelly: rooms with private baths. But at the Hub, none were available, so I shared a hallway biffy. That made for a few flustered encounters with sleepy, half-dressed men in the middle of the night. The shock was entirely theirs.

Mearl Boyer has lived in room 1 at the Hub for about a decade. He is typical of the men I met at these forgotten inns: born at the Royal Alexandra Hospital in 1928, widowed, retired tradesman, self-sufficient, alone but not lonely. He likes the Hub because it's central. We talk hockey as an NHL game unfolds on his little TV. He never liked Wayne Gretzky, always thought he was a sissy. And he doesn't like how Northlands sells the name of the Coliseum to lift companies and pharmacies. "That's a bunch of garbage."

A loud clanging like hammers on railroad announces the radiator coming to life. A pair of brown loafers prop open the door to his private bathroom and zippered rubber galoshes sit next to a half-dozen coats on a rack. He has a ship tattoo on his left forearm and a woman under a palm tree on his right—remnants of 1944. He used to live in McKernan, back when there was a lake there. He used to play right wing when people played hockey outside. He used to be married until his wife, Caroline, died in 1991. He used to work on the railroad, checking cars for inventory. Now he lives the life of a widower in a room that costs him $390 a month. Cigarettes and TV.

Mearl has a dusty dignity, like the Hub itself. At 3 AM I wander the halls and drag a chair to an iced-up window overlooking Jasper Avenue. Inside, thin carpets and hissing radiators pin me to the past. I sit with the ghosts and peer into a frosty April morning, which car exhaust and spring moisture have rendered a surreal, ice fog grey. I squint to blur the street lights and imagine the Calgary stagecoach pulling up six hours from now to disgorge its wayfaring cluster and to scoop up another: preachers, monied gentry, salesmen, carpenters, young brides, and politicians. Everyone tethered to the Western dream before Mearl was even born.

In the eastern and western quadrants of the city, which used to be their own towns of Beverly and Jasper Place, a feeling of rapid development, of fleeting years and notions, lent an added air of transience to the Jasper Place and Beverly Crest hotels. Built after 1950, Edmonton's middle years still lingered here.

I didn't stay at the Crest proper. A new chain franchise agreement and fancy renovations to the forty-three-year-old workhorse have ruined the rooms with new furniture and modern fixtures. I was looking for 1960s shabby. The Jockey Motel next door, which the Crest owns, offered the kind of dry, stale-smoke atmosphere I sought. My room, overlooking 118th Avenue, faced a tombstone factory outlet store and every time I passed my window, I thought of layoffs, divorce, overdose, and death. I drank cheap beer from the hotel liquor store and read Bible passages during *Sex and the City* commercials, feeling lonelier than a Jew at Christian camp.

People used to raise chickens in their yards around here. People used to dig for coal. Duck-filled sloughs lined 118th Avenue when it was a dirt trail, and Beverly was a small town. The men in fedoras I met at the Crest tavern told me all about it, said the mines attracted labourers from all over Europe. The old guys occupied the bar during the afternoon, usually relinquishing the nights to the dance crowd. The portion of the tavern behind the back bar is now an air-conditioned games room full of VLTs, a lucrative revenue replacement for hotels who nixed the strippers in the early 1990s. The old lads used to sit back there, at one long bench table known as "death row."

Jasper Place was the largest town in Canada in 1964 with thirty-nine thousand people. That year, after protracted political debate, the town voted with a narrow margin to join Edmonton. But some Jasper Place residents never accepted the annexation. Some still don't, regarding 149th Street as the dividing line between home and away.

The Jasper Place Hotel VLT room was once the "henhouse," the bar where women and escorts drank separately from the single men, a practice that endured in Alberta until Canada's centennial in 1967. The hotel, built in 1951, was the centre of Jasper Place entertainment for decades, drawing hundreds of patrons to its main-floor tavern and downstairs nightclub. The club closed in the late 1970s and is now occupied by moths and auction-bought hotel furniture.

My room, though renovated, has no hot water and looks across narrow, bustling Stony Plain Road toward a nightclub and a massage parlour. It has a cable TV guide but no Bible. I'm immediately uneasy. God doesn't live here. In the bar, I meet long-time hotel guests and area residents, First Nations and Caucasians in equal measure. I hear about barbershops and clothing retailers that used to occupy the street. Within four blocks of the hotel, I count seven cheque-cashing joints, three pawnshops, five porn stores, and two liquor outlets. A person could get into a lot of trouble around here.

Bar staff at the hotel tavern tease the regulars, stock their favourite beer—in cans, if they prefer—and have assembled a dozen or so funeral cards on a shelf to remember those who've died. Next to them is a spittoon-cum-urn which contains the ashes of Hubert "Hubie" Rossum, a roofer and "travelling man" who died in 1998. "The thing about this place is they remember you," says Pete Christensen, an ex-junkie sheet metal worker who currently resides in room 217. "Sometimes you come here and it's full of ghosts." Our conversation lulls and Meatloaf fills the silence with "Bat out of Hell."

Many of these old hotels are turning to chain franchises to survive, or closing down. The Cecil, the Cromdale, the International—all downtown hotels which once offered Salisbury steak and cheap rooms for the unlucky and the unwanted—are now closed for good. Rundown, crime ridden, roach infested, they succumbed to the drug users and prostitutes, leaving fewer havens for those average folks escaping the doleful world inside their heads or the one outside.

Historian Lawrence Herzog, who writes a heritage column for *Real Estate Weekly,* laments the slow expiry of old hotels—the intimacy of sharing bathrooms, the built-in network for newcomers. "There was that communal sense of sharing," he says, "a deeper sharing where people made connections. And there was a greater sense of trust back then. We are social creatures. We have a need to share and make connections."

You don't make those connections in a Super 8 motel. You don't make them in a nightclub. You don't make them sitting in front of your home theatre system. The independent hotel and tavern was once the centre of the community, the meeting place. A few still are. They survive thanks to thirsty university students, VLT drones, and karaoke. The Transit just got a new facelift. So did the Jasper Place. Their endurance in the face of faux Irish pubs and chain motels is commendable. Edmonton is still a place where people chase the Western dream; where desperate people come for work and a bit of dignity, like they have for a hundred years. For now, at least, they can still find a cheap place to stay and a tavern where workboots are welcome.

THE MAGNIFICENT "ROGUE"
OF THE MIRACLE MILE

RUTH DYCKFEHDERAU

It would occupy too much space to tell in detail what union men think about it, but very definitely the majority of them are wholeheartedly in favour of it, and find it difficult to understand why certain interests are opposing it so strenuously. . . .

And yet, knowing Edmonton, it is not hard to understand. Edmonton is a paradox, and always has been ever since she was born. Old-timers well remember that when some scheme was mooted for the benefit of the town, opposition would immediately develop, and many times the deal fell through.

. . .

Now comes the Miracle Mile, and immediately groups of citizens square off for and against it in the customary Edmonton manner. That was only to be expected, the Edmonton tradition must be maintained!

The year was 1950 and Edmonton was mushrooming at an alarming rate. After years of growing at the perfectly respectable pace of a few thousand people a year, Edmonton's population in the late '40s had begun to balloon at an unheard-of rate of over ten thousand people a year. From June 1949 to June 1950, Edmonton had gained 11,392—nearly a thousand people a month. With growth rates like this, journalists noted, census figures became obsolete just days after being released.

Of course, most Canadian cities were expanding: The War ended, the boys came home, the baby boom boomed. But Edmonton, now, Edmonton was growing faster than any of them. Edmonton stood proudly as the new Gateway to the North, and the North bristled with ripe, erect, straight-backed lumber just waiting to be cut. Jobs galore. Edmonton rubbed shoulders with Leduc, home of the oil well that had burst through rock and soil three years earlier and then spawned a refinery in nearby Clover Bar. More jobs, and it looked like more were on the way: folks wanted natural gas as much as they wanted oil these days, and Alberta had plenty of both. Even the Texas oil people wanted to tap the Alberta and British Columbia fields for gas to carry to the Pacific Northwest in their new pipeline. The upshot was this: while cities and newspapers elsewhere considered ways to combat post-war unemployment, Edmonton offered more jobs than anyone could have anticipated. And money too: the 15 February edition of the *Edmonton Journal* states that the surplus for the last nine months of 1949 was "$14,429,061, a new all-time record for the province and seven times that for the same period last year." Immigrants, eastern Canadians, the Boys who had passed through the Edmonton military training ground on their way to The War, they heard the news and came in droves.

The sense of abundance, imminent prosperity, and untapped potential throbbed everywhere here, as if that oil well spurting out in Leduc presented the perfect metaphor for what was to come in Edmonton. The city could already support two major newspapers: the *Edmonton Bulletin*, a staple since 1880 and the outspoken voice of Liberal Frank Oliver, and the more conservative young upstart, the *Edmonton Journal*, a respectable paper in its own right despite its humble 1903 beginnings in the back of a fruit store. The possibilities of the region had even caught the attention of New York City. On 3 January 1950, the New York World Telegram announced that "if any spot on the globe could be called a land of promise . . . the claim would be firmly tied to Canada," and "in particular [to] the oil development of Alberta and Saskatchewan." Rest assured a summary of that report took pride of place on the front page of the *Journal* that same day. And a short nine months later, hundreds of international and national geologists at a Banff convention heard that, if oil was what they wanted, Edmonton—and not Calgary— was the place to be.

But Edmonton's sudden prosperity didn't come without frustrations. The city had an urgent housing shortage, the worst of any western Canadian city (war veterans alone made for sixteen hundred people needing homes), and that affected everything. People were living—and sometimes squatting—wherever they could find shelter: in garages, in basements, in buildings never intended to be homes. And they were building houses in areas where town planners never planned houses to be. City administrators and engineers scrambled daily, borrowing money where they could, just to install the bare necessities of sewers and power and waterlines and roads for the scores of families flocking to Edmonton.

Managing the basics meant that other important projects had to be set aside. The downtown civic auditorium, for instance. Despite the embarrassment that came with asking sophisticated international acts to perform on a rickety high-school stage (or in a drill hall, church, or—as longtime downtown furniture merchant Mr. Easton once suggested—cattle barn), the civic auditorium committee recommended on 3 October 1949, that the much-anticipated civic auditorium project be scrapped and all available money, labour, and energy go into establishing the services and utilities needed for the three thousand new Edmonton homes each year. The auditorium—and all other non-housing-related projects—would simply have to wait. It was a succulent mushroom, this lovely city, and it was growing out of control.

Edmontonians had another frustration, too: they wanted to be taken seriously in national and international arenas. They weren't backwoods rural folk who just happened to have stumbled onto an oil well, and they didn't want to be seen as such. It wasn't 1913 anymore—discussions about city centre developments should no longer be shoved into the margins of Edmonton's newspapers as they had been then, sharing a side column with the prize Pennsylvania hog that swallowed the two-hundred-dollar watch of an exceptionally well-heeled judge, while the rare flowers being terrorized by "militant" suffragettes in Kew Gardens, London, got the central headline. It was 1950: Edmonton had made important global contributions of natural and military resources. The time had come for Edmonton to be recognized and appreciated, both at home and abroad. Sure, city council had appointed a committee to summon national and international attention and to put the multicultural and increasingly urban Edmonton "on the map." But, well, really, how much can a committee do?[1]

◆◆◆◆

Into this stew of simmering potential and ripe frustration, stepped a man, a slick, dapper, debonair man. His name was Mister L. Edgar Detwiler, he was from—of all places—New York City, and he was smitten by Edmonton, Alberta, Canada. Here was a man of the world! He had, or would come to have, extravagant development projects on the go in Ghana, England, Congo, and the Atlantic Shipping Zone. He had at his fingertips intimate details of planning and development in the world's finest cities. He could see the BIG picture; he had vision. He knew what an important role Edmonton could play in the new post-war global economy, and he had the connections to foreign investors to make it happen. He represented the energy and money that were out there and that wanted to come here. He made promises. He lavished compliments. And he swept Edmonton off its feet.

The newspapers described his style, his panache. He was the "broad-shouldered and tough, yet smooth-talking, greying and distinguished looking New Yorker" whose "credentials have been closely checked by the city and they were verified in New York, Washington and Boston." But mostly, the papers described the way this haphazard, cold city delighted this shiny cosmopolitan man. Edmonton "can't miss being another Houston, Dallas, Miami, or even Los Angeles," he said. "Edmonton Seen As Second Dallas" splashed across page one of the *Journal*. Edmonton offered possibilities unparalleled elsewhere, he said. In other cities, his company demolished and reconstructed buildings in heavily developed downtown areas in order to eliminate traffic congestion. But Edmonton was different—it was, he said, "the only major city, with such a future, not too deep in congestion mistakes to

---

[1] The publicity booklets the committee distributed to industries and other cities did raise Edmonton's profile, but even more effective was the Edmonton Mercury hockey team, which travelled Europe that year, beating every team it came up against to take the world amateur hockey championship.

be resurrected before it is lost." Edmonton, he said again and again, was exceptional. Edmontonians smiled; someone had finally noticed. Most important of all, Mister L. Edgar Detwiler claimed to know "seventeen major outfits interested in Edmonton," investors from "top banking, financial and insurance houses, architectural, engineering, merchandising and commercial experts," all of whom wanted generously to help Edmonton realize its obvious potential.

And what Edmonton needed, Mister Detwiler said, was a distinctive, bustling civic centre. It was common sense, really. When you thought of the truly fabulous cities in the world, you thought of the distinctive centres and architectures at their hearts: London and Big Ben, Paris and the Eiffel Tower, Cologne and the great Cathedral. If Edmonton was to be taken seriously in global arenas, and if it was to focus this sprawling conglomerate of old and new citizens into a cohesive, distinguished, newly minted *city*, it needed a congestion-free, functional, and spectacular civic centre. It needed, he said, a Miracle Mile.

Edmontonians couldn't agree more. The newspapers had long kept the issue of the civic centre at the front of the Edmonton mind. In its early years, the city had set aside several blocks of the choicest land at the heart of the city for a civic centre, and although many plans had been drawn up and considered, nothing had been done with the land. There had been the 1912 plan drawn up by architect C. Lionel Gibbs; the 1913 plan drawn up by A. U. Morell; the 1913 plan drawn up by R. H. Knight, of Driscoll and Knight, Surveyors; the 1947 plan of Cecil S. Burgess, Architect; and the 1947 plan of city architect M. C. DeWar, to name a few. The most recent plan, the Glenton Hotel plan, finally failed on 16 January 1950, as Colonel J. C. Boright, the man behind it, didn't come up with the two million dollars needed to pull it off. Often empty and frequented by people upon whom upwardly mobile businessfolk frowned, the civic centre land had become either a "'blight'" or a "'pigsty,'" depending on whether the mayor or the town planner described it, and it contributed to declining property values in the larger downtown region.

Well, Mister Detwiler had the solution. He knew of a way, he said, for Edmonton to get the perfect civic centre. His solution would even be politically savvy. Any civic centre plan, he said, must not crowd out local businesses—they made a city unique. Nor could it overlook women. He confronted the stodgy men of town council with numbers: "Eighty-five percent of the purchasing is done by housewives. . . . Women also own 66 percent of all savings, hold 71 percent of the securities, and are beneficiaries to 80 percent of the insurance policies." Women, he insisted, "cannot be overlooked, so must be provided with the most convenient, modern, and attractive commercial areas." Needless to say, Edmonton women took an immediate liking to this intelligent fellow who considered seriously their financial power, their physical comfort and convenience, and their lives outside the home. He provided welcome relief from "experts" like University of Alberta zoology professor William Rowan, who rationalized and encouraged women "trip[ping] about in forty below breezes with nothing covering their lovely legs but a pair of nylons," arguing that the body fat which gave them "sex appeal" also protected them from the elements.

After three short weeks of intensive research, Mister Detwiler and his associates, the First New Amsterdam Corporation of America, presented Edmonton with a surprisingly comprehensive set of plans. "Nothing like it has been attempted anywhere in the world," Mister Detwiler said. "We are still looking for the bug in this thing. . . . Everything works out almost too good to be true. Never have we met such an amazing series of coincidental breaks from an architectural and engineering viewpoint. Ground levels, grades, all important matters suggest their own solution on this site."

The always conservative *Edmonton Journal* immediately cautioned Edmontonians against being misled by Mister Detwiler's effusiveness, reminding them that, despite Edmonton's obvious advantages, business is still business. Mister Detwiler's corporation, the editor said, "is looking for a profitable investment like any other firm of its kind. There is, or should be, . . . nothing surprising in this." But Detwiler meant what he said, and to prove that he meant it, he made Edmonton a promise: for an astonishingly low sum—for *no actual money at all*, in fact—he would give Edmonton the Miracle Mile.

◆◆◆◆

The first version of the plan squeezed, into the blocks of land between 101A and 104th Avenues and 99th and 100th Streets, a twenty-five-hundred-seat auditorium, thirty storeys of office space, six storeys of retail space, a four-storey market, parking for sixteen hundred cars, at least one lengthy covered strip of shops, a pool, landscaped courts and mini-park areas, monumental decorative gates, and a huge fresco covering one wall of the auditorium. The buildings, covered largely in glass, would shine in the sunlight by day and glow under floodlights at night. Over the following months, the plan became still more grandiose. It grew to include a museum, child care and play areas, sixteen additional storeys of medical and professional offices, rooftop gardens, an extensive underground shopping complex and art gallery, both of which could function as bomb shelters, and parking for eighteen hundred (instead of the previously proposed sixteen hundred) cars. And parkland. Lots of parkland. The plan, Commissioner Hodgson thought, would turn out "a sight for the gods."

As for the money, well, Mister Detwiler was as good as his word. The Miracle Mile wouldn't affect the credit or the finances of the city at all. All he and his associates wanted was a ninety-nine-year free lease on the land (with eighteen months to secure funding) and the opportunity to offer the city 25 per cent of net profits on the project instead of taxes. After all, the land had been empty and unused for decades already; a tax concession and a free lease on it wouldn't actually cost the city anything.

The plan was perfect. Edmonton would have a distinctive, functional, income-generating civic centre, complete with plenty of parking and the long-wished-for auditorium. The land value in the downtown region would inevitably rise and stabilize, increasing business taxes in the area and, subsequently, city revenue. Important foreign investors would come up to Canada to see the Miracle Mile they were funding, and of course they couldn't help but be impressed. Inevitably, they would invest not only in the Miracle Mile but in surrounding businesses as well. Most importantly, though, Edmonton would finally be able to attract foreign interests and tourism; the Miracle Mile would just keep on bringing in money. And all this for nothing. Mister

Detwiler "may just possibly be," the *Bulletin* noted (just above the sermon of the day), "Edmonton's fairy godmother." What could possibly go wrong?

Absolutely nothing. The Miracle Mile machinery immediately began whirring its oil-slicked gears. The New York financiers gave Mister Detwiler permission to proceed on 24 January 1950. In a letter received 20 March 1950, the federal government gave city council permission to build the federal building, originally planned for the area of the civic centre, in the government centre east of 109th Street. And the council approached the Alberta legislative assembly for permission to grant tax concessions for projects that offered public services. Even the *Edmonton Bulletin* helped pave the way for the new civic centre, periodically publishing articles about other local projects that had received or were receiving similar tax concessions to the ones Detwiler requested, along with rousing calls of loyalty:

> Mr. L. E. Detwiler of New York has presented a magnificent plan for the improvement of downtown Edmonton.
>
> It does him and his colleagues credit.
>
> For we are convinced that Mr. Detwiler is reliable and sincere.
>
> We are convinced that his associates are sound and trustworthy.
>
> We are convinced that the proposed centre would enhance property values in downtown Edmonton and give a tremendous lift not only to that section, but to the entire city.
>
> We are convinced that the development would give Edmonton new publicity all over the North American continent.

And so forth and so on. Everything was going according to the Miracle Mile plan.

••••

But quietly, from somewhere in the midst of all that enthusiasm, a nearly imperceptible puff of resistance pushed its way out and planted itself firmly on the front page of the *Edmonton Journal*. On 15 February 1950, beneath the article about the new anti-Communist Finn president, the *Journal* remarked that a fabulous civic centre had been proposed "—but not promised—," a tiny phrase enclosed in dashes that rang a different tone than anything heard thus far, that whispered the slightest hint of suspicion of the Miracle Mile and the ability of its slick benefactor to make good on his plan. No one seemed to notice. For a month or two, Edmonton's attention seemed to drift to other issues: the new racetrack, the ever-widening embrace of the Cold War, and the accusation made against Premier Manning in the legislative assembly that he was the Judas Iscariot of the Social Credit movement, as he was "praying for the poor" so that he might be "dining with the rich." Behind the scenes, however, the sides were lining up. While the *Bulletin* continued to publish editorial calls for loyalty to and support of the Miracle Mile, the *Journal* quietly nurtured the dissent it had sown with further questions and suspicions about Mister Detwiler and his plan.

Until 27 March 1950, when the *Journal*, in tall, bold letters, announced on the very front page that a "snag" had appeared in the Detwiler plan. The previous evening, it reported, a group of downtown businessmen had appeared before the municipal law committee of the Alberta legislature. The original purpose of this meeting had been to consider amending the city charter to allow tax concessions for plans offering public services so that city council might seriously consider the Detwiler plan, and to decide upon a route that the process of consideration might take. One gets the impression that the municipal law committee was genuinely surprised to find nearly one hundred local businessmen at this otherwise routine meeting. Ostensibly, the businessmen requested that they, like Mister Detwiler, receive the option of paying 25 per cent of their profits to the city in lieu of taxes. Those who had survived the Depression, when taxes swallowed up meagre profits, feared another Depression lurked just around the corner and they wanted similar tax concessions. It soon became evident, though, that the businessmen's presentation was less a request and more a part of an elaborate strategy of resistance to the Detwiler plan. They bombarded the committee with criticisms of the plan, many of which were completely irrelevant to this meeting. The plan was still too vague, they said. How could the city make an informed decision on something that still had wrinkles to iron out? And why had no other offers been invited or considered? What is more, Mister Detwiler was an American; his proposed market would probably not be a public farmer's market, as Edmontonians expected, but an American-style supermarket. And what would happen then to all the good Alberta farmers who currently used the civic centre area for a weekly market space? They would suffer double, first from the lack of market space, and second from supermarket competition. And speaking of competition, the city economy couldn't possibly accommodate two more department stores, they argued. What was Mister Detwiler thinking? The proposal should not be accepted outright but put to a vote of the taxpayers, they said. And the taxpayers, the *Journal* implied, should vote against it.

On the very same day, the *Edmonton Bulletin*, in an editorial entitled "Bewildering Logic," mused:

> We confess ourselves bewildered by the extraordinary arguments with which the *Journal* newspaper casts doubts upon the Detwiler civic centre proposal.
>
> . . .
>
> The Miracle Mile does not cost the city a cent. But it does save the city millions.
>
> . . .
>
> The only persons who can possibly be hurt are a few speculators in property who have gambled on the city growing in another direction.
>
> We cannot believe that the *Journal* would wish to represent a greedy minority.
>
> It would be folly to say that their interests are to be placed above the interests of the majority of common men.

The *Journal* appears to regard the Detwiler proposal with suspicion because it is too good to be true.
We cannot understand such naïve distrust.[2]

••••

And with those words, the fight began in earnest. The municipal law
committee disregarded irrelevant arguments, approved the plan in
principle, asked Detwiler for a few more details (and a few changes,
including an annual fixed ground rent of fifty-thousand dollars), and
forwarded the matter to city council. While Edmontonians awaited the
council battle, Detwiler revised the plan as requested, City solicitor
Thomas Garside analyzed it, and the *Bulletin* continued its campaign,
urging city council to "Get On With It," dedicating large front-page
spreads to the Miracle Mile that would make Edmonton "the most
modern city in the world," and, of course, calling down the opposition.
Those opposed had a "personal axe to grind," were "utterly puerile,"
"narrowly reactionary," and (in an unusual front-page editorial), com-
parable to "certain ancient bigots [who] used to say that no good could
come out of Nazareth." The *Journal's* criticisms, the *Bulletin* insisted,
were "[sour]," "suspicious," and ultimately "laughable." And when the
Labour-Progressive Party opposed all plans that granted tax concessions to private businesses, the *Bulletin* decried the move with a headline especially contentious in these Cold War times: "Obstruction
From the Communists." In reply, the *Journal* stated baldly that tax concessions of any sort amounted to "a form of discrimination and
favouritism." It continued: "How anyone in civic office in Edmonton
could favour tax concessions and exemptions to a corporation which
boasts of its access to the massed millions of Wall Street, while our
home owners are taxed to the limit, is beyond our understanding."

On 19 June the matter came before city council in a three-hour
meeting that would go down as one of the most vigorous in
Edmonton history. Dominated by accusations of lies and misrepre-

[2] Ironically, the *Bulletin*, just two months earlier, on 21 January 1950, had noted
that "Nevertheless one entertains an uneasy feeling that [the Detwiler
plan] is all too good to be true . . ."

sentations, the meeting heard supporters insist that the plan would solve countless Edmonton problems and cost Edmonton nothing, while opposers criticized tax concessions and presented new sets of numbers that suggested Edmonton would lose money on the scheme. At the end of the evening, nothing had been resolved, and the group continued the fight later that week and in subsequent weeks.

But of course the battle spilled over into the arena of newsprint. Both papers noted the way Mister Detwiler had directly attacked the *Journal*: "This is the only city where we've been in which the leading newspaper has taken an attitude against downtown parking, while all other newspapers from coast to coast are screaming for it." And both papers noted the pertinent details of the evening. But there the similarities ended. The *Bulletin* presented an intelligent, considerate, and generous Mister Detwiler, and noted his willingness to continue negotiations despite being "thoroughly convinced there is a group of persons in this city who . . . will oppose any kind of agreement for the project, even if we offered to do everything for nothing." The *Journal*, on the other hand, described Mister Detwiler as petulant, arrogant, and patronizing, all at once. Waving his arms, pounding his fists, and speaking in "a wide vocal range," he claimed to be "so surprised at opposition to the project from businessmen that I am almost losing confidence in your city." "I haven't got time to teach everybody in Edmonton the planning business," the *Journal's* Mister Detwiler said, "but the city must create street space it hasn't got now. Do it now and save millions, or do it later and cost hundreds of millions." The *Journal's* Mister Detwiler "did not want to be held to decision by inexperienced people [who] might want gold doorknobs." And the *Journal's* Mister Detwiler was not altogether honest, as he asked to be exempt of Canadian expropriation laws while simultaneously asking the city to expropriate current citizens on his behalf.

When the *Journal* subsequently recommended city council deal with the Eastern Canadian firms interested in negotiating similar deals, minus tax concession requests, the *Bulletin* cast barbed aspersions upon the integrity of the *Journal's* writers:

[K]nowing that the *Journal* newspaper is violently and

unreasonably opposed to the Detwiler city centre plan, Edmonton citizens will look with some suspicion at the story carried by the *Journal* to the effect that Eastern Canadian interests are prepared to make a similar offer on better terms.

They will be all the more suspicious of the *Journal's* glowing story when spokesmen for the city call it "absolute nonsense."

We are not suggesting, of course, that it is absolutely impossible that such an offer could be made by Eastern Canadian interests.

But it seems odd that a representative of such interests, visiting this city only casually on his way back from the north, should talk to the executive secretary of the Chamber of Commerce and say nothing about it, should talk to the City Commissioner John Hodgson and say nothing about it—and then unload almost a detailed proposal to a reporter of the *Journal* newspaper.

It would be a queer and furtive way of doing business. And the circumstances do not increase public confidence in anybody who has had anything to do with it.

In the end, on 15 July, city council passed the motion 5-4 (the *Journal* insisted a few days later that the motion wouldn't have passed if one of the councilmen hadn't been on vacation; the *Bulletin* responded by accusing the *Journal* for a second time in as many weeks of dishonest journalism), and the matter was turned over to the provincial Public Utilities Board, the next step in the approval process.

Two weeks later, on 31 July 1950, the hearing before the two-person Public Utilities Board began and the ground rules were set. Once again, the two sides lined up, each with its now-refined arguments and radically opposed sets of numbers. They disputed the legalities of profit-sharing, they argued about the ways in which the tax concessions might limit or enhance the ability of Edmonton to borrow money, and they nearly came to blows over whether the Miracle Mile might hurt or help the existing business community. The mayor testified, past and present city architects testified, local businessmen testified, businessmen from other cities testified, the chair of the department of political economy and the president-designate for the University of Alberta testified, professors from other universities testified, and Mister L. Edgar Detwiler himself testified.

As they had all along, both papers reported the lengthy cross-examinations, but this time they threw even the costume of objectivity out the window and reported the proceedings with overt biases.[3] The *Journal* swept aside arguments of the Miracle Mile defenders by focusing upon the pointed questions of opposing council and upon how the chairman "rebuked" defenders for speech-making. The *Bulletin* emphasized that the project couldn't bring even "one disadvantage to the city," and took sympathy upon the Public Utilities commissioners who had to listen to the "pretentious drivel" of the opposition lawyers whose tactics were "discourteous," "mischievous," and "definitely obstructive." When the opposition tried to prove Mister Detwiler a rogue, claiming he had lied about developments in Los Angeles, the *Journal* clearly sided with it and pumped up opposing arguments in the paper. And when Mister Detwiler calmly produced the Los Angeles paperwork to substantiate his claim, the *Bulletin* smugly remarked that, despite the best efforts of the opposition, "no evidence has been submitted . . . to indicate that the city will be bamboozled, hornswoggled, or gypped."

Certainly, one thing had changed since the first civic centre discussions some forty years earlier: Edmonton downtown developments no longer took a back seat to national and international events. Steel shortages and pipeline construction, railway strikes and funeral arrangements for Mackenzie King now often appeared in the side or lower columns while civic centre developments took the larger and

---

[3] I should note, however, that the *Bulletin* published a regular column by Stan Ross, a highly visible and vocal opponent of the Detwiler plan. Although few of his columns addressed the Miracle Mile, his very presence in the paper would have mitigated the *Bulletin* bias to some degree.

more prominently placed headlines in the papers. And major publications in other cities—Calgary, Toronto, and Ottawa newspapers, and *Time* and *Financial Post* magazines, to name a few—now watched Edmonton and commented on developments here. It was about time.

But, like everything else in Edmonton, the opposition, aided by the relentless daily campaigning of the increasingly popular *Journal*, was mushrooming, and under its considerable weight, the slick Mister Detwiler (whose only mistake to date had been an occasional burst of frustrated arrogance) cracked ever so slightly, though the crack didn't come to light for several days. While on the stand, he claimed to be mid-negotiation for similar tax-concession-based projects with Vancouver and Montréal, noting that "plans were more advanced for the Montréal projects than for here due to the fact that in Montréal there is nobody to convince and they are trying to convince us to come in." Both papers mentioned this reference in their reports that evening. A few days later, though, Vancouver alderman George Miller testified to council that Detwiler had misrepresented his meetings with Vancouver and that, "The day is long past since Vancouver has given tax concessions to propositions of this kind." Mister Detwiler's exaggeration made the front page of the *Journal* two days in a row in headlines charging him with inaccuracies and misrepresentations. But the *Bulletin* dismissed the accusations as "More Red Herrings" in a debate now thick and sluggish with red herrings, and once again offered sympathy to the good gentlemen of the Public Utilities Board, who surely had better things to do with their time.

Indeed, the red herrings had done their work. The opposition had presented so many increasingly dire sets of numbers, each of which had been countered by yet another set from the defenders, that even those who calculated them had grown confused:

"I don't see how you came to those figures," said Mayor Parsons.

"I don't either, Mayor Parsons," replied counsel, "but they're your figures."

Furthermore, an important detail had come to light: whatever the state of Mister Detwiler's affairs in Vancouver and Montréal, Edmonton was not exceptional after all. At best, it seemed to be nothing more than an experimental ground, or "guinea pig," for similar First New Amsterdam of America projects on Canadian soil. Mister Detwiler's earlier compliments had simply been *shtick* tumbling gracefully out of the slick mouth of a wealthy American salivating for Canadian oil money. The naysayers had clearly gained ground and they stepped up the intensity of their attack, accusing Mister Detwiler of one thing after another, and finally closing with this summary: "[Mister Detwiler is] almost entirely the story of the salesman and promoter painting a glowing picture as to what will be done. There are inaccuracies and sweeping exaggerations in his evidence and in the representations previously made by him. His evidence should be greatly discounted."

The hearing adjourned on 18 August and Edmonton awaited the decision.

The Public Utilities Board, however, could not provide it. The two-person board, like the city around it, "finds itself with a divided opinion," it announced on 12 September, one member believing that the Miracle Mile would benefit Edmonton and the other having serious reservations. Once again, the final decision would be deferred, this time to a vote of the taxpayers. And because of the charter amendment under which the deal had been considered, the voting question had to be in the form of a money bylaw and needed a two-thirds majority to pass.

Once again, the weary sides lined up. Once again, the arguments for and against were stated and restated in the newspapers. Then, on a foggy 1 November 1950, a record 19,484 people (just under 60 per cent of eligible voters) turned up to vote on the Miracle Mile civic centre and other money bylaws. At day's end, the Miracle Mile took a 60.78 per cent majority—but it needed 66.7 per cent to pass. In an enormous headline at the top of the 2 November front page (well above the death announcement of the famous and beloved playwright George Bernard Shaw), the *Edmonton Journal* announced: "Detwiler Scheme Rejected By Voters."

The opposition had won.

♦♦♦♦

And with that, Mister L. Edgar Detwiler, of New York City's First New Amsterdam Corporation of America, was gone.

His schemes in Vancouver, Montréal, and, two years later, Hamilton would never come to fruition. His mineral oil scheme in Ghana would allegedly prompt a Ghanaian official to say, "if he comes here again, we'll kick him out." His two billion dollar development plan in the Congo would bear similar fruit as it allegedly "embarrassed the United Nations." His massive steamships carrying passengers across the Atlantic and back again for sixty-two dollars per round-trip ticket would never sail. And his Protestant Vatican in Canterbury (complete with fake sunsets and motels alongside the pilgrims' path) would never be built.

And in Edmonton, well, there would be other civic centre plans, schemes, and scandals. There would be the 1962 plan drawn up by another American firm, Webb and Knapp, rejected and then blatantly plagiarized by Edmonton city council and employees. In eight years of negotiations and legal battles, the case would eventually be dragged all the way up to the Supreme Court of Canada, where Edmonton would be charged with copyright violation and have to pay out a settlement. There would be the 1965 plan that proposed an all-seasons centre that included pools, waterfalls, a winter ice rink, and a Jetsons-like bubble in Churchill Square through which one could look down into a shopping complex below. And there would be the 1984 Parks and Recreation design-competition-winning plan that called for a multi-tiered, many-treed Churchill Square.

Would Edmonton have benefited from Mister Detwiler's Miracle Mile? Who's to know? One thing is certain: Edmonton never did become the oil capital of Canada, or even of Alberta, as it hoped to be back in 1950. That title would instead go to Calgary.

But perhaps the most significant development of all is this: it would turn out that Edmonton could not yet support two major newspapers after all. The Detwiler battle would be one of the last great hurrahs of the always feisty, never dull *Edmonton Bulletin*. It printed its last paper on 20 January 1951, just eleven weeks after the Miracle Mile vote.

The opposition, it turned out, really had won.

CLARENCE RICHARDS, FONDLY REMEMBERED

TONY CASHMAN

Clarence Richards (1895–1963) was hardly a man of his time; time could hardly keep up to him. With a few interruptions, including service with the Royal Air Force in the First World War, he taught physical education, biology, geology, and geography in Edmonton schools from 1915 to 1961—the final thirty-five at Victoria High School—on the premise that he and his students were on a treasure hunt, out to capture knowledge. But when the bell rang at twelve o'clock or four, Clarence didn't relax. He was off and running on a round of extracurricular activities, enhancing the quality of life wherever he saw need for enhancement, in Edmonton or in the country beyond, where two of three Albertans lived.

In 1919 he saw a need to enhance his own education, and as a "spare time" student spent seven years earning a university degree. While teaching at Westmount, the Technical School, and three years as art supervisor making a round of Highlands, King Edward, and Scona elementary schools, he rode his bike to enough lectures to become a Bachelor of Arts. With this he began his long tenure at Victoria High School, where a typical former student observed that he couldn't exactly recall anything Clarence taught him, but he remembered all the comments.

As he reached his final teaching destination, he was deep into his first major after-school activity—founding president of the Kinsmen Club of Edmonton. The Kinsmen ideal represented everything he believed in, a unique "only-in-Canada" movement which began in Hamilton in 1920. It called to action young men from twenty-one to forty, just what Edmonton needed, he thought. In 1925 he was granted Charter Number 8 and the Edmonton club stands forever eighth among 598.

In 1925 Walterdale was a lively river-level hamlet with residents like

Red Pollard, the jockey of Seabiscuit fame, a brickyard, a Presbyterian church built by John Walter himself, and a one-room school which became the original Walterdale Theatre. In the years since, the Kinsmen Sports Centre has grown to fill the whole of Walterdale, an idea so good and so big that the city had to take it over.

As Clarence was firing up the Kinsmen Club, his concerns were ranging beyond the limits of the city of seventy-thousand to high-school kids with no high schools to go to. The department of education was supplying correspondence courses to elementary students in rural areas through the heroic efforts of a single employee, Mrs. Elizabeth Sievewright, but the program ended at grade eight. Though Alberta had been twenty years a province, and education was a provincial responsibility, Ottawa had held on to the natural resources, revenue from which now enhances schools, roads, hospitals, and other good things. Clarence rushed in where the province was financially unable to tread. He got teacher friends to write courses, which he sold to eager farm kids. One of his customers, a lad of the Peace River country named Edward McCourt, earned university entrance, worked his way through the U of A, and went on to Oxford as a Rhodes Scholar. And what did the minister of education think? He called Clarence a bootlegger. Clarence laughed. He was busy filling another void. Teachers (in both town and country) were also short of course material. The impoverished department issued them a diploma but not much else. Again, Clarence turned to his friends for guides and aids for which there was a ready market—a shining example of enlightened capitalism in a dark world, most might think, though the minister called Clarence a "red," colour-code for communist.

He was having so many guides and lessons printed—by other people—that he saw a need for his own press, and this was the beginning of the Institute of Applied Art, a unique meeting place of private enterprise and public service, on the west side of 109th Street, on what is now a vast parking lot reaching from almost 100th Avenue to almost Jasper. The Institute Building was a narrow brick affair, a few steps down to the press in the shallow basement, a few steps up to the Institute office and rooms rented out to three piano teachers and a dance-and-fitness studio. Clarence's father ran the print shop. After a busy life as a Calgary contractor, the elder Richards found that retirement wasn't the great adventure he'd expected, and he was glad to move to Edmonton and tackle the printing business.

Clarence was never averse to a risk if he believed in a project, though he didn't tell Mrs. Richards that to start the Institute he had put up the bedroom furniture as collateral. Teaching from nine to four and running the Institute from four to whatever hour should have been enough activity for any man, but Clarence saw another civic need. Edmonton needed a football team, for the fans, but more for the players. So he organized the Hi Grads, echoing the name of Edmonton's world champion women basketball players, the McDougall Commercial Grads. Today's children of prosperity cannot imagine Clarence's football team, except in a comedy of the silent film era. The uniforms were anything but. He apparently scrounged four odd lots of equipment from various sources, judging from the sweaters, but the appearance of the Hi Grads was as fully representative of Edmonton in the tattered '30s as today's Eskimos in Commonwealth Stadium. Contrary to an impression given by a pervasive two-word rhyme, the '30s were not dirty, just tattered. The club was so poor, Clarence couldn't afford to buy shoelaces, and the only player he ever kicked off the team was a lad who refused to replace the laces he had broken. The Hi Grads played with all the fire and determination Clarence instilled into them. They played the University Golden Bears, the Calgary Ponies, and the Lethbridge Bulldogs, a team that would arrive at the varsity gridiron in a Trailways bus of such antiquity it seemed to predate the invention of the motor car. They played hard and they learned, and when conditions improved and a local brewer revived the Eskimos in 1938, the nucleus was made up of graduates of the Richards school of hard knocks.

It was characteristic of Clarence that when something became established, it was no longer interesting to him. With football secure, he sensed that the Edmonton of 125–150,000 should have a recreation commission, with resources to promote recreation in all its forms, from games to the arts. The city created the commission in 1944 and he served as chairman until 1951, when the junior chamber of commerce named him Citizen of the Year. He left then because he was deep into a new campaign and because the commission was firmly established and would evolve surely to the Parks and Recreation Advisory Board and then to the Edmonton Arts Council, which has seven employees and three hundred members, and each year distributes three million dollars in grants to the arts. About the new campaign: as an educator, Clarence was becoming uncomfortably aware of books on Canadian history which weren't being published, and because they weren't being published weren't being written.

It was clear that Edmonton needed a publisher. This career began when Jim MacGregor brought him the manuscript of "A History of the Saskatchewan River," a study of the fur trade posts along the original water highway to Edmonton, the Scots who ran them, and the First Nations people with whom they traded. Jim had done much of his research "on location," in days off from his work as an electrical engineer, running power lines for Canadian Utilities. He visited the sites of vanished forts and poked among the ruins for artifacts. And he wrote with the pioneer authority of a lad who had come with a family of Scottish townspeople to clear a homestead near Westlock. *Blankets and Beads* turned the Institute into a publishing house. That was in 1949. It was soon followed by Jim's tale of the Peace River country, *Land of Twelve Foot Davis*. Grant MacEwan was a member of the legislature in those days. Up from Calgary for one session, he brought in a biography he'd written of Bob Edwards, fabled editor of *The Eye Opener* in Calgary's young days. Clarence was all interest. In his youth he had delivered *The Eye Opener* to households where Edwards' racy commentaries were appreciated (in many, they were emphatically not). He was delighted to publish *Eye Opener Bob*. I had the good fortune of joining this process when Clarence took a chance on sixty scripts from a radio series called "The Edmonton Story"; the Institute brought my first book into existence. Type was set on an antique letterpress by a wonderful old-timer named Bill Gimblett, who was allowed to work two days a week without damage to his pension. Gutenberg, the inventor of moveable type, would have felt at home in that shop, though the type moved slowly. Bill was deliberate at the speediest of times, and if he disagreed with the writer, he would stop altogether to detail his objections. And if he laughed at a story, he would stop to tell some from his personal collection.

Bill was slow but sure. When Clarence passed away unexpectedly in 1963, some twenty books had gone out of the shop carrying the name Institute of Applied Art. They are out of print now but not out of mind, in demand by patrons of used book stores and libraries across Canada. At current count, Edmonton has fourteen publishing houses. As in many things, Clarence Richards led the way.

AN IDEAL LOCATION

ANNA MIODUCHOWSKA

The rectangular three-storey walk-up on 112th Street might not invite a casual passerby to stop and reflect on the lives that unfold behind the red brick and white board facade. It's a nearly exact replica of the building beside it, and there are three more across the street. One of the balconies sports a bicycle, another a barbecue. Yet the mellifluous name—Allison Arms—displayed above the numbers on the address plaque bestows a distinctiveness on it that, ironically, brings to mind British period dramas, a connection that is reinforced by the name of the community: Queen Mary Park. It is ironic because images of elderly gentlefolk, who rarely if ever change their address or their daily routines, are at such odds with the reality here. Statistics indicate much of the population in this community is young, single, and transient. Over 50 per cent are new immigrants attracted by the relatively low rents and central location. People from over forty countries, and speaking more than twenty major languages, are purported to be living in this area; just standing on the corner of 112th Street and 107th Avenue, one can see Acajutla Mexican and Salvadorean Restaurant, Pho Huang Noodle House Restaurant, Than Thao Video, Tuyet Mai Café. . . . They can't afford to cultivate too many routines, as flexibility is their key to success, and most move on as soon as their finances allow. What remains are the buildings, though even they have a relatively short lifespan.

Allison Arms, along with the tall, graceful pine that partially shields it from prying eyes, has occupied this spot for almost forty years, twice as long as the modest house which previously stood here, and carried the same address, and which, along with the rest of the single-family dwellings in the neighbourhood, was demolished in the mid-'60s. The last to inhabit the white one-bedroom bungalow was a family of five, newly arrived from Poland. After six months under their sponsors' hospitable roof, they were on their own for the first time, in a tiny house rented from Tadeusz Niziol. The middle one of three children, I was in Grade 8 the winter we moved in, and it was here, at 10633 – 112th Street, that I participated in the dramas associated with new beginnings. The only remnant of that period in this block is the attractively landscaped comfort-pink stucco house with lime-green window and door frames—Union Street Hair and Tanning—located on the corner of 112th Street and 106th Avenue.

When I park my car by the curb on a cold sunny day, the street—the whole city—is covered with a thick layer of fresh snow. Snow is a great equalizer. It conceals, it smooths out, it provides the same glittering finish to dissimilar surfaces. It brings out the same need for warmth and safety in all of us, no matter what our financial status or how long ago we have claimed a particular spot for ourselves. I have good memories of this neighbourhood; of the house, which for three winters kept us comfortable; of the backyard, where we could throw down a blanket and our swimsuit-clad bodies on a hot summer day; and of the garden, which yielded a good crop of raspberries and vegetables. Under the power of these images, the functional, severe angles around me blur, soften. Yet I'm not here on a sentimental joyride. I have not forgotten the small daily humiliations stemming from the ignorance of language and custom, the yearning to belong, my parents' exhaustion, the bouts of homesickness so severe the body refused to get out of bed. I am also aware that this is a very different neighbourhood today. There are no green spaces between the walk-ups for the children to play. A liquor store and a pawn shop stand just half a block away on the corner of 107th Avenue. In the evenings, a young woman dressed inadequately for the cold shivers under one of the attractive lampposts.

The address first appears in Henderson's Directory in 1943. Most of the block is a green space, and Ella and Arthur Turner, who move into the house that still smells of fresh paint, must feel like pioneers. Their brand new home is located on the Hudson Bay Reserve, much of which is still undeveloped. There is only one other bungalow in the short block between 106th and 107th Avenues, six bungalows on the unpaved 107th Avenue east of the intersection, and five west of it.

Although located on the wrong side of the CNR tracks, next to an industrial area, this is not a bad location. The red and green street cars running every ten minutes along 107th Avenue between Calder and Rossdale connect them with the downtown, and with their jobs. Rationing is a way of life but aside from an occasional sugar shortage, it hasn't made life too difficult. Dairy products, eggs, and bread are delivered to the house; other groceries are available only a short walk or bike ride away at Kirks Grocery at 11023 – 107th Avenue, or at Sunlight Grocery on the corner of 109th Street. Ella can have her hair cut and permed at Susanne's Beauty Parlour. A shipper at James Brody's shoe shop, Brod-Ease Shoes, at 10127 – 104th Street, she probably takes care to look her best at all times. The city is swarming with good-looking American soldiers, who do not stint on appreciative glances.

Previously employed as sign painter at Henderson's Signs, Arthur now works for Northwestern Utilities. He likes his paintbrushes well enough, but like most young people, he dreams of moving up in the world. He puts his spare energy into yardwork. Ella wants a place where they can sit outside on hot summer evenings, watch the tomatoes and peas ripen in the garden. Arthur is planning a square, flat-roofed gazebo by the side entrance to the house, with benches running along the side, a project he will eventually bring to fruition. The only inconvenience is the roar of airplanes continuously taking off and landing at Blatchford Field just north of the neighbourhood.

They probably don't have much in the way of furniture, but there's a war on, and they're just starting out. The kitchen is equipped with an icebox filled with fresh ice twice a week by a man from the Arctic Ice Company. Four chairs surround a simple wooden table. The bedroom contains two tubular metal-frame beds pushed together, a chest of drawers, plus a wooden box for blankets and wool sweaters. The living room's best feature is a luscious fern, a gift from Ella's friends at the shop. The coils in the worn Winnipeg couch serve to ground the radio, their main source of news from the Front. Arthur has pinned a map of the world on the kitchen wall and religiously marks all the battles taking place in Europe and on the Pacific. They don't have a phone, but not many do. There is no mention of children in the directory, and until the mid-'80s, Ella is listed as working outside the house.

On Saturday nights during the war years, the tram might convey the Turners downtown, where they will either go strolling along Jasper Avenue or take in a new show. War hasn't dampened people's appetite for a good time, and Hollywood obliges with musicals, comedies, and satisfying war dramas. Ella makes sure to take along a jam pail of bacon drippings she has been saving for the war effort. After the show, coffee with pineapple or cherry tarts at Picardy's. In the winter, they walk to the skating rink on Jasper and 112th Street, where a live band entertains the skaters on Sundays.

In the post-war years, the neighbourhood steadily fills up with houses, as well as new businesses along 107th Avenue, which is paved in 1948, the same year the red and green streetcars are replaced by trolley buses. In 1950 the Turners have the option of shopping at 7th Avenue Pharmacy at 11023, and between 113th and 114th Streets: Crown Food Store, Seventh Avenue Cleaners, Howard Drugstore, and Sue's Grocery, joined two years later by Shirley's Beauty Salon, and Central Cycle and Hardware.

The late '40s and '50s see the area bloom along with the rest of the oil-rich city. In 1952 Ella and Arthur witness the official birth of the Queen Mary Park Community League. It takes up residence in the no longer used Prince Rupert Golf Course clubhouse, and soon becomes a vibrant entity. Families flock to the box socials, regular dances, talent shows, bridge nights, Christmas parties. There are children in almost every house; one can see them on the streets, playing hopscotch and tag, pitching snowballs or baseballs at each other.

In 1953 Arthur Turner, promoted to foreman at Public Works, and Ella, a sales clerk at the Holt and Renfrew (jobs they will retain until the mid-'80s), sell their little nest to Joseph Pierce, retired CN Express Messenger, and his wife, Susan. It is the beginning of a general move of the local residents to the better-appointed homes in new residential areas, a trend which will eventually result in developers buying out whole blocks of single family dwellings and replacing them with the low-rent walk-ups and apartments that are there today. In 1956 King Size Photo, a shop that will survive until the mid-'80s, opens on the corner of 112th Street and 107th Avenue. Three years later, the long-awaited Loblaws establishes itself between 114th and 115th Streets.

The Pierces have lived frugally all their lives and the new prosperity does not greatly affect their lifestyle. Their children are grown and on their own, so the new house is large enough for the two of them, and small enough to keep in perfect order. Even so, Susan worries about the near future, and looks on with raised eyebrows at the cars which grow longer every year, the electric kettles, and drive-in restaurants. Still, she's happy for her children when they get nice things for themselves, and likes to watch Ed Sullivan when the neighbours invite her and Joe for an evening of television. Joe has a hobby, the result of which will delight and exasperate the next inhabitants of the house.

In 1960 Joseph and Susan celebrate their golden wedding anniversary. Two years later, they sell their house to Tadeusz Niziol, and transfer to an apartment.

The location is ideal for the new family who move in. The trolley bus takes Jan Wojno, my father, to various manual jobs the first few years until he secures a position of technician at the University of Alberta. It carries Jozefa, my mother, a former teacher, to a garment factory, where she will work until, ten years later, arthritis puts a stop to her new career. There are no ESL classes, no organizations to ease immigrants into the new life; the bus carries my parents to their weekly private English lesson with Mrs. Dunn, who along with English grammar and vocabulary feeds them tea and cookies, much appreciated on cold evenings. She also provides a shoulder to cry on when my mother finally breaks down after she had been flying high for days on the amphetamines the doctor had prescribed to cure her fatigue. The children are expected to absorb English in school, as if by osmosis.

Saturday mornings, my mother also travels to the Polish Hall, just north of the Prince of Wales Armory, to her other job as teacher in the Saturday Polish School. Sundays, the family boards the trolley bus to attend mass at St. Andrew's Church on 124th Street, or the Holy Rosary Church on Princess Elizabeth Avenue. The dentist, Dr. Batiuk in the Tegler Building on 101st Street, and the family doctor, Dr. Szerman on Jasper and 110th Street, are also easily accessible. Luckily, both the St. Catherine Elementary/Junior High and St. Joseph Composite High School are within easy walking distance.

Only those who do not possess a car can truly understand the importance of a good grocery store in their neighbourhood. Loblaws is close enough for the groceries to be pushed home in a shopping cart on a Saturday, a luxury not available to the present tenants of Allison Arms, as Loblaws moves out in the early '70s. Gone, too, is the NADP milkman who delivers fresh milk, cottage cheese, and buttermilk in the summer.

With Father's help, Tadeusz Niziol, a caring landlord who drives one of the Edmonton Public Library's three bookmobiles for a living, builds a room in the basement for my sister Basia and me. Mother curtains off part of the long, narrow living/dining room for our brother. The furniture consists of metal fold-out beds at first, and an arborite-and-chrome kitchen table with vinyl-covered chairs. Father buys two sets of legs for the donated round tabletop. The short set transforms it into a coffee table, and the long set into a wobbly dining table used for special occasions.

Three of the wooden chests that had crossed the Atlantic with the family become desks—a chest stood up sideways with the lid nailed on top is just the right height. The other chests become bookcases. Wood-patterned wallpaper takes care of aesthetic needs, as well as protects from slivers. As soon as the first purchases are paid off, the living room receives a burgundy sofa, for which seventeen dollars must be delivered to Eaton's twice monthly. Every penny is accounted for in the family budget, yet there is always enough to send Christmas parcels with good tea, coffee, raisins, chocolate, and other delicacies to the closest relatives and friends in Poland.

As if to make up for the absence of television, the house offers its own attraction to the children. The walls and the ceiling in the basement, as well as in the garage, are covered with pictures that had been clipped out of magazines by Joe Pierce, and over the years glued into an infinitely fascinating collage. Faces of royalty, politicians, movie actors, photos of ships, airplanes, cars, monkeys, strange ceremonies, have a way of reaching out and snagging whomever is passing by. We recognize some of the personalities—Roosevelt, Churchill, de Gaulle, Princess Grace, Clark Gable—and gaze in wonder at the unfamiliar landscapes. They become a vehicle to take us away from the constricting and problem-ridden worlds of school and home. This wallpaper offends our mother's aesthetic sense, however, and she spends her rare free moments patiently soaking and peeling it off.

We long for good bread. A slice of the white toast bread from Loblaws can be rolled between one's thumb and fingers into a hard little ball. The slogan "It's Not Bread, It's McGavins!," printed in bold letters on trucks and billboards around town, becomes a family joke. To assuage the longing, Mother buys Graham flour and on weekends bakes a few moist brown loaves. They are always slightly caved in but that does not detract from the taste. I instinctively understand that like the unorthodox living arrangements in the house, the bread is best kept private, and since I come home for lunch, it's easy to keep it that way for a while.

Since 1966, over twenty single individuals and/or families have lived under the flat roof of Allison Arms at any one time. Multiplied by the building's age, that adds up to a whole village. Like the Turners and the Wojnos, many of the people who move in are making a new beginning, yet each one follows a distinct path. In the '70s, additional businesses appear on 107th Avenue to serve the now more densely populated neighbourhood. Between 111th and 112th Streets: Sky Chief Service Station, Seventh Avenue Car Wash, and a two-floor business building. The appearance of Catholic Social Services, followed by Native Outreach, within a block from Allison Arms reflect the shifts taking place in the area.

The community league, whose membership drops dramatically as the houses give way to apartments, goes into hibernation for over a decade, to wake up to an entirely new set of challenges in the '80s. Eighty-nine per cent of the community's population is listed as living in rental units, and schools are threatened with closure. Homeowners look on with doubt at the apartments; many of the tenants come from virtually every corner of the world, and most don't join the league and attend its functions. They don't hold block parties. *You don't know who they are* is a refrain as old as humanity itself. For most of the newcomers, the language barrier, the lack of hours in days filled with work outside and inside the home, study, the ongoing search for better employment, does not permit extra-curricular activities. There is talk of gangs, and prostitutes have moved in on 107th Avenue, unofficially referred to as the Ho Chi Minh Trail because of the large Vietnamese refugee population in the district. It takes a concerted effort on the part of the league and of organizations such as The Avenue of Nations Business Association, the Seventh Avenue Community Enrichment Project, and the Immigrant Neighbourhoods Community Planning Association to start cleaning up the area. Today, 107th Avenue, called the Avenue of Nations, is so brightly lit that many of the prostitutes have moved on, but the community is still far from becoming the cohesive, influential unit it needs to be to make this a healthy and attractive area.

There is at least one day in the year when representatives of the various groups in the neighbourhood of Allison Arms come together. Every November, St. Joseph High School organizes a ceremony to honour those of its students who went off to fight in WWII. In the centre of the long courtyard, covered with a glass roof, stands the War Memorial containing two plaques with 575 names. On the day of the ceremony, veterans and their families and friends, dressed in their best for the occasion, fill half the courtyard. Facing them, children from the nearby St. Catherine Elementary/Junior High sit cross-legged.

Among the first group, seated in rows of plastic chairs, many remember the 1920s and the '30s. They are mostly descendants of European immigrants—Irish, French, Italian, Ukrainian, Polish, Scandinavian—or are themselves old immigrants. Some have lived in this community all or most of their lives. The second group forms a much more intricate mosaic; every part of the world is represented here. Several of the children don't speak English yet and attend ESL classes offered in their schools. There is a number of aboriginal children.

The high school students crowd along the balconies that ring the courtyard. Dressed carelessly, they look on with poker faces. They come from different parts of the city, and again, many were born in places as diverse as Cambodia, Vietnam, India, Somalia, Columbia, Iran, former Yugoslavia. In a year or three they will be looking for further education, or for work, and an affordable place to live in a community that has access to groceries, health services, child care, recreation programs, green spaces, and a low crime rate. I fervently wish them luck.

City Traffic

POSTOUTPOST

LISA MARTIN-DEMOOR

737

Out my window, black humus,
the skin of the land, peeled back.
Light, enough to see the fallow
fields rich from the moisture this year,
and pale umber patches, torn-up like asphalt;
the ground harvested into the ground.

Late, enough to see the pale blue
haloes of houselight going on
in farmhouses that look like toys: unreal.
What lives threshed out in these kitchens, stories
like mine, too real, landing in this land-
locked city, with its gestures toward creeks,
amnesia of the river that cracks it open

while in Vancouver another plane lands without me
past the scars of Rockies
and crooked shadows of blue
herons like lost fishermen
stabbing the shallows where they last saw the sun.

November 11, 2003
Edmonton, Alberta
bus route #4

outpost, *n.* 1. A post at a distance from the
body of an army; a detachment
placed at a distance from a force, when
halted as a guard against surprise.
Oxford English Dictionary

His overcoat, navy lapel spiked
with a straight pin through the black
heart of a poppy.

He is the only one
on this bus who looks old

enough to remember. His own landmarks
white hair, white skin,
stretched thin and watery
over the dark lines of blue that map

his face. Moments caught in those
veins like barbed wire

that even he doesn't recall.
These days, there aren't many veterans left
from the old wars, so we're manufacturing more.
Edmonton has its share of empty

beds: vigils held around them nightly.
The ironed sheet smoothed with a firm hand.
She still keeps this embassy open, all night
this patch of foreign land

for him to come home to.

Deferrals for the Word "Home"

i.
The outpost of an idea.
That same, colonial moment
made comfortable. You're curled up in moccasins
and mugs of black coffee by the frosted
window that looks back out onto the world.

ii.
This square of land. Your vulnerabilities
drawn back inside its borders, hopes
charted through hallways with stickpins—their coloured knobs
map the degree of drift: here, generosity has lost ground.
Ambition is taking over the bathroom.

iii.
Home is intersubjective, a truth that subsists
among friends, like a private joke.
It rests in a past you've long forgotten.
When your mom calls to say, *It wouldn't be Christmas without you,*
you hear, *We need you to sustain the ruse.*

iv.
So many homes by the time you've grown.
You carry this word outward
into the world, like Sisyphus' rock: when alone
it is the refuge you take. Among strangers,
the fear you feel is the earthquake of its walls.

v.
Home has begun its retreat from you
like God. You don't want to find it.
Deferrals in the heart.
A boundary you can't think past, like nothing.
You know it only by imagining

vi.
absences you couldn't bear.

Band Number 2021-38531

Ovenbird. Male. After hatch year. Wingspan 24 cm. Weight 19.5 g.

Fall migration. The nets at Strathcona Science Park
drooped with the weight of passerines heading south.
Another ovenbird tangled in the net.

We took an aluminum bit. Pliers.
Clamped the braille-small band
around your leg, and let you go.

You flew to the top of a spruce. Looked south along the river.

Then you flew the country,
the skiff of your wings carrying you far
from wintering-down aspen scrub. You fled
the 1200 miles

to Iowa, broke your beak there
on a picture window.

Someone picked your body up.
The number on your leg, a message
in a broken bottle. They phoned the code in:
We've got one of your bands down here.
Ovenbird. Almost made it home.

"City of Champions"

> Love, what is night?
> Is a man thinking in the night the night?
> Is fruit ripening in the night the night?
> —Li-Young Lee

Love, what is this city, surfeited on snow?
Full in the winter months of exhaust that freezes and
falls back to earth. No vents, despite industrial stacks.
Vertical highways for the fumes that go nowhere
and stay there. Where? Away. *There is no Away.*

This is not a city to look around in. Have you ever looked up?
On Whyte Avenue the only thing up is the green peak of the Dominion
Hotel building and occasional windows of second-storey housing
above restaurants and outdoor stores, windows hidden beneath the eaves
at a level the eye usually does not travel.

The skyline is two-dimensional, a trace of a trace.
Outskirts disintegrate, going up in smoke
stacks, dispersing among the dormant
seeds of grasses that follow the Yellowhead east.

Is it only a gathering, this city? Reference points
that transmogrify the landscape? Is it a dream—this city,
that subsists between us—from which some wake hungry
holding their mittened fingers out for change?

The river runs past us—wearing the debris of snow, in spring.
It pushes ice up its banks with a terrible weight
rips roots from the ground, demolishes bridges,
washes out the footpaths that steal through
the valley like varicose veins.

Can it tell us a story? This river?
What will it contain when it is through with us—
outfalls along the highways leading away
from town, and the "Welcome to Edmonton"
signs, all rubbed out in a sudden flood.

A flat town, no Sinai. Just a prairie, refuse for building with.
Love, in the dream you and I meet in the outskirts.
Is this city ours? Are the letters used in the sign, the sign?
Love, the grooves in the wet wood are familiar.
My fingers find 'Map;' The rest, 'Scion.'

City Traffic

> outpost, *n.* 2. A trading settlement situated near a frontier
> or at a remote place in order to facilitate
> the commercial contacts of a larger and more
> centrally situated town or settlement.
> Also, by extension,
> any of various other kinds of remote settlements. . . .
> *Oxford English Dictionary*

Jasper Ave ushers you past AM congregations that squat
all week on Mustard Seed steps. Higher than McCauley's
streets. You cleave the river, split the difference.

Meanwhile McCauley is packed with people.
Labour Day. The Union is theirs.
Though the man with the BBQ and bullhorn
may not know their names. He screams like he does.

Across the street, the Italian grocery sells me Jarlsberg
while rally-goers wander past: they don't look
like they're one day off work. They're wearing frayed
nylon coats, fumbling through for the free
food, and skin is the colour of their land.

You can drive away without witnessing
the crowds disperse, or crumpled papers
litter the lawn. That empty park
a sanctuary, after the others close.

There is more traffic here
now that this century's imploded
along the banks of their river.

**Edmonton, Directions
to East of Centre**

To Experience Downtown, one day you should
get lost in the Arts District on foot,
trip out the wrong doors
of Canada Place, or pause in humid Citadel
gardens to ask the man asleep
on his tropical bench to leave.

Then you could follow him east
to the edge of Chinatown where he is more
at home in neighbourhoods of closed shops,
abandoned facades in logographs
you can't read.

Let your metered time expire here.
Pawn your watch in one of these shops.
Do not be afraid for your safety.
Trust only the soles of your feet.

Deferrals of "Homelessness"

> **outpost,** *n.* 3. The furthest territory of an Empire,
> especially in the phrase, outpost of Empire,
> now occasionally used in a nostalgic or ironic sense.
> *Oxford English Dictionary*

Home is the first premise of the city,
the New Empire, whose furthest territory
is this fission of the human heart:
the other side of the coin—to be without
a home. Enter the Alberta Advantage—
its subzero climate. That's how Premier Klein
does it. He's a man of refined, Northern sensibilities.
That's why he promised all of the homeless among us
not Peace, Land, or Bread, like our circumpolar neighbour,
but bus tickets to Vancouver.

Still, he is not the only one among us to use
this tried and true solution—if you don't like
the problems in the Old World,
send them into the New.

Postscript

Outposts: dendrites that lead nowhere.
Postsynaptic axons. One body, postdiluvian,
discovers it is its only survivor. Post-trauma.

Posts: outranked, outsourced. Spine
without limbs, postaxial. And on the outskirts,
everything else: outsiders, outcasts; outbred.

Posthypnotic postlude. An outcrop to posterity.
The outfall postponed until the blackout.
No, white-out. Post-consonantal silence.

BRIBING THE BOUNDARY GOD:
EDMONTON'S MYTHIC PROGRESS

ERIN KNIGHT

In nature, the new is mythic, because its potential is not yet realized;
in consciousness, the old is mythic, because its desires never were fulfilled.
—Susan Buck-Morss, *Dialectics of Seeing*

it's only by our lack of ghosts we're haunted
—Earle Birney, "Can. Lit."

prelude to a city

The first of the upturned stones, city
marker. The airport shuttle, Yellow cab & Remus's
wife's minivan carry visitors through the swollen Gateway;
they've heard that from the Edmonton International
you can see the curve of the earth.
A heeled rumour commutes Highway 2, merges
between CKUA's pledge drive and the insulated furnace
of Ed's new Explorer in the frosted AM rush: a theatre
with screens that'll be as wide as the prairies,
seats like La-Z-Boy recliners, a royal
blue fortress borne by the flexed tricep of that empty
field off Ellerslie (it's true—those seats will be to die for).

I. Disorientation
leges sacratae & Cineplex Odeon

memo: invite Terminus for ~~coffee~~ cocktails: La Ronde,
        sunset, seduce him with city light vista, the revolution
        of a celestial eye respectfully wait
        until dessert

You see, they say, *we know how to house the universe
in reels of film, projected light, it's all in the flickering
of images only, slightly, infinitely doubled the way visuals
are transmitted (the focal centre) wouldn't you want
to be guardian of that?* Terminus adjusts his tie, the light
catches the diamond filigree of his watch (Eros gems,
straight from the Canadian Arctic) Terminus
folds his hands about his distinguished paunch
(*And how was your filet mignon, sir, rare
enough for you?* asks the well-tucked waiter
*Yes certainly, nothing like Alberta AAA) and what about
the leges sacratae* says Terminus, but it's all
for show, he's been bought before: *Yes well ahem*
—the couched whisper—*and what if I told you
we'd found a way around it, that divinely troublesome
earth land & sky contract, yes.* One of them pushes a blueprint
across the table, *but see: we've designed
our own set of stars.*

meanwhile

Thera mother of cities finishes her shift at the Stanley Milner
turns her key in the lock behind her and shudders
through the turnstile teeth at the mouth of Churchill
station. She sits on the cold stone cube and opens her book.
Thera, says a voice behind her, sluice hiss, *you're looking ravishing,
going home to dine alone I suppose. Pity.*
Shut up Hades says Thera, trying not to think
about the etymology [to ravish], *in fact
I am on my way out to dinner and am rather late
I'd appreciate it if you left me alone thank-you.* Hades smiles.
He curdles down the platform. This time
Thera hasn't even lied; it was in her e-mail this morning:

> To: thera@mundus.net
> From: terminus@shaw.ca
> Cc:
> Re: formalities
>
> Thera:
> Happy hour meeting with board tonight
> Sorry I haven't called, very busy lately—
> Request your presence (legalities, I know)
> La Ronde at 5.   PS Janus still
> acting hostile any suggestions
>   Yours, Terminus

Thera has read about operations
for short-sightedness with a laser on your cornea, they freeze you
with a derivative of cocaine and yet
it doesn't always take, meanwhile on they go
slicing away. This is how she felt in front of her computer
this morning, the cursor blazing into her eye.
The impersonality, formality, and then of course
the anachronism 'yours' when in reality—

(Thera harbours a leaner memory of Terminus)
and Janus, Oh—
Thera mother of cities hopes her LRT train arrives shortly.
She'd like to have time to shower, revitalize
herself: lately she's been feeling so dour.

the trouble with two heads

Janus has a hangover. Janus
wonders vaguely what the point is
waking up each new year to a singed headache
and the contradictory desires: to go for fried eggs
or else throw up. Janus pours a glass of orange juice.
The obnoxious red light of his father's answering machine
mimics the twitching muscle behind Janus's second left eye.
>   *Janus honey it's your mother*
>   *I haven't heard from you for a while*
>   *how's your asthma I—*

Janus presses 1-to-erase-this-message
thank-you-from-Telus. He looks out the window.
Years ago Terminus bought him a swing set.
Weekends at his father's Janus's asthma acted up.
The unreined wind gathered free dust
from the newly zoned lots next door, so instead
Janus got a Nintendo and a ventilin inhaler.
On the fridge Janus finds:
>   J—
>   *Important* meeting this PM (i.e. presentable pls.)
>   La Ronde, nice if you could come (taxi? $60
>   on table) if not there's Pizza Pops
>   Dad

Janus cuts a corner off the note and folds a small square.
He sits on a bar stool at the island (open concept), his elbows
on the black marble counter and rolls a joint.

II. Boredom
these great streets exhale boredom

The napkin on Terminus's lap is stained
with spots of watery blood. He's surprised
at his embarrassment; it wasn't long ago
that sacrifice was hardly so delicate.
Terminus can we get you another Manhattan?
Terminus looks across the table with bloodshot eyes.
They're still talking about the Cineplex, the multiplex,
the googolplex; two million square feet of retail space.
Yes from time to time we may have a foreign film
but you know what's really getting popular, those epic
trilogies, streamlined Jungian allegory etc.
we've got the inside scoop. For a long while now
Terminus has been enduring
small speeding cars tearing along his prone spine
at midnight, he's had enough of Ellerslie,
its black solitude, the outskirts could use a little floodlight.
It's just a modernized boundary rite Dad, said Janus
about the racing, when he still spoke to Terminus
in full sentences, but lately Terminus has been considering
renewing his appreciation for ancient ritual.
What about my son, he says, *he's getting older now*
maybe deserves some recognition.
Why certainly; we call it the Gateway Underpass.

the collective sleep

Thera's hair leaves a veined oil fringe
on the dim windowpane of the LRT train. Eavesdropped
strains buckle under the cement guns of the runners.
Thera watches the grey walls slip past her ear.
She reads the back of a red-toque's newspaper:
Klein to Discuss For-Profit Health Care
Thera sighs. That man's manipulated the oracle again,
wealth over health, she suspects
she'll be getting a weepy collect call from Delphi soon.
A woman across from her narrates
Thera's waking dream . . . *down in Calgary, they say those clusters*
of suburbs will reach the Rockies one day . . .
Suddenly Thera opens her eyes.
Dead yellow and evergreen frost
rising over the river—*damn*—thinks Thera,
I've missed my stop.

cast your own shadow at the sixth hour

Winter is sweating already. Janus stands
and stands at the bus stop. His jacket is open and
large gaps of chinook pocket under his arms.
All his ears are cold.
He watches several magpies assess his cat.
A dovetail fold of geese passes baying over the unset
moon-ghost. Janus shudders at this criss-crossed portent
(his nausea renewed) *what month is this?* he thinks.
Janus, Terminus had said after an early annex,
in this city right fortune can follow
sinister designs. After that Janus parcelled any latent pater-worship
and neatly chucked it into south Mill Creek.
Once Janus wrote a letter to the mayor:
          Mayor Jan, what about the prairie dogs
          who were there before Mill Woods Town Centre
          don't you think there should be a relocation
          program, maybe development restrictions

Janus cried himself to sleep
thinking about the First Furrow, the collapsing
tunnels and overall prairie-dog panic. *It's like Moses*
said his mother, rubbing his back, *they relocate, a whole parade*
it's called diaspora D-I-A-S- . . .
Janus believed her for about a day.
Janus spits synchronized lugies onto his shadow, he wishes
the goddam bus would come.

III. Guilt
the town's foundations carry the burden of guilt

Terminus listens to his own wheeze.
He belabours over the dessert menu and tries
to ignore the vacuum pressure of the two empty seats
beside him. For the moment he is backlit
by the sunset like a sinus headache.
What about traffic? he manages to ask.
Traffic? What? They are genuinely surprised. Terminus
has never shown even relative resistance. *Alberta
is the shining star of the economy we expect that to translate
to the cash register.* Terminus falters.
He was once quite fascinated by translation theory
yet he finds he is inexplicably saddened
by their seizure of the stars. Terminus shakes himself.
One should always be wary of reifying metaphor.

a river to follow the axis of sky

Thera examines the rounded bulb of her face
in the stairwell mirror. She leans
against pebbled drywall that is clouded
with a dubious stain. Thera
is generally quite adept at getting through the day: crisp baguettes
and the small racket of coffee-shop meetings
momentarily consume the blanket loneliness
that begins to smooth over her skin around four o'clock.
She's glad this rendezvous with Terminus
is at an hour still sufficient with detour, on the cusp
of the work-a-day traffic. *Thera*, she hears whispered
(she'd forgotten about Hades). She hurries upstairs
to break the surface. Thera wonders about these months:
she seems to be walking always into the slant
of the setting sun. Thera gets free transit
(during business hours) but instead
she garners the dusk, paces the High Level Bridge:
a truth lost long ages ago may be sought with confidence
in the thousand years yet to come.
Sometimes Thera disbelieves this river.

the quartered body

We are now accustomed to give the name of 'Common' to
a tract of uncultivated waste land alone, but at a comparatively
recent period the name . . . still continued to be applied `
to fields, pastures, meadows . . .
—E. W. Robertson, 1872. (*OED*).

Janus inhales sharp corners of air he
pounds up the stairs tiny fibres
in his quads tearing releasing
heat. Some people believe that visions
of the future would be like carefully packaged gifts
tied in a silver ribbon they could touch to their cheeks.
Janus slips once, hauls on the slivered wooden railing;
ice climbs the stairs up McDougall Hill.
The small pouches of his bronchi tighten.
Future is not always wrapped in brown paper
packages in fact today it was served to Janus
on the edge of a knife, the edge of a city. Janus inhales, the knife
is poised along his left windpipe. Janus looks up
at the tall buildings, hundreds of winking eyes
square stars he tries to orient himself each time
he blinks he sees beige monoliths an orthographic
maze at the mouth of the city a bitter taste—
the riddle setting monster Janus
pushes through the doors of one particular highrise,
collapses in front of the elevators not dying
just triangulating his lungs: breathe.

IV. Banishment
catacomb fairies

Terminus wanders the new dark.
He has never felt quite so small. He's always found the city centre
pretty viscerally disorienting but at least
he knows exactly what he'll say to her.
Terminus wouldn't you like a ride home? they had said,
grins like grinches as they capped the heavy pen. Terminus
rested his temples momentarily on the soft tips of his fingers
I'll be fine, meanwhile feeling mildly queasy in the navy lighting.
(His doctor had warned him about cholesterol.)
Terminus stood in the concrete bowels of the parkade.
There was an echo like an empty body around the corner,
sullen false light and expensive cars. A particularly sweet dose
of panic was fed to Terminus on a spoon he passed
a hand over his eyes he couldn't find his car
anywhere. Terminus reached out for a crooked girder,
bracing, he shouldn't have been driving anyway so
he came to the cold surface and now wanders the new dark.
Suddenly the slick aftertaste of his Manhattan speaks
a smooth caress at the back of his throat it says:
Thera. He already feels
the thick mass of Thera's anger. *What do you mean
you agreed to the power centre? (Power Common,* he would protest)
You revolve around power she will say,
*power-bars power-suits power-plays
power-centres, haven't you got enough?*
She should hear it from me first, Terminus himself says;
the Manhattan ghostie croons in his throat again:
Thera.
Terminus repeats this to himself as he mounts the grey stairs
(he despises elevators, cubic enclosures make him feel
inadequate) he rests his head on his knees
after the eighth flight, continues
his incantation: *Thera this thing of darkness I
acknowledge mine this thing of darkness I acknowledge
mine.*

V. (En) Compass
limitatio

Janus lies underneath the lintel.
He has slept here before, sometimes all he needs
is a certain proximity. Terminus escapes the stairwell
of Thera's apartment and stumbles over his son.
Jesus Janus what are you doing here? Janus
looks small and crooked (he is folded
in an awkward fashion). His eyes open
through the fog of their cotton sleep.
I was waiting for my mother I guess I forgot
my key. Terminus says nothing.
He sits in the dim hallway beside Janus. He puts his hand
in the hair of one of Janus's heads.
Tonight guardians of a smaller post.

find an unobstructed view of the horizon

Of course Thera meant to go to the dinner
but things have a habit of coming up. Nervously
Thera changes lanes. She's never been
a confident driver, doesn't even have insurance but the city
lights shine so brightly it isn't often
she gets the chance to see the northern.
Thera grips the steering wheel and continues
her discussion with an imaginary Terminus:
furthermore the arteries of mundus and terminus
can't flow in isolation, also my dear
you have BBQ sauce on your chin.
Imaginary Terminus replies *Thera, I've been sprawling*
without you I am one single catastrophe forgive me.
She crosses the unguarded threshold slams the breaks
and stops along the shoulder of the waning Calgary Trail.
Thera turns towards the tiny square stars of her cityscape.
The sky swells green and mauve with northern bruises.
Imaginary Terminus says *this is where I live*
beautiful & lonely & large, Thera: this
is how I can believe it doesn't end
Thera mother of cities is used to a vertical horizon,
she hears only an aurora silence.

keys to the city   (the augur's epilogue)

The augur's act in drawing his diagram on the ground changed the earth he
touched from anywhere to this unique and only place . . .
—Joseph Rykwert

We want to know how to translate wolves.
How to map fluid borders onto the muscled plain.
Remus never believed in fortifying walls,
instead: feel for the ridge
of a tendon. An elastic tension
in the adolescent ligaments, the city's
long-legged sinew. Hold your hands
around the taut boundary strings, cat's cradle
and rope burn. Lift the tangled mesh:
there is a city under there.
Acknowledge it yours.

Love thou thy land, with love far-brought
From out the storied past
—Tennyson

Family Recreation Centre, Rundle Park

LOST PLANS AND PURPOSE FOUND:
THE STORY OF RUNDLE PARK

SCOTT DAVIES

Often described as one of Edmonton's best-kept secrets, Rundle Park has many secrets of its own. Back in the 1960s, city officials began to look seriously at the possibility of developing a park in the area south of the Rundle Heights neighbourhood, and in 1969 a grand plan was presented to city council. As it was conceived, the creation of Rundle Park would eliminate the deficiencies of the park system while introducing new, imaginative recreation concepts to the citizens of Edmonton. It would be nine long years before the park opened, and when it did, it lacked many of the amenities and attractions originally planned for the site. Yet, in spite of what seemed to be missing, Rundle Park was clearly a successful project, becoming an essential element of Edmonton's park system. This, then, is the story of a city park designed with forward-thinking vision, built with its community in mind, and programmed to flourish in the spirit of providing quality, one-of-a-kind recreation experiences for all.

On 28 January 1969, an *Edmonton Journal* article by Guy DeMarino announced that plans for a "major, new park . . . which could rival Copenhagen's famed Tivoli area" had been presented to city council the previous day. DeMarino's words paint a beautiful picture of the construction of Rundle Park, which meant "the disappearance of the Beverly dump under a mantle of grass, trees, and recreational buildings." The park would fulfill a dual role, with accommodation for both district-level sports facilities and city-level attractions. As a major city park, its location was perfectly balanced with the popular Mayfair (today's Hawrelak) Park, though the site itself did present some concerns. For one, it was startlingly close to refinery row and set, in part, atop the Beverly garbage dump. Planners felt that the odours of the garbage dump were of greater concern than the odours of the refineries, and that the odours would become irrelevant with the closure of the dump. Another problem presented by the proposed location was that it did not have obvious access points, though this was to be addressed by extending Ada Boulevard into the park and providing a neighbourhood entrance at 111th Avenue.

Planners divided the Rundle Park site into three. It was recommended that the highest ground be used for a golf course, as its construction and use would be unlikely to disturb the soon-to-be-covered landfill in that area. The grasslands further south in the park were suggested as a site for the other district sports facilities, with plans calling for a pool, tennis courts, an arena, a track, a wading pool, change facilities, and a restaurant. On the lowest ground, closest to the river, plans called for the development of an area with unique opportunities for structured family activities, a concept the Rundle Park Master Plan refers to as "a new kind of family experience." A fascinating array of facilities was planned here:

- a problem-solving area, consisting of games, tasks, and an illusion course
- creative play structures, like "build-your-own-environment" and "old fort" play sets
- the use of an old mine to have a children's sand pit and crane operation
- mini-car riding and driving courses
- a theatre for educational films and children's movies, concerts, and shows
- a model boat basin
- a log flume ride
- a Teen Centre for singing, theatre, drama, games, and a discotheque
- an Adult Centre, with a giant checkers game and meeting rooms
- "the old lighthouse" and "Swiss Family Robinson Tree" play structures
- a fire engine ride
- a pony ride

- the Geological Interpretive Centre
- a train, with tunnels
- a cable car to what would eventually be Gold Bar Park
- a self-propelled boat ride
- a Rondvaart boat ride
- a restaurant and concession
- an information booth
- a small marina
- horticultural displays and water features.

Developed with the needs of the entire city in mind, this all-inclusive "family recreation area" would be accessed by the Ada Boulevard entrance and joined to the sports facilities and the rest of the park only by the train ride. The varied terrain here and in other park areas also offered possibilities for year-round programming including tobogganing, skiing, skating, snowshoeing, snowmobiling, and sleigh rides. The total estimated cost of developing Rundle Park over a ten to fifteen year period was 6.7 million dollars, an extravagant price today, let alone in 1969! But at the time, Edmonton was still in the process of finding its identity and taking shape as a major city— a facility like Rundle Park was surely justifiable.

In spite of these exciting plans, it took some time to get construction going in Rundle Park to the point that the public was confident it would be finished. Covering of the landfill began in 1969 and took two years to complete. The first stage of construction began in 1971, as the city started spending relatively small amounts of money on the park. As the need for district parks and recreation facilities increased, the Beverly-Rundle Heights Action Committee began lobbying the city for increased funding and community involvement in the long-range planning of the park, which was perceived to be of low overall priority. In the early 1970s, Rundle Park was, indeed, little more than some rough trails and distant dreams, but by 1974, some progress could be seen. Part of the main road was established, with the drop-off circle and two parking lots for the sports facilities under construction, along with the tennis courts and some playing fields.

Rundle Park, as envisioned by its original planners, was starting to take shape.

Part of the reason for the increased construction in Rundle Park is attributable to the Capital City Recreation Park (CCRP) project. The provincial government partnered with the City of Edmonton to conceive the plan, which was announced on 26 April 1974. The project involved spending 30 to 35 million dollars from the Alberta Heritage Trust Fund on creating a unified, comprehensive park system between the High Level and Beverly Bridges. The CCRP plan included the adoption of the concepts presented in the Rundle Park Master Plan, which had already guided development since 1969. One of the new (and ultimately notorious) ideas brought forth by the CCRP plan was to install a weir on the North Saskatchewan River. It was to be primarily accessible from within Rundle Park, and was intended to make the river safer for city-sanctioned boating, fishing, canoeing, and other activities. There was great concern among both experts and everyday citizens that the seven million dollar weir would create a toxic "cesspool" and possibly even erode the banks of the river itself. By November of 1975, the weir idea had been scrapped, and planners began shifting the emphasis on water-based recreation to the interconnected lakes planned for Rundle Park. Some were uncertain about "digging a lake out of garbage," but it was made clear that these would be built in the lower regions of the park, where gravel pits had previously operated.

Further development was influenced by plans for a one-of-a-kind facility to be located in Rundle Park. Late in 1974, the Associated Canadian Travellers (ACT) organization announced its intention to build a facility aimed at providing recreational opportunities equally accessible to persons with and without physical disabilities. If the city were to donate the land, ACT would then put up the money to construct the facility. Plans were unveiled on 30 January 1975 and involved three phases of construction, all of which would dramatically shape the development of Rundle Park. Each phase would be paid for using money from yearly star-studded teleramas. Construction of the first phase began that September, and saw the creation of an arts and crafts space, a library, a small greenhouse, a reception area, and a cafeteria. The second phase, started in the following year, included the facility's gymnasium. The third phase, an accessible swimming pool, was added several years later. By siting the facility close to the proposed family recreation area, and by including a pool in the plans, the shape of Rundle Park and its developments changed significantly. The road leading to the sports complex was extended deeper into the park than originally planned, effectively eliminating the need for the undesirable Ada Boulevard entrance and the train connection. Furthermore, the swimming pool originally planned for the sports complex became unnecessary. These changes were merely cosmetic, however, since the idea of the ACT centre fit in perfectly with the creative, inclusive recreation philosophy of the original plans for Rundle Park.

As park development pushed forward, guided by the CCRP plan and under the influence of the ACT project, community concerns began to surface in the newspapers. In 1976 a bid to stop construction on the parking lots was launched. Residents were worried that the park would draw thousands of people into the neighbourhood daily, and that the roads and parking areas were going to be too close to their houses. One resident was especially concerned about the "carnival atmosphere" that would be created by the midway rides and lake activities. A city commissioner responded that only three or four rides were planned and were still awaiting council approval. The community later presented its concerns formally to city council, leading to the removal of one leg of the park road and further landscaping of the parking lots. Otherwise, councillors "refused to downgrade the park" by adopting the other requested changes, suggesting that a reduction in parking and attractions would hurt the city as a whole. Further changes desired by the community included the relocation of the maintenance yard and removal of the rides, and though these changes were initially rejected, the community would ultimately see these wishes fulfilled.

Despite these protests, ACT construction was on schedule and the Rundle Park Golf Course was quietly nearing completion. It was opened with little fanfare on 25 June 1976, as a nine-hole course, with the back nine under construction. The first phase of the ACT Recreation Centre officially opened on 9 January 1977, with great optimism. Playing fields, tennis courts, dressing rooms, ponds, and roadways would soon be completed, with construction beginning on the other buildings. Among these was the Family Recreation Centre, designed to provide space for skate-changing, kite and model boat-building, storage, and ticket booths. The building was celebrated as being more than double the size of the pavilion in Hawrelak Park. The lake outside the centre was flooded in the fall of 1977 for its first use as a skating pond, with visions of canoeists on the same lake the next summer. The Geological Interpretive Centre, designed to preserve and promote the geological features of the river valley, was under construction in the building that later became the Trail House. Bridges linking Gold Bar Park and Strathcona Science Park were nearing completion, and with a grand opening scheduled for July 1978, excitement about Rundle Park was growing. Yet, compared with the original plans for the park, much seemed to be missing from the almost-finished product. There was no pool (yet), no arena, no running track, no wading pool, and the family recreation area was lacking just about everything that had been planned for it. The Family Recreation Centre under construction only warranted a few lines of description in the newspapers of the day. On the eve of Rundle Park finally opening, what would the public think of how the park turned out?

◆◆◆◆

On 9 July 1978, the entire Capital City Recreation Park system was officially opened with a massive all-day celebration, culminating in a spectacular fireworks display spanning the entire CCRP area. Rundle Park, with its golf course, seven ponds, sports fields, trail system, geology centre, and more, instantly provided the most complete park experience in the city of Edmonton. The ACT Centre featured a craft room, library, plant room, cafeteria, social room, banquet room, lounge, and gymnasium. Complementing it was the Family Recreation Centre, featuring a park office, first-aid services, a snack bar, lockers, a firepit, and various recreation equipment rentals, including skate rentals and sharpening in the winter. The park was a success. A reported 8,355 people rented paddleboats in July and August of that year, and around two thousand people converged on the park every Sunday. Park officials expected this number to grow as people found out about the variety of services available in the park.

Following newspaper articles of this time, it becomes clear that, even though Rundle Park lacked many of the facilities described by the original plan, the philosophy of providing unique recreation opportunities was indeed fulfilled by the programming of the two recreation centres. For instance, a snow-fort playground was created in the park and used daily by school and community groups. Other winter activities included a cross-country skiing program launched by the Family Recreation Centre and a sledge hockey workshop organized by the ACT Centre. The ACT Centre also offered courses in pottery, ceramics, cross-country skiing for the disabled, sign language, astronomy, and much more. In the summer, the Family Recreation Centre had the power to transform an ordinary picnic by renting out earthballs, parachutes, tug-of-war ropes, gunny sacks, Frisbees, and balls, all at minimal cost. The centre also rented out rollerskates, paddleboats, and canoes for use in the park, and river raft trips were organized regularly. Other park developments included the wheelchair-accessible playground behind the ACT Centre, an outdoor minigolf course (which opened in 1987), and a lake dedicated to remote-control model boats (something from the original plan). For more than a decade, Rundle Park and its facilities provided countless important and popular services to its community and to the city of Edmonton as a whole. Some of the many events held in the versatile park over the years have included the Women's Cultural Harvest Festival, CHED's Bicycle Picnic, Muk Luk Mardi Gras, a ski swap, an Edmonton Opera production, the Penny Picnic, the Learn to Golf Tournament, Cub-A-Ree, Spring Awakening: A Tribute to Moms, boomerang clinics, sleigh rides, New Year's Eve celebrations, and the AMA School Patrol Picnics.

Most of the Rundle Park story is upbeat, but some darker subjects bear mention here. For instance, given the fact that the park is near refinery row and that part of it is built over an old dump, pollution has long been a concern. Today, the most obvious sign of the old dump is the park road, which shifts and sinks dramatically with every spring thaw. In fact, Edmonton Transit concluded in 1981 that regular bus service of the park would not be possible, limiting access for many people. In 1990 concerns were raised over apparent seepage from the dump (the moisture was later determined to be groundwater). Besides pollution concerns, there has always been concern over vandalism, which has occurred regularly over the life of the park. Some of the earliest instances of vandalism occurred throughout the Capital City Recreation Park area just months before it was completed. Damaged light fixtures and handrails on the bridges and immobilized construction equipment cost tens of thousands of dollars to repair. The darkest story Rundle Park has to tell happened in 1980, when a helicopter used for distributing fertilizer had a mechanical failure and its rotor decapitated one park worker and crushed another, breaking the leg of a third person. Many Edmontonians can recall this horrifying accident.

What has affected Rundle Park more than anything else, however, is the cessation of Family Recreation Centre services and staffing around 1998. Lacking the recreation opportunities and park presence once provided by the centre, the public's experience of Rundle Park has suffered. There seems to have been a shift from drop-in park visitors to those who come only for certain paid activities, like swimming or minigolf, and then leave. The Family Recreation Centre, on the other hand, attracted people such as seniors who enjoyed coffee and a walk in the park, or teens who needed something to do. Having staff in the park at most hours of the day also provided an informal policing of the park, and it is harder now to prevent vandalism. Most of all, with the Family Recreation Centre sitting mostly vacant, the park lacks a focus, though the ACT Centre has worked hard to fill the void. There continues to be a significant demand for the services once offered by the centre. As some of the only regular onsite staff, workers renting paddleboats and running the minigolf course are relied upon to assist the general public, often beyond their abilities.

Still, today's Rundle Park has found other ways to meet many needs of the community and the city, while continuing to provide unique recreation opportunities. The disc golf course, for instance, is the only one of its kind in Edmonton, and has broad appeal. The accessible ACT pool is also unmatched, and continues to provide an extremely valuable service. In the winter, the shinny pond is always busy, and the baseball programs enjoy great success all summer long. The new Paddling Centre is beginning to open doors for many clubs and interested citizens. In sum, there is still more to do in Rundle Park than anywhere else. But what remains of the imagined Rundle Park of 1969? There is a landfill nestled safely under a charming golf course, a grassy expanse turned into a sports facility for the community to enjoy, and inviting facilities and spaces developed for people from all walks of life to enjoy together in spirited recreation.

Thus, while most of the amenities and attractions described by those early plans never materialized, what did materialize was a park built by taking into account the needs of the community, the city, and society at large. Many of the community's concerns were addressed in the final product of Rundle Park. Had it opened with its amusement park rides and attractions, planners would have frustrated and alienated the community that Rundle Park was very much designed to serve. The city as a whole also had needs, and by finding ways to compromise and still provide ample facilities, parking, and open space, planners allowed for Rundle Park to become a significant Edmonton attraction. Most importantly, by introducing creative recreation concepts at the Family Recreation Centre, and by integrating those with physical disabilities at the ACT Recreation Centre, Rundle Park has produced significant benefits for society as a whole. Though the powers of the Family Centre have been diffused, the memories and inspiration undoubtedly remain in those who benefited from its services. Today, Rundle Park remains relevant in new and old ways. Perhaps it is the spirit of the original plans and intended purpose of the park that will continue to guide positive future development for Rundle Park.

Restoring the Mural

MURAL ON CONTRETE: DIGNITY UNVEILED

CHERYL MAHAFFY

"Since 1983, a total of 23 Edmonton women have been found murdered.
All are described by police as being prostitutes or having high-risk lifestyles
and only five of the cases have been solved."
—Justin Thompson, CBC *News Online, 8 April 2005*

A strong, determined Aboriginal woman gazes clear-eyed from the centre of a mural standing sentinel at Alex Taylor School, 9321 Jasper Avenue. Unveiled 28 January 2004, this addition to Edmonton's expanding array of art in public places is a work whose journey echoes the two-steps-forward, one-back reality of life in the inner city.

The vibrant seven by eleven foot painting began life a decade earlier, indoors, created by Eugene Demas to help transform a notorious drug den known as the Fortress into Kindred House, a drop-in centre for women and transgendered individuals in prostitution. Painted directly onto fortified concrete walls, its blanket-like zigzag border opening to an expansive backdrop of mountain and star-studded sky, the mural infused a measure of beauty and hope into what had been a place of evil.

The mural is one of three the artist painted inside the house on 103rd Avenue near 96th Street between December 1994 and January 1995, as work experience for a YMCA employment program. A woman in joyful dance, now mounted in the foyer of Alex Taylor School, was painted on drywall in an upstairs room. The third mural, a simpler portrait of a young woman, was painted on concrete in the stairwell.

A quiet, unassuming Lakota Sioux from Manitoba, Eugene Demas gained local notice when he joined three other artists in painting murals for the Bissell drop-in centre at 10527 – 96th Street. His work, *The Guardian,* sets a Sioux warrior on a cliff watching out for his tribe, backed by rich turquoise. Displays followed at such venues as Orange Hall in Old Strathcona. As he worked on the Kindred House murals, the artist expressed hope that those using the drop-in would gain life-changing courage from living with his art, just as he was trying to do in creating it.

Twin Fortress: Evicting Evil

For those who knew the Fortress in its darkest days, the events surrounding the mural's birth and rebirth involve redemption far too long in the coming.

"It was an evil place," says Dawn Hodgins, a survivor of prostitution who ventured inside the steel-reinforced concrete walls and bullet-proofed, steel-barred windows for drugs when other sources failed to come through. "For me, it was almost like a defeat to go there." Indeed, the loop of reality clips that finally shocked Hodgins out of her downward spiral includes at least one scene from the Fortress: a mother shooting up while her children played with used needles on the filthy floor.

Nor were the Twin Fortresses alone in causing community angst as the '80s marched into the '90s, a time when prostitution and drug dens were rampant in the neighbourhoods of Boyle Street and McCauley. "Everyone knew what was happening but seemed powerless in the face of this evil," recalls Kate Quinn, who hated the fact that needles and condoms littered the streets where her two young boys should be free to play.

Neighbours banded together, seeking solutions, encouraged by grassroots facilitators such as Ed Laboucane. Initiatives such as Communities for Controlled (later renamed Changing) Prostitution earned media attention, then municipal action through such venues as a multi-department Safe Housing Committee and an Action Group on Prostitution chaired by then-Mayor Jan Reimer. Partnering with housing, fire, and health officials, a police task force shut down nearly two dozen drug houses. But the heavily fortified Fortress and its next-door twin, connected by an underground tunnel through which drugs could be passed to avoid detection, defied numerous raids. "By the time we came in through the roof using a chainsaw on a fire crane, all the drugs were disposed of," recalls Dean Boyer, who led the task force.

One of the Twin Fortress houses burned down in 1991, but the second remained open until fall 1993, when tactics ranging from cutting off power to bylaw enforcement of a too-big back porch closed its doors. "The City was trying to be creative and apply any tool it could," Quinn recalls. "It takes everyone working together from different angles to create solutions for tough problems."

As a city whose drug houses were the most fortified and the most persistently battled, Edmonton attracted inquiries from across the country, adds Quinn, who sat on a panel arranged by then-MP Judy Bethel to inform legislation. "Edmonton's unique experience had a national impact through the creation of a legal tool to prevent the fortification of drug houses."

Kindred House: Reclaiming the Space

The Fortress closure in 1993 came just as the Edmonton Social Planning Council began shaping its response to an on-the-street survey funded by Health Canada's National Drug Strategy that indicated people mired in prostitution needed a place of refuge and safety. Communities for Changing Prostitution suggested the empty drug den be claimed for that purpose, and Kindred House was born.

Transforming the dark, splattered hellhole into a welcoming space took immense energy. Kate Quinn recalls walking in one day to find Centre Coordinator Sandi Morrison deeply discouraged, wielding a broom that made barely a dent in the mess. Several phone calls later, neighbours were out in force, equipped with chili and buns, scrub brushes and paint. Just as Eugene Demas worked miracles on the interior, Rick Jones, a construction worker who'd begun Action Against Johns, painted the exterior green—for hope.

Overcoming initial skepticism among clients made cynical by the streets, Kindred House became a place of rest, healing, and camaraderie. Clients began dropping by, surprised to find they didn't need to pretend they were leaving the street to be treated as humans with soul. "We had lots and lots of room. The basement we used for laundry, we could go upstairs to sleep, and in the attic was a clothing trading place," says Tammy, a daily visitor who fondly recalls the larger-than-life murals as a welcoming backdrop. At the suggestion of Sister Marion Garneau of Edmonton's Inner City Pastoral Ministry, a member of the Sisters of Charity of the Immaculate Conception whose steady presence proved the centre's lifeline, clients formed a council to guide what happened in the house and wrote proposals to obtain tools such as computers and a backyard barbecue.

With the Social Planning Council's seed money for the project due to run out, the Boyle McCauley Health Centre agreed to take Kindred House under its wing in 1995. The match provides a way to reach a population whose well-being had been nobody's business, says Colleen Novotny, now coordinator of internal operations.

Within three years, however, property owners evicted the drop-in centre to make way for a rooming house, raising the spectre of a return to earlier habits on that inner city avenue. Forced out of the Fortress in August 1997, Kindred House spent five months shoehorned into the toe of the Women's Emergency Accommodation Centre on Jasper Avenue, where close quarters and shared bathrooms made transgendered individuals feel particularly out of place. Finally, a small suite was found above a Jasper Avenue tattoo parlour. Again it's a haven of support—physical, legal, medical, and especially emotional.

Crossroads Duplex: From Fortress to Hope

After sitting empty for four years, the Fortress and a related lot next door came up for sale, amid growing realization that lack of safe, affordable, supportive housing is a key barrier keeping people from exiting the streets. Addressing that reality became a priority in Edmonton's first Community Plan on Homelessness, setting the stage for Edmonton City Centre Church Corporation to purchase the lots in 2001 for transitional housing. Unwilling to harbour ghosts of a bleak past, ECCCC demolished the Fortress to make way for the Crossroads Duplex with space for fifteen residents.

Initially, some who'd experienced the Twin Fortresses as drug dens were horrified by plans to use that land for transitional housing. "Why would you put a safe house on the site of the old Fortress? Evil was done there. People died in there. It won't be a good place for people to start over," one survivor insisted. From that insight grew a ceremony to heal the Fortress land and set free the spirits of broken lives. Having held a memorial each August since 1999 to remember people who've died, the partners involved in this work knew the power of ceremony.

On a November day about a week before the wrecking ball arrived, a small circle gathered outside the Fortress. Pastor Faith Brace and Sister Marion Garneau of Inner City Pastoral Ministry led them in sprinkling the land with cedar branches dipped in water. Penny Summers, then coordinator at Kindred House, drew on her Cree traditions to offer a smudging of participants and the land. Prayers and reflections involved survivors such as Charlene Johnson. The ceremony, Johnson says, "put a sense of closure on that life. My anger at the people who caused the turmoil in lives of women and transgendered people could be behind the ball that would wreck the house. I walked away feeling, 'Right on. When we come back sometime in the new year, there will be something positive here.'" Johnson had often walked up those stairs desperately needing a fix, afraid she might never come out. "So for me it was a very spiritual blessing, to see there are steps you can walk up that lead to dreams come true."

Before the demolition, workers rescued two of Demas' inspiring murals: the clear-eyed portrait and the joyful dancer. On 15 January 2002, a bitterly cold day, concrete torches and drywall cutters extracted the murals painted seven years earlier to help clear the air for Kindred House. A crane was required to hoist the larger-than-life portrait, fused as it was to a two-tonne block of reinforced concrete on a main floor outer wall. The dancer on drywall proved easier to move, although more fragile. Faded, cracked, and rough-edged, both murals were painstakingly restored and prepared for their new settings.

After three moves and outdoor storage, the concrete mural required major patching before it could be installed under a protective overhang at Alex Taylor School. Eugene Demas could not be located for the restoration, so artist Christine Frost set to work, her task complicated by the fact that the murals incorporated a mixture of indoor house paints, artist acrylics, and tempera. Unlike the interior mural, whose most severe damage occurred in large colour fields that were easy to patch and match, the mural on concrete sustained damage to the face and hair, especially details added with water-soluble tempera. After sanding repaired areas, Frost carefully cleaned each section, then applied a water-based primer. Referring to pictures taken prior to the damage, she returned all sections to their original colours with multiple layers of Benjamin Moore premium outdoor latex and Grumbaucher artist acrylic medium. Finally she rolled on One Shot UV Protectant Anti-Graffiti Topcoat to safeguard the mural and highlight its vibrancy.

The site those murals once graced, meanwhile boasts a modest duo of duplexes. Operated by Edmonton City Centre Church Corporation, the rooms inside provide housing to a dozen or more inner city residents. The story of these four units in itself reflects challenges met in serving Edmonton's most vulnerable. Opened in 2002, "the Duplex," as it was called, originally offered not only housing but a network of support to adults intent on exiting the street. Termed transitional housing, it added a key piece to Crossroads, which began in 1989 as an outreach to people caught in prostitution and soon expanded to include housing for youth and mothers with children. The Duplex extended that support to adult women and transgender persons, with success. More than 58 per cent of clients discharged after a month or more at the duplex had stopped prostituting, while 42 per cent moved to stable environments. Six months later, 39 per cent were holding to their resolve. "For this particular population, those are good results," says Crossroads manager Kourch Chan. What's more, clients were reaching that independent stage faster than anticipated, meaning the house could serve more adults than first thought.

Despite such testimonies, no funder would step forward when pilot funding for the Duplex ran out. Lacking operational dollars for the round-the-clock staff and other resources residents need to piece together the skills and connections to move from homelessness to a stable home of their own, the Duplex reverted to unsupported housing.

Minus this key resource, Crossroads soldiers on, offering on-the-street outreach, follow-up support, liaison to other agencies—and housing for certain populations. One of several interlocking programs offering safety and hope to people whose life sadly includes prostitution, Crossroads touches more than five hundred lives a year, including many children's. It's among the reasons why ECCCC earned the 2003 Honourary Member Award from the Vanier Institute of the Family.

Tapping Potential: Culture Shift

Finally pulled out of the shadows, the strong images created by Eugene Demas call us all to heed the dignity of those living in danger on our streets. Like the women he depicts, those individuals face the world head-on, with determination and savvy. "I truly believe you can't be stupid on the street," reflects Dawn Hodgins, a survivor who works with the Prostitution Awareness and Action Foundation of Edmonton, a community-powered initiative known for its "john" school. "You have to be on top of your game. If you're going to make it and you're going to survive you've got to be smart and you have to have a game plan. I always say if you could take that amount of energy that people use to *use* and get them to use that for something else—man!"

Potential, indeed. But also deep scars. Rape, abuse, incest, fetal alcohol, lost childhood, pimping parents, failed fostering, racism, sexism, poverty, greed, addictions—their litanies span all classes, all orientations. To cope, those impacted enter a culture with its own allegiances and rules. Quitting that life means severing those ties. Emigrating, in a sense, to a foreign land.

What does it take to emigrate—to exit the street? For Hodgins, a series of sorrows, including multiple losses as Edmonton's rash of street deaths claimed some she knew well. Plus the friendship of a man named John who was anything but a "john": a man who didn't chase her away from the corner next to his work but brought her soup, bought her coffee, listened to her all-too-typical story of stolen childhood. Asking nothing in return.

It took Charlene Johnson a summer in the bush, grounded by Kate Quinn and other steadfast friends. "This was the best thing that ever happened to me," she says now. "It gave me the kick in the butt I needed, but it also helped open my eyes to what others are going through."

What she needed—what those still selling their bodies most need—is to connect, human to human, Johnson says. "Everybody on the face of this earth has problems, whether that be raising your children or reaching a different level of education or managing a new job. But the women who are out there, because of the environment that we grew up in and the life they live now, feel like they're the only ones in the whole wide world who can't let you in on what's going on for them in their world. They feel so misunderstood—so alone."

Intent on spanning that chasm, the partners who midwifed the Fortress redemption push ahead, fuelled by an inter-agency osmosis of insight and energy. Both Crossroads and PAAFE are part of a streetwise network that has launched interlocking initiatives ranging from a Diversion Program urging those charged with soliciting off the streets to a Distinctive Employment Counselling Services of Alberta (DECSA) Transitions program that blends training with counselling about sexual exploitation and addiction to street life.

In many ways, appearance included, Johnson could be the strong, clear-eyed woman depicted in Eugene Demas' concrete mural. Perhaps that's fitting, for the portrait now stands as a public reminder that women and transgenders, whether on the street or exiting the street, are individual human beings. Their gifts, if accepted by those of us who drive by with eyes averted, could enrich us all.

WHY IS SQUAW SUCH A BAD WORD?

NAOMI MCILWRAITH

I work as a historical interpreter at Fort Edmonton Park. This work has taken on much deeper meaning for me than merely a "summer job," as I have ancestors who laboured for the Hudson's Bay Company and participated in the Canadian fur trade in ways the historical record largely ignores. My education on this gripping history is enriched by the increasingly challenging questions about Native–White relations in Canada posed by visitors to the Fort. I want to tell you about a number of recent challenges, including the question, "Why is squaw such a bad word?"

The Fort Edmonton of the 1840s depicts a community of approximately 120, all engaged in furthering the fur trade through their daily activities. One room in the Fort provokes questions from visitors about the families, women, and children living there. A sign saying "Married Men's Quarters" identifies the room. Visitors often express confusion because they want to know why all the married men lived together. I explain that the quarters to the south of the arch might more accurately be labelled the Married *Families* Quarters, though the Hudson's Bay Company failed to articulate the presence of women and families in their naming of these lodgings. Visitors frequently respond with incredulity when we clarify that the small room accommodated three families, because there is only one hearth to prepare meals and the room is only half the size of the Great Hall in Rowand House. It is difficult, frankly, imagining so many people squeezed into such a small space. Recently, a man from another part of the world, but now living in Montréal, led a group of international visitors to Fort Edmonton. The group was learning English as a second language and their leader astutely wanted to give them an experience of local history. I conversed with this group in the Married Men's Quarters. I explained that men who had acquired neither a trade nor the ability to read, write, or numerate were compelled to work as labourers and to live in closer quarters with their families. The leader of the group of international visitors asked if "they swapped women" in the fur trade. I was surprised by this question, raised by an intelligent man. I responded by accurately describing women's vital roles in the community and economic life of the fur trade, and by explaining that, yes, sometimes women of the fur trade just as women throughout history received negative treatment and destructive representation. I found it difficult to hide my reaction to the implications of his question and the man said apologetically that he meant it only as a joke and that he, too, understood the legacy of imperialism in his personal experience. I elaborated, with some restraint, on the intricacies of the myths and stereotypes so difficult to correct, and the group readily received an important lesson on the Canadian fur trade.

Some weeks previous, in the Married Men's Quarters again, an elderly man showed an interest in the barrel filled with the long, thin Red Osier Dogwood willow sticks. I showed him the leather double-ball and explained that it was a game similar to lacrosse, but that the players used these slightly curved sticks rather than webbed sticks. The man picked up one much thicker stick from the barrel; it was longer as well, and I explained that it was better used as a walking stick. He turned to me and said, "It's a wife-beating stick." His wife, standing by the far door, said, "I'm his wife. It's okay, he means nothing." The man's son-in-law stood at the window and offered, "Don't mind him. In this day of political correctness, gee, you can't say anything anymore." I chose not to retaliate because of the sensitivity of both racial and gender issues and my responsibility to engage visitors professionally, despite what they may say. Instead, I responded with a question: "What do you expect me to say?"

A week later, I discussed the Made Beaver system of trade and the overplus with another visitor. These are very complex concepts, developed by the Hudson's Bay Company and their Native trading partners. Another male visitor came from around the corner and interrupted by asking, "Are we selling women today?" On yet another occasion a colleague told the story of a woman who asked, "Which tribe of Indians provided the prostitutes for the fur traders?"

Those of us who return to this seasonal work year after year do so because we enjoy history and we like people. We recognize the important role we play in public education. As an optimistic person, I hope that the ignorance represented in these cases can give way to the gentle awareness that historical interpreters work so hard to effect.

Near the end of the summer I guided a group of people from the United States on a "Sunshine Tour." Beginning with the Native Encampment, just outside the Fort walls, I explained that Natives were integral to both the survival of the Europeans and the success of the fur trade. As we walked toward the North Saskatchewan River to view the York Boat, a kindly older gentleman asked me, "Other than referring to a woman of ill repute, why is squaw such a bad word?" His question surprised me, and his genuine curiosity inspired me. His was an elderly group and many of them walked slowly, so several did not hear his question. I asked the man if he minded if I waited to answer his question until after we looked at the York Boat and went inside. He agreed. My guests all enjoyed learning about the York Boat, the Fort walls, the Indian Trade Store, the Made Beaver system of trade, the Fur Press, and Rowand House.

I chose to respond to the important question raised by the curious man when we settled into the Great Hall of Rowand House. While explaining the other aspects of the Fort, I did not have much time to organize my thoughts. Fortunately, however, in my research and thinking about the complex relationships between the fur traders and their Native trading associates, and the integral contributions Native women made to the success of the fur trade, I had prepared for just such a query about Native women and was now able to provide my most educated and perceptive response. As I finished explaining that John Rowand's wife, Louise, was a Métis woman, I shared the man's question with the group and said I could give them my most thoughtful insights on the fur trade if they all had the time to commit to a discussion that would last more than a couple of minutes and the curiosity to understand the intricate nuances of relationships between women and men of the fur trade era. I told them I would express my own opinions and concerns, not those of the City of

Edmonton or Fort Edmonton Park. My guests waited expectantly for my answer.

And this is what I said.

I explained, knowing that my words were not the typical material of historical interpretation at fur trade sites, that the question was simple but its answer complicated. According to American Indian theorist and activist Ward Churchill, the word "squaw" arose from the inability of European men, in New England, to say the word "sunksquaw" in the Narrangansett language. They corrupted it to "squaw." I described the similarity between the Cree word for woman, "iskwew," and the word squaw. For Cree, like Narrangansett, is an Algonquian language. In my personal research to enhance my work as a historical interpreter, I have read a number of inspiring books on Native–White relations and women's economic roles in the fur trade, including Ward Churchill's book *A Little Matter of Genocide: Holocaust and Denial in the Americas, 1492 to the Present* (1998), Sylvia Van Kirk's *Many Tender Ties: Women in Fur Trade Society, 1670–1870* (1981), and Jennifer Brown's *Strangers in Blood: Fur Trade Company Families in Indian Country* (1980). Until very recently the chronicle of my maternal ancestors has been neglected, and my own understanding of this vital social history necessitates such scholarly investigation.

I said that everyday people don't always agree with scholars where questions like this are concerned. When I shared my reflections with my dad, who grew up speaking the Cree language, he told me that the word "squaw" is not always used in a derogatory way. He cited an example where someone came into a restaurant in Elk Point, Alberta, downstream of Edmonton on the North Saskatchewan River, and asked for a certain Native woman. The waiter, a Native man, gestured toward a woman and said, "That squaw over there." Black people object to non-Black people using the word "nigger," but may use the word themselves in an ironic and self-referential way. Perhaps they use it in a privileged way as well because of their historical experience with slavery; possibly Native people, even Native women, use the word "squaw" for similar reasons. Indeed, I know a woman who sometimes refers to herself as an "old squaw," without suggesting anything at all of a woman of ill repute. I have learned that "nohtokwew" means "Old Woman" in Cree and expresses all the respect that such a term should. In different contexts and used by different people, words and labels take on different meanings. Squaw may be such a word.

Sometimes we act in ignorance of what a word means, ignorance meaning both "unknowing" and "demeaning." Here is an example of our sweeping ignorance of the subtleties of relationships between Native women and European men. I deepened my response to the elderly gentleman and his friends that evening by revealing how a schoolboy adeptly chose a moment when one of my Native colleagues had her back turned as she tended the fire at the Native Encampment to point and shout, "Look! There's a squaw!" My colleague hurt the rest of that day, and then some, and now I shared this with my respectful visitors. Where does a young boy learn this behaviour and how do we change it? People from every curve of the planet visit Fort Edmonton Park, from the very young to the very old, and I take seriously my responsibility to correct such misconceptions as expressed by this boy and to share my best understanding of the truth. I ask you now to appreciate my concern for this subject and that I have learned to temper it and articulate myself intelligently. My guests continued listening intently.

I briefly explained that when fur trading empires competed most fiercely with each other, this was good for Native people in one way and bad for Native people in two ways. It was good because competition meant better prices for the Natives. But it was bad because both liquor and women were traded. Liquor was destructive for all involved and trafficking in Native women was most especially bad for Native women.

I took some personal risks in my response, but I owed it to the man who had taken a risk in asking the question.

I expressed my frustration that I have ancestors who worked for the Hudson's Bay Company as boat-builders, interpreters, and labourers, yet I know little about them. Their surname was Sabiston, as they were Orkneymen who worked for the company; and though my maternal grandmother's maiden name was Sabiston, definitive genealogical connections are difficult to determine as the honourable company would not have seen the merit, for at least its first century of operation, of recording the role of an indentured servant's wife in fur trade social and economic life.

Just three days previous, I elaborated, I viewed a disturbing story on the news about residents of the Shamattawa Indian Reserve in northern Manitoba, descendants of the first Natives to trade with the Hudson's Bay Company. Sadly, the Chief of the Shamattawa Reserve appealed to the federal government because three of his people had committed suicide in nine days. I explained to my guests that to those who do not understand the difficult history, Native Indians might seem inferior. But this is not so, I said. Several factors contributed to the deterioration of relations between Natives and non-Natives, as the fur trade declined. The near extermination of the Plains Bison devastated many Plains Indian groups because the bison provided more than food for these tribes; the buffalo also contributed to shelter, clothing, footwear, culture, and spirituality. The fur trade declined as the land was taken up by settlers and homesteaders, and as governments forced Natives onto reserves and to sign treaties. Some residential schools, not all, I emphasized, did substantial harm to Native people by abusing the students in many ways, and that abuse cycle sadly continues in some of these Native families and communities. Now, as I think back on my talk with these elderly visitors, I would add that residential schools, whether or not the students suffered abuse in any way, were based on a racist, patriarchal assumption that our Native Indians needed "civilizing" to a European standard.

I trust that my guests saw me express my concern most passionately when I talked of the more than sixty women who have gone missing in Vancouver in the last fifteen or twenty years. Many of these women were Native, worked in the sex trade, and were addicted to drugs. It seems that the trafficking in Native women has not abated. Only in the last two or three years have the families of these women successfully summoned the authorities to re-examine these missing persons' cases. They believe the authorities ignored their female relatives because these women led dangerous lives, but to know that is not enough. These families declare, "My sister is a human being;" "My daughter is a human being;" "My wife is a human being;" "My mother is a human being." Now, the families reach toward closure in their ordeals, hoping that the remains of their female relations will be found and their murders solved. At the time, I could not predict that here, too, in what the Cree call Amiskwacîwâskahikan, at least eight *more* Native or Métis women would go missing and that their bodies would be found in the vicinity of Edmonton, in wooded or industrial areas where danger often lurks. Just yesterday, as I waited for my bus on Stony Plain Road in our city's west end, at 7:30 AM on my way to the university, I watched a Native woman walk by me with a bruise on her face. I wondered how this woman came to have that bruise on her face, whether she was part of the sex trade along this busy avenue. I wondered whether that bruise was the visual remainder of her historical circumstances, the travesty of colonialism that left her with few options other than to seek whatever value her flesh provides. I did not say these things to my visitors because it may have been too much misery to share and because they had not yet happened. But I did speak of what I knew at the time.

I knew how heavy my words were, as I concluded my passionate plea for understanding to my elderly guests. I said that these are profoundly complex issues and that there are good and bad in all cultures. I warned that not all Native people suffer; many Native people in Canada thrive and lead, are strong and accomplish much. But too many continue suffering and we must ask why and what can we do about it.

I finished by taking a deep breath and saying, "That is the best I can do for now. I thank you, sir, for asking this important question and I thank you all for listening. I hope I haven't belaboured the issue, but there you have it."

The sincere man who asked the important question responded, "No, your answer is outstanding. Thank you so much. We really appreciate the heart you have put into your time with us." My eighteen guests clapped quietly and I smiled as well as I could under the burden of my words.

Just now, as I reflect on Amiskwacîwâskahikanihk, the city of my birth, I think about its recent one hundredth birthday in October of 2004. Birthday parties are a lot of fun, and I remember many cakes spread with blue icing and prisms of candied sprinkles, in the communities of Norwood, Parkdale, McQueen, and West Jasper Place where I ran through the neighbourhoods with my young friends, until the sun went down and I could no longer ignore my mother's calls to come home, "Now!" As an adult, I have lived and worked many years away from Edmonton, but now as I commit to making it my home, I realize both my rootedness in this city *and* my sadness that I walk home along Jasper Avenue and Stony Plain Road rather than through MacKinnon Ravine, an intriguing wooded gully leading into the swiftly flowing waters of the river I love. Some years ago, while retracing a historic fur trade route with five friends, I canoed this same kisiskâciwani-sîpiy from nearly its headwaters in the Rockies to its mouth at Grand Rapids on Lake Winnipeg, on my way to Kaministiquia, also known as Thunder Bay or Old Fort William, on Lake Superior. The North Saskatchewan River is an artery along a vital waterway that linked such important fur trade centres as Fort Edmonton and Fort William. Indeed, this same river connected Fort Edmonton to York Factory on Hudson Bay, where the Home Guard Cree, the forebears of the Shamattawa Cree in Northern Manitoba, helped Company employees stave off scurvy, producing pemmican from caribou, hunting geese, and fishing when starvation threatened.

The reconstructed Fort Edmonton now sits on the south shore of the North Saskatchewan River, south and west of MacKinnon Ravine, even though Rossdale, the Ross Flats, and the current lawn bowling greens of the provincial legislature were three of the previous five sites of Fort Edmonton along the north shore. Notwithstanding the impact of West Edmonton Mall on our cultural history, many people still experience a thrill at visiting Fort Edmonton Park and the sensory awakening such an outing allows. The park signifies much of the historical development of our city, from its beginnings as a meeting place between Natives and Europeans, through its growth into a town and eventually a city. I hope by sharing my concerns with you I have honoured the memory and presence of nehiyâskwewak (Cree women) and women of other groups, whose histories continue to pulse through our city in much the same way as our river.

Makeshift Memorial

EDMONTON'S "FORGOTTEN" CEMETERY

PAMELA M. CUNNINGHAM

On 8 July 2004, City of Edmonton Streets and Transportation workers arrived at a small yet busy road junction in Edmonton's river valley. They placed road barricades and signs on the far eastern lane that snakes past the EPCOR power plant, causing traffic to detour approximately one hundred feet north before making a hard right turn. With those barricades came the City of Edmonton's first physical recognition of the existence of a historic fur trade cemetery and Aboriginal burial ground in the centre of the city. It did not complete the story of the Fort Edmonton Cemetery/Aboriginal Burial Ground—only in the distant future will we truly be able to see the consequences of the road closure. However, the closure of a small portion of Rossdale Road is a significant step. The continuing conflict in Rossdale is not easy to explain. It involves understanding, or attempting to understand, a complex relationship between the City of Edmonton and its history. The story of the burials on the Rossdale Flats is also about the conflict of memory and its usage by two very different parties—the City on one hand and descendants on the other. What I want to do here is explore the site, its history, its people (both historical and contemporary), and its importance.

The Meeting Place at the Bend in the River

In their 2003 report on the site, *Fort Edmonton Burial Ground: An Archaeological and Historical Study*, Calgary-based archaeology firm Lifeways of Canada noted the presence of archaeological material dating back eight thousand years. This material, consisting of what was determined to be a bison bone showing evidence of butchering, indicates that the site on the Rossdale Flats has one of the longest presence of human occupation or use in what is now known as Alberta. Further evidence shows that the site's occupation, while not continuous, occurred consistently for thousands of years before a quasi-permanent settlement was established.

It surprises many people to learn the following: Fort Edmonton as it currently exists in Edmonton's river valley off of Fox Drive is not the "real" Fort Edmonton. The structure that attracts thousands of visitors each year, including numerous school outings, is a replica based on an 1846 painting by Paul Kane, an artist who is widely noted for his works and the embellishments they contain. Fort Edmonton Park is also not located anywhere near the site of the original Fort Edmonton. In its various incarnations, Fort Edmonton (the real working fort) had at least five different sites in and around the Edmonton area. The first location, or Edmonton House I, was opened near Fort Saskatchewan in 1795. As was usually the case during the earlier years of the fur trade, Edmonton House was built by the Hudson's Bay Company at this setting as a reaction to the building of Fort Augustus by the North West Company. This competition between the rival companies continued and in approximately 1802, the two companies uprooted themselves and built Fort Augustus II and Edmonton House II on the Rossdale Flats. Here the companies remained until 1810 when they moved onto the White Earth Creek, where a brief stay was marked by the return to the Rossdale Flats during the 1812–13 winter. This would serve as the home of the two forts until they merged in 1821; the final move for the rechristened Fort Edmonton (now Edmonton V) was in 1830 to the higher ground now occupied by the provincial legislature buildings.

A review of the extant historical records indicates that the first mention of a possible burial on the Rossdale Flats occurs on 27 March 1814. The Edmonton House Post Journal for this date records the following: "A Free Canadian arrived at our Neighbours [the North West Company's Fort Augustus IV] bringing with him the dead Body of his Companion, another Freeman, who left this Friday in Company with three Southward [Cree] Indians." While it cannot be stated with complete certainty, it can be inferred that a burial likely took place and it was probably in the area. According to Lifeways of Canada, this was the first of ninety-one historically documented burials in the Fort Edmonton Cemetery/Aboriginal Burial Ground. However, it must be noted that the historical record for the Hudson's Bay Company's Fort Edmonton (and the North West Company's Fort Augustus) is incomplete—years and sometimes entire decades of post journals have been lost. This, along with the early scarcity of missionaries and their accompanying records in this area, means that it is not entirely possible to ascertain the extent of the Fort Edmonton Cemetery/Aboriginal Burial Ground usage during the 1800s.

There are, however, many things we do know about the burial site through the documentary record. In their analysis, archaeologists and historians for Lifeways of Canada report the following: "36 per cent died in the winter . . . 46 per cent were under 18, and, of those, only five were over the age of 10 . . . 65 per cent [of the recorded 91 burials] were male . . ." (2003:82-83). While it is not always possible to determine the ethnicity of the people buried at the site, a review of the historical documents indicates that while the majority of the interments are people of First Nations and Métis ancestry, the site is in fact indicative of the multi-nation and multinational composition of Fort Edmonton during the 1800s. Reflected in the burial record are people of Métis, Cree, Blackfoot, Dene, Tsuu T'ina, French Canadian, Scots, English, and Norwegian ancestry.

The Fort Edmonton Cemetery/Aboriginal Burial Ground was in near continuous usage from the early 1800s until the early 1870s. The apparent "abandonment" of the site was gradual and occurred for numerous reasons. The establishment of Lac Ste. Anne Mission in 1842 under the direction of Father Thibault does not appear to have affected the burial rate or patterns of Fort Edmonton's Catholic population. In fact, burials of Catholics still occurred on the Rossdale Flats as indicated by the Forts des Prairies Burial Register. However, the founding of the St. Albert Mission by Father Lacombe in 1861 (a move that was precipitated by the superior arable land located around the already established Big Lake settlement) had the opposite effect—Catholics ceased to be buried on the Rossdale Flats after 1864 and the deceased were instead transported to St. Albert for burial. The Methodists under Rev. McDougall placed their mission on top of the hill behind the fort (near the present-day McDougall United Church on 101st Street south of Jasper Avenue) in 1870. From this point forward, recorded burials in the Fort Edmonton Cemetery/Aboriginal Burial Ground ceased.

Since burials stopped in the 1870s, it is not uncommon to hear the burials on the Rossdale Flats referred to as forgotten or abandoned. However, a review of the newspapers produced in Edmonton from the early 1900s until the present contradicts this. For instance, a 1943 newspaper bears the following headline: "Workmen find bones of five by river side." The article continues: "The discovery was made in the vicinity of the 105 Street bridge. All were in decayed coffins that crumbled to dust when air penetrated to them . . . City Commissioner R. J. Gibb stated that inquiry would be made to establish whether or not a graveyard existed at this location, and also to endeavor to determine the identity of the remains." A 1958 article in the Edmonton Journal by reporter Ted Bower is entitled "Pioneer finds timbers from fort; reveals site of Indian cemetery."

As previously mentioned, Fort Edmonton IV was relocated in 1830 to the grounds now occupied by the provincial legislature. The land continued to be held by the Hudson's Bay Company until 1899, when it was sold to the Edmonton Industrial Exhibition Association; in 1903 a small portion of this land was resold to the Town of Edmonton "for $1,000, for use as its power and water treatment plants" (HLUS 2004:104), construction of which began in 1902. The industrial development taking place on the site had many consequences for the burials the site contained; chief among them was the disturbance of the graves. Perhaps one of the most poignant stories of a disturbance occurred early in the development of the power plant. In the University of Alberta libraries, you can find the following recollection by female pioneer Mrs. McQueen:

> One vivid memory Mother has is of Cecile coming in to the Manse at the time the Edmonton, Yukon & Pacific Railway was being built. The men were digging along near the hill in front of the Fort. Years before a child of Cecile's had been buried in this location. She knew the exact spot, and when the men left, went and took the bones, which she wrapped in her apron to Mother, and asked her to fix a little coffin. She showed she wanted the box covered with black,

like the dress she wore, and lined, with white, like her apron, on the inside. Mother did this for her, and the little coffin, was taken out to the burying place on the Reserve at Stony Plain.

Over the next decades, the number of disturbances increased, culminating in 1967 with the installation of a gas line in the area, which resulted in the removal of six people from the Fort Edmonton Cemetery/Aboriginal Burial Ground. The removal took place as part of a field school conducted by the Department of Anthropology at the University of Alberta. Today, these individuals remain at the university. Many descendants are concerned that the remains of their ancestors have been subjected to scientific study. Lifeways of Canada reports that twenty-four people have been disturbed, removed, and relocated to various sites, or lost.

". . . our greatest and best chief, Lapotack"

To some, the idea that people are concerned about the fate of individuals they never knew, buried under a roadway and industrial development, is unreasonable. How can the desecration of the graves of people who existed before you were born cause pain?

To the descendants and activists involved in the struggle for recognition over the sacredness of this site, these are more than human remains. They are people. Some of them have names that are now lost to us. They all have stories.

On 10 February 1861 the Edmonton House Post Journal notes that the "remains of Cree Chief Lapotack were interred. . . . The funeral was attended by all the Protestants, Rev. Mr. Woolsey reading the burial service." Lapotack's body had been brought back to the fort two days earlier by John Cunningham and his party of hunters who relayed the story of how Lapotack's band thought he had been poisoned by a rival group of Cree. However, the Freemen who composed the hunting party believed instead that he died of a ruptured blood vessel. Lapotack is further described as "a good man in every way and [he] always did his best for the whites. . . . Never touched a drop of liquor. His loss to Edmonton House is irrepairable. His family are left for the charity of the HBC and right well do his children deserve to be taken care of." Our first introduction to Lapotack occurred in the 1840s through the diaries of Rev. Robert Rundle—we learn of the struggle Rundle went through to keep Lapotack (or Le Petet as Rundle calls him) in the Protestant faith in which Rundle had baptized him and away from Father Thibault of the Catholic persuasion. Through Thomas Woolsey, a later Methodist minister, we learn that he not only considers Lapotack to be "the leading Cree Chief in this section of country," but that Lapotack and his wife (whose name unfortunately is not recorded in this section, though she is referred to in the Lifeways report as Maria Kitimakenakoos Moses) were married on 18 October 1858. Woolsey further writes that he "had not mistaken the sincerity of Joseph Lapotack's profession at his baptism, he having ever since conducted morning and evening prayers in his own tent for the benefit of any who were disposed to attend."

During the 1850s and 1860s, Lapotack appears often in the writings in the Edmonton House Post Journals. This alone is a rarity, as Indians are rarely named in the business records of the post. The importance of Lapotack is recognized by the fort and on 6 October 1856 the clerks write:

> The Chiefs Lapitugne and Maskepetoon with their respective bands came this afternoon on a trade, they were received with a salute of 3 guns each, Lapitugne has been recognized as a chief of the first rank. After the customary speechifying & smoking the Calumet was gone through the Chiefs got a present of a suit of clothes & a keg of mixed Rum each. They appear to be well satisfied with their treatment & Lapitugne has promised to be one of our Hunters. He gave in a horse on arrival.

However, approval was not always granted Lapotack's behaviour. Only five days later, Lapotack is reported to have taken one of the ferry boats, untied its mooring, and let it float down the river when he arrived at the fort in the middle of the night and there was no one awake to trade with him. The fort decided to wait out the punishment, as they believed an apology would shortly come forward. Indeed, on 13 October 1856, two fort hunters, Meskootewakus and Appetaw, brought in a "humble apology from Chief Lapitugne for his misdemeanors in setting adrift a ferry boat."

Lapotack was a person who mattered to Fort Edmonton, its inhabitants and the missionaries. His body was buried in the Fort Edmonton Cemetery/Aboriginal Burial Ground after his death and it is possible that Lapotack remains there today. It is also possible that Lapotack is one of the many people whose mortal remains have been removed from the site. Today, many of the descendants of Lapotack, whose Christianized name was Joseph Morin, live on the Enoch Cree First Nation west of Edmonton; he is considered by many people to be the founder of their band.

The Rossdale Flats Aboriginal Oral Histories Project

In August 2001, Gene Zwozdesky, then Alberta's Minister of Community Development, wrote a letter to Edmonton's former mayor Bill Smith. In this letter, Zwozdesky reiterated the need for a comprehensive history of the Rossdale Flats site. In particular, he stressed:

> While archival research will no doubt shed much light on the situation, in particular from a non-Aboriginal perspective, no historical investigation of this type could be considered balanced and complete if the large, parallel body of knowledge that resides in the minds of people most closely connected to the deceased were not included. This oral history would need to be garnered from First Nations, Métis and non-Aboriginal communities. . . . Therefore, I would urge you to add an oral history component to the research proposed for the Rossdale area.

In September of 2002, the City of Edmonton's Planning and Development department proceeded with the Historical Land Use Study. The terms of reference for the project did not include oral history. The Edmonton Aboriginal Urban Affairs Committee (EAUAC), an advisory body to the mayor, council, and administration for the City of Edmonton, stood firm in its belief and support of the necessity of an oral history project. Through a series of negotiations, EAUAC was able to secure partial project funding from the Community Services Department of the City of Edmonton and additional funding from the Alberta Historical Resources Foundation. With funding in place, EAUAC devised terms of reference for the project that allowed them to proceed with the hiring of a contract team to complete interviews with descendants, activists, and others with knowledge of the Fort Edmonton Cemetery/Aboriginal Burial Ground. While the project name made specific mention of Aboriginal oral histories, early in the project's inception EAUAC determined that in order to have a complete oral history, it was necessary to include descendants of other ethnicities. To this end, the project was opened to include people of French-Canadian and European ancestry.

In the six months between June and December 2003, the contract team, led by a volunteer project manager seconded from EAUAC, struggled to overcome preconceived notions of distrust that many descendants and community members had toward the City of Edmonton. For the most part this struggle was successful and a total of twenty-seven interviews were conducted. Interviewees were broken into two distinct categories—descendants and those with a professional or more recent connection to the site. The project team adopted a standard protocol (a gift of tobacco, blanket, and honoraria) that was used for all interviewees. If a person felt uncomfortable accepting the offered protocol, they were asked for advice in how they would like to proceed. Interviews were primarily conducted in the interviewees' place of residence or another place they would feel comfortable and the project team travelled to many locations within central Alberta. Where necessary, interpreters were available for Cree, Blackfoot, and French translation.

An analysis of the interviews illustrates that knowledge of the site was passed down within some family lines, while in others (sometimes within the same family) it was not. One of the more intriguing revelations was that a number of people who are, or may be, descendants of people buried in Rossdale had no knowledge of their ancestors' burial place until recent media attention encouraged them to conduct personal genealogical research. During the interview, people were asked what they hoped would happen to the site. The majority indicated that they wanted to see the road removed and possibly even the power plant; almost all interviewees wanted to see the site, and those involved in working to protect the site, treated with respect. Another major theme that emerged from the interviews concerned the location and size of the cemetery and burial ground. Many interviewees expressed the belief that there is more than one cemetery on the flats—one for Natives and one for non-Natives. Some further believe that burials extend to the east of the approved commemoration site under not only EPCOR property but possibly to the northeast under Telus Field.

Perhaps the most difficult portion of the interviews involved the discussion around the disturbance and removal of people from their graves at the site. Numerous interviewees expressed the need for the immediate repatriation and reburial of those removed. At the time of writing, this has yet to occur.

And From Here . . .

The final report on the oral histories relating to the Fort Edmonton Cemetery/Aboriginal Burial Ground was submitted to the City of Edmonton in February 2004. To date, the findings of the report have not made an impact on the size or direction of the commemoration site. A small portion of Rossdale Road was closed in the summer of 2004 and it has been promised that in 2005, the year of Alberta's centennial, the repatriation and reburial of those removed from the site will take place on the Rossdale Flats. Perhaps one of those returned will be Lapotack. Perhaps he is still there. Perhaps he is one of those who is now lost. What remains to happen from here is still to be determined. What is known is that those that have been actively involved will continue to be. It is hoped that no one will be removed from the site again and that the site will be recognized for what it is—an important piece of Edmonton's history that cannot continue to be ignored and neglected.

Snowy

NATURE IN OUR OWN BACKYARDS

DAN RUBINSTEIN

Mr. Rabbit, Mr. Rabbit
Your ears are mighty long
Yes by God they're put on wrong
Every little soul must shine
Every little soul must shine.
—*Paul Westerberg*

We called him Snowy, because of his white fur. We still don't know if our long-eared muse is indeed a "he," mind you, but we have learned plenty about the white-tailed jackrabbit who's been basking in our backyard sanctuary for much of the last two winters. Snowy likes to dig a shallow pocket in the snow beside the firepit and sleep all day. The spot is halfway between his escape route to the street and his well-trodden path to the back alley, and the "form" he rests in provides shelter from the wind. Even when his eyes are closed, Snowy's ears remain alert. He looks annoyed when the police helicopter flies overhead and flexes a paw when curious magpies get too close. He usually wakes up just before dusk, stretches and preens for about an hour, then meanders over to the cone-rich ground beneath the skirt of our giant pine. It's where we leave the carrots. After a snack, Snowy's off for another night of foraging.

Our carrot budget soars over the winter, but the extra expense is worth it. We spend hours at the kitchen window cradling a pair of binoculars when he's here, watching Snowy drift off to sleep and fighting our own urge to nap. We collect his sloughed-off fur when increased daylight triggers his moult from white to brown: there's an envelope labeled "Snowy, spring 2003" in my filing cabinet. We even started keeping a log to record his habits. On 12 March, for instance, he was at the firepit at 7:45 in the morning and slept there all day. On 18 March, he remained in the same spot from 9 AM to 8 PM before beginning his evening ritual. He showed up eleven times in March (a record month!) but never on a Monday.

Sometimes, in each of the last two winters, there have been a pair of white-tailed jackrabbits in our yard at the same time. We initially called the smaller one Mrs. Snowy, but my wife insisted "she" be given her own name. So we called her Fluffy. Again, we're not sure if Fluffy is a she. We didn't even know whether they were mates or just friends. But after observing their jousting one afternoon, and later reading in a science text that the "courting behaviour of white-tailed jackrabbits consists of a series of aggressive charges and jumps," we understood. We tell friends about Snowy's behaviour. "You *really* need a pet," they say.

But despite our anthropomorphizing, Snowy is no pet. He's one of a thousand or so wild white-tailed jackrabbits in urban Edmonton, according to King's University College biology and environmental studies professor John Wood, who has been researching the city's *Lepus townsendi* population since 1992. Walk, bike, or drive around Edmonton long enough, especially at night or during the winter, and you'll probably see one. Most Edmontonians have a jackrabbit story: a friend and his girlfriend saw two in the parking lot at 109th Street and Whyte Avenue one night this past winter; the next night, after my friend's girlfriend had flown home to Mexico, he saw a lone jackrabbit in the same windswept lot. Anecdotally, we know these small gnawing mammals have a strong presence in the city, particularly around the University of Alberta campus. But Wood and his students, after conducting population counts for more than a decade, have put together some hard data.

"The interesting thing about this species is that our activities have actually favoured it," Wood says, looking out over a large, grassy field from his second-floor office in the King's building on Fiftieth Street. Wood has watched jackrabbits sleeping and eating in the field, which borders an industrial park. He's also watched foxes and coyotes "working the field," hunting their prey. But because fewer predators prowl the city core than the outskirts, jackrabbits have thrived in Edmonton. They've been known to dodge under fences to escape swooping hawks and owls. They're fast enough to evade dogs, cats, and people (they've been clocked at fifty-five kilometres per hour and have the hops to cover five metres in a single leap). And most of the time they're smart enough to avoid the city's biggest danger: cars and roads. "What we've done in the city is create a bit of a predator shadow," Wood explains. "We've reduced the predation pressure for them. And these jackrabbits have the capacity to learn."

Years of beer and TV notwithstanding, I too have an ability to learn. Although rabbits and hares are relatives in the family *Leporidae*, white-tailed jackrabbits are not actually rabbits, I discovered; they're hares, formally the white-tailed prairie hare. There are many different varieties of each, but rabbits are generally smaller, live in burrows or warrens, and are sociable. Hares, on the other hand, are solitary, rest in above-ground forms, and use their speed—not cover—to escape predators. The biggest distinction is that rabbits are born naked, blind, and helpless, while baby hares (or leverets) are "precocial," born with fur, open eyes, and, in the words of U of A Museum of Zoology assistant curator Wayne Roberts, are "ready to go to work right away."

Edmonton's jackrabbits live in residential neighbourhoods, parks, and industrial districts. But they rarely venture into the heavily-wooded river valley. That turf belongs to the slightly smaller (and smaller-eared) snowshoe hare, the *Lepus americanus*, whose traditional range covers virtually all of Canada and most of the northeastern and northwestern states. Snowshoe hare populations grow and recede in cycles, and Roberts hasn't seen many in the river valley over the past couple of years. But jackrabbit numbers seem relatively stable. By calculating hare density in residential and industrial areas and parks, then extrapolating outward to account for Edmonton's three hundred square kilometres of land, Wood's students counted 1,302 hares in 1992, 973 in 1994 and 1129 in 2001. It's unclear how accurate these figures are, he says, but there is a consistency to the results.

Jackrabbits are relative newcomers to Edmonton. Wood uses the German word *kulturfolger*, or culture-follower, to describe their migration. Their natural range includes southern tracts of Alberta, Saskatchewan, and Manitoba, plus the American plains west to

California and east to Wisconsin. Because Edmonton used to be boreal forest, it wasn't jackrabbit habitat. According to Wood, the first in the area was spotted southeast of the city around New Sarepta in 1922. Since then, as the city was deforested and developed, jackrabbits have shifted here from the open prairie to the south and east. Roberts says he's noticed an increasing number of jackrabbits on the U of A campus since arriving thirty-six years ago, explaining that other animals like prairie shrews, plains garter snakes, and northern pocket gophers have migrated north and west as well. "The city is food rich because of all the different plants and shrubs," he says. "They're not only prospering in the city—they're colonizing."

When Wood came to Edmonton sixteen years ago from the US, he wanted to continue studying urban ecology. He did his undergraduate work in Chicago, where he learned how to identify birds in a stream that was "almost an open sewer" of street runoff and rats. Wood earned his Ph.D. in Berkeley, California, studying aquatic insects at the bottom of steep ravines choked with discarded bicycles, tires, and TV sets, and getting grass clippings dumped on his head from the houses above. "Those experiences," he recalls, "taught me that urban systems are more ecologically alive and viable than we can imagine. We don't look at the city as nature. We think of nature as somewhere else. But the city *is* a natural area."

After starting his tenure at King's, where he's now the director of environmental studies, Wood began looking for a research project for his students. He was gazing out his office window at a field embroidered with hare tracks every winter when the idea struck. His students were better at identifying the animals and plants of Africa's Serengeti than those native to Alberta, so Wood wanted them to focus on their surroundings. "We live in an age of marketing," he says. "If it's not marketed to us, if it's not flashy, it's really hard to appreciate what's in your own backyard."

My southside backyard, Roberts speculates, is a safe haven because hares are creatures of habit. We surrender the yard to Snowy and Fluffy when they're here—taking out the garbage can wait—and they repose undisturbed until it's time for their instinctive nocturnal roaming.

"They have a tendency to use the same spot over and over again," Roberts says. "They're naturally shy, but they can probably tolerate things they see every day that don't bother them." Snowy often keeps on eye on us when we're watching him through the window and his ears perk when we make noise inside the house. "He probably recognizes you," Roberts says. "You too have habitual patterns," Woods adds, picking up the trail. "He knows you come home at 5:30 PM and are quite noisy banging around for an hour while making dinner. Does he respond to *you* individually? Hmmm . . . But he habituates to your patterns."

Although his students have compiled numbers, Wood says one needs at least a thousand hours of observation to begin understanding an organism's behaviour. He doesn't know of anyone studying white-tailed jackrabbit that intensely (and is still looking for funding to attach radio collars to track their movement). But by watching the hares both around King's and his home, Wood has developed a few theories. Because they feed "a little bit here, a little bit there," eating buds, branches, grasses, and shrubs, the jackrabbits don't seem to harm vegetation in the city; he hasn't heard many people complain about their gardens being raided. "I've walked down a sidewalk following a bunny for three blocks," Wood recounts. "He went up to every shrub, tree, and large object, just to investigate." But hares won't trace the same route every day—just once or twice a week. "It's like working a trapline," Wood says.

Winter routines change once the snow melts. Jackrabbits know they stand out more against the brownish green ground and are displaced by pesky humans reclaiming their yards. "Suddenly, during the daytime, you see bunnies running all around the neighbourhood," Wood says. "They don't know where to go." In fact, they don't really go anywhere. We may see them much more often in winter, but in spring and summer they just find new hiding places—beneath shrubs and trees, in city parks, but not in the forested river valley, because open prairie is where they're safe. In spring, as well, the young are born, generally around mid-April, in litters averaging three to six leverets. Within two weeks, the young can forage for themselves. They reach adult size in three or four months (bodies eighteen inches long, ears six inches, weight five to ten pounds) and at eight-months-old are sexually mature. Yes, even in the city hares breed like rabbits.

"It's interesting that an animal can live side by side with us and do well," Wood concludes. "That actually represent a significant part of the natural world. Most animals are not pests; they don't cause us problems and they don't particularly benefit us. They just are. We're a culture that's fixated on everything having a worth, a purpose, and a meaning. Here's an animal that just is and can teach us some lessons. We need to learn a lot more about how the natural world works and every animal is a window into that world. I think we can look a lot deeper into this animal. White-tailed jackrabbits can teach us that nature is not just 'out there' outside the city. It's where we live. And if we start acknowledging that we live *in* nature, then we might change some of the decisions we make about land use, planning, transportation, about how we live—about everything. It's about living with nature, not living against nature."

RAILROADS AND RAVINES

CATHERINE KUEHNE

We didn't live in suburbia—where nothing happened. We lived by the Gainers meat processing plant. We lived where trains ran and whistles announced them like the trumpets that heralded arriving dukes and duchesses, kings and queens. We lived where diesel-smoke-darkened engines pulled long freight trains driven by seasoned engineers. The trains came from faraway places and we wondered what the crews had seen, what adventures they had experienced.

But no matter how worldly they were, they still looked for us. They waved to us. They waved to us! And we never missed a chance to wave to them.

In summer we would disappear from our homes to the empty lot or the ravine bushes, only to emerge at the sound of a train. In the midst of hide-and-seek or Mother-May-I, we would hear the call of the train when it crossed at 69th Avenue and 96th Street. We would quickly assess who was winning. But when we heard the second whistle as the train was crossing 69th Avenue and 93rd Street, we started to run. We ran to the crest overlooking 76th Avenue. It was an overhang, where the road dug into the hillside as it descended into the ravine.

The final whistle blew as it crossed 76th Avenue at the bottom of the ravine. We couldn't see the train until it lunged onto the black oiled trestle bridge. Steel scraped against steel, the thick metal bands straining against the weight. But we loved the sound of the thump, thump as the wheels passed the joints at either end of the bridge, built sixty years before. We stood there, each hoping that we would be the first to be seen by the engineer or the man in the caboose. The man in the red caboose always seemed to be especially on the look-out for us.

The engineer couldn't always look up. He was often focused on the sharp corner—a natural place that the creek had cut over years of

Childhood in Ritchie Ravine, circa 1965

spring torrents. The sharp turn meant that they were almost there. It would have been a welcome relief for the crew. They could unload their cargo of angry cattle and pigs at Gainers.

Yes, we lived by Gainers processing plant, a hub of activity and noise. And because of it, we had trains and cows and trucks and pigs.

The Gainers building was an enormous white concrete structure. It stretched over two city blocks and its shadow blocked three stories of sunlight. We could easily see it from the crest. People came from all over the city to work there. We watched them arrive on buses and in cars and disappear into the building, carrying their tin lunch boxes. It was an important place. We did not know about blue-collar workers, market value, or the stigma of living close to an industrial railroad track or a meat-packing plant. The whistle from the train and smells and sounds of Gainers were as much a part of us as the ravine and our friends. This was our neighborhood.

There was action in our neighborhood. We were city children but we saw and heard cows bellow at each other and at their masters. We heard the indignant grunts of the pigs, and their squeals at the injustice of forced walks up the ramp. We could smell their manure on hot summer days. We witnessed the renegade cows that escaped from their captors. We were almost country kids. We knew a lot.

The open fields were the closest thing we had to farmland. The forest was new—still bearing the ravages of years of farming. There were no trees blocking our view. We broke trails through the low-lying, dense Saskatoon and poplar bushes that weren't even tall enough to be fighting for light.

There was an empty lot next to our house: the original Ritchie farmhouse. The house had a sprawling front porch partially hidden by a scrawny old spruce tree that challenged the height of the two-storey house. There was a suite on the top floor with dormers facing each direction. When tenants left, we wanted to be the first in there before my mother could clean away the clues of the people. They would leave treasures, the cast-off possessions they thought unworthy of a trip to their next home.

There were many children in our neighborhood. Some anchored the neighborhood: Muellers, Wrights, Schmidts, and Lees. There were many other children who came for a while, perhaps a summer or two. We didn't understand rent or why the children came into our neighborhood for short periods. We only knew that they came to be here because it was so special. For a while they could be in this place that was part country, part city, part forest, part concrete.

The trains would leave Gainers at the end of the day, but the squeals from the pigs and the mooing from cows could continue for days. We could see the holding pens that contained the animals until the building was ready to consume them. Then there would be silence. We noticed the silence more than the noise of the animals waiting to be slaughtered. It was as if the sound of imminent death was more natural than life.

However, the silence would soon be replaced by a stench and a gunmetal grey cloud, a tribute to the animals being offered as a sacrifice to our insatiable appetites for meat. Our youthful minds did not connect the slaughter to the boiled hot dogs we had for lunch.

My younger brother and I also were the source of a neighbourhood secret. Our teenaged brother had done something no adult would approve of. When the concrete sidewalk was poured in front of the Gainers building, our brother and a friend had hid behind the green *Edmonton Journal* newspaper shack.

The timing was perfect. The truck had already delivered the bundled newspapers and the *Journal*s had been carried away for distribution in their canvas sacks. When the cement truck and crew finally left, the young teenagers moved in to write their initials in the barely damp cement. My brother's were H. K.

To the younger children it was a sign of defiance that proved my brother and his friend were bold and daring. Yet still the child in them needed to cloak their true identity by using only initials. Slashing the sidewalk and all that adults said should not be done, they uttered a challenge fit for a Hardy Boy mystery, the books my brothers feasted on at night.

Our neighborhood also boasted a launch pad. In the empty space behind the rental house next to ours, my parents had built a large frame from two-by-eight-foot planks. It was filled with dumptruck loads of sand to buffer our jumps off the highest crescendo our swings would reach. This sandpit was the site of many a rocket launch. Launch days were chosen for their wind. We needed a northerly wind that would take the remains of the rocket boosters by parachute into the ravine past the tracks and the trestle bridge. When the countdown started, children from both sides of the block would come running to the sandbox and wait until the rocket was ready to launch.

After the launch the search for the white plastic parachute began. The farther the distance from the launch site, the more perfect the rocket design. The noise from the cows and pigs cheered the search on.

The sound from the animals was less frequent in winter. Yet on the days that the animals came and the plant ran, the sound carried further and clearer on crystallized air. It pushed through the walls of our homes, reminding us of summer, when our children's laughter would join in the animal choir.

Our childhood didn't slowly fade, though. It was slaughtered.

We were warned about strangers. We were told to stay together. At the time it seemed like a silly adult rule. Why would friends ever be apart?

Little did we know that sexual predators seemed to be quite nice people and liked following the paths that years of children's short-cuts had created. They liked exploring in the bushes like we did. We were excited when adults shared our interest and we were willing to befriend them much too quickly. They liked to play hide-and-seek. We hid and they sought. And they found us.

The trains stopped running soon after. We did not run as eagerly toward things that came from outside our neighbourhood. More and more we played in the safety of our own backyards. We heard the whistle but we ignored it, and soon it became a white noise filtered through the sounds of animals.

Then the Gainers plant closed down. The name was taken to a more modern building on the north side of Edmonton. Only the city-block-sized cement shell, metal-gated holding pens, and wooden unloading ramps remained.

The old Gainers building stood abandoned for years until the area's property value increased. Then they tore it down. But the building didn't leave. It sleeps quietly in the neighborhood, buried in the hillside under the high-end adult housing complex. Occasionally a sinkhole appears on the hillside as the building continues to consume anything close to it.

The thick steel tracks where our heroes drove their trains are now covered with asphalt. The trails that rest upon them are treasured by young and old travelling by bike, foot, wheelchair, and cross-country skis.

The ravine bushes are no more. Now the trees stand tall and bare, the lower branches wasted by the majestic tree crowns. The forest is so dark that no grass grows. Small bushes attempt to grow, then die out. The clearings make for a safe refuge for the many homeless people who live there, at least until a strong wind or heavy wet snowfall breaks the tall trees at their weakest spot.

The sounds of the animals can't be heard anymore. But on hot summer days the old trestle bridge still bleeds black oil.

QUEEN ELIZABETH AND THE VICE
OF THE CURVED WOOD

MINISTER FAUST

When I was six years old, my vice almost got me killed. It wasn't guns, it wasn't crack, it wasn't smack—it was tobogganing.

I lived on Saskatchewan Drive at 105th Street, back before developers had torn up the street to make room for shoebox-yuppie apartments. My family's house was one of those old houses, worn and comfortable, like an autumn sweater, and it overlooked the river valley and the modest Edmonton skyline. There was even a brewery in our line of vision back then, built up larger than the possibly vacant building that stands there now. Its top was ornate, strangely so for a brewery, and it looked like a castle. That was how the area was. For a six-year-old, it was magic better than anything in Tolkien.

Down a shaft of wooden steps, the valley unfolded and revealed Queen Elizabeth outdoor pool. When school was out for the year, Queen E. served as a beacon for the summer-drunk, for picnickers, for families and teenaged puppy love couples on walks under fat, green July leaves. And when school returned and Halloween fell and winter came, the river parks were covered with frozen marzipan a foot or two thick, and the brown of trees stood out in honest nudity against ice cream hills and valley.

When I was six, the area seemed endless. I had only the vaguest mental map of it all. Back then, I guess the part that one could label "Here there be tygers" would have been 105th Street and 99th Street wrapping around Queen Elizabeth Park, with cars zooming lethally up and down those slippery roads (yes, *up*, too, for the city was only a year or so into the Purvis mayoralty and many one-way mainstays were still bidirectional). Any tobogganner (tobogganeer?) foolish enough to fly near the edges of the park, or to avoid laying down the foot brakes in time, could find himself quickly cadaverized.

My tobogganing partner was Jeff Park. Tobogganing partners

didn't have to be your best friend, but it helped. Jeff lived with his family on top of the Hainstocks' funeral home, where his parents were the live-in directors. I've never gotten over the feeling that there's something just a little *off* about living above a funeral home. Even the name, "funeral home," seems bizarre. Not that we ever saw any dead people, mind you—even if our toboggan pilot careers almost saw us as customers of Hainstocks' a thousand times.

Jeff and I were your typical six-year-old Edmonton boys of 1976. Well, your typical *south side* boys, anyway. *Star Wars* hadn't yet come out, nor had Micronauts, and you could still get five gumballs for a nickel at Don's Grocery across from Mount Carmel Catholic Elementary and Junior High School. And we didn't need much to be best friends, other than sharing a few gum balls, and a few ice cream sandwiches, and a few Hot Wheels cars, and dutifully dragging Jeff's toboggan the six blocks north from his house to mine and my toboggan and his the half block and down the staircase to Queen Elizabeth Park. When you're six, there really are a billion worlds of wonder, and a trillion things to talk about, though for the life of me I can hardly recall what.

Certainly there weren't girls. That wouldn't come for another few years. There were probably rival boys, especially the barbarians of grade two. And of course, there was always, always, just how fast and from how high a dangerous hill we had gone and would go. And the fact that Jeff was White didn't seem strange, either, for so were most of the kids at Mount Carmel. Jeff might've been a little taller than I was, and I might've had a smarter mouth, but all in all we weren't so different.

Sometimes Jeff's older brother Jim would even come along to supervise us. Keep in mind, this was before the public even imagined assaults against children or lurking molesters behind every water fountain. So for the most part, Jeff and I tobogganed with only ourselves for guidance. In fact, it was probably one of those days that Jeff and I started to slide down Walterdale Hill, the one that connects 109th Street to the 105th Street bridge. We had started out all right, each of us gliding gently and accelerating down the hill along the snowbanks on our own 'boggans, an overly cautious two metres or so from the roadway of pick-ups, cabs, and buses. Somehow or other, perhaps due to a groove in the snow or the juice of acceleration, Jeff and I lost formation, and as he was sucked off to the right ahead of me, I zoomed off and into the road, flying directly beside, and matching speed for speed with, a few tons of automobiles headed for the bridge. I have no idea how I got out of that one, incidentally. I just remember it as being a thrill, and laughed about how exciting it had been. It never occurred to me that I would have been a parka-rhubarb burrito if my thrusters had failed me or my stabilizers had given out.

But that's not the incident I want to tell you about. No, in fact, the day in question should have been extremely safe, as Jeff's brother Jim, who was probably in grade six, was with us. As I recall, it was after school, and the sky was cast over, slate. The day was fairly typical, not too cold, although at six you've still enough baby fat that winter rarely has much of a bite. I doubt we were dressed up much, probably just boots and parkas and such, with hoods or balaclavas instead of toques. And of course, no six-year-old ever wore gloves; it was mitts—the woolen kind your mother makes you. When you used them the way you're supposed to when you're six, namely, to make snowballs and snow forts and snowmen and snow angels, well, the mitts would tend to get soggy, especially when it was only a few degrees below zero— but they'd also sprout these crazy little ice berries across the netting of the wool. Periodically you'd have to rub your mitts against a chain-link fence if you wanted to maintain any semblance of dexterity.

Anyway, that afternoon, we'd been tobogganing long enough that our mitts were veritable ice-berry bushes, but as there were no fences around, we just kept our engines roaring and flew all over the park in our wooden AVRO Arrows. When we'd find a really good stretch of hill, Jim would hop on with one of us, and the extra mass would give us a massive push, shooting us dozens of metres farther than our puny sixty-pound frames could.

Now, the thing about tobogganing is that it's intoxicating. With every tree narrowly dodged (and the more narrowly, the better), with every bump or jump slid over, with every wipeout wiped out, the thrill becomes greater, yet the risk seems to melt away. I think that was why I decided to sail on and ignore the command, "Pull out!" that day.

It's funny, because even as I'm now writing this, the exact memory of what happened has just popped into my head. Jeff and I backed up some considerable distance. We were going to make a northward trajectory, sweep in low and fast past the picnic tables and between a few eye-trees, then pull out with a double lean and swing to the west. It was a simple manoeuvre for two on a single toboggan: the pilot would lean into the curve and the rear-seated helmsman would lay down a foot into the oncoming snow on the side of the turn. We had made the manoeuvre dozens of times. It should have been simple.

Jim stood on the side, probably checking his watch, probably thinking it was time to return home for *Happy Days*. Jeff and I backed up, got far enough up the incline to pick up the necessary speed we'd need. As a last thought, with barely a nod between us, we backed up some more. Pilots and helmsmen understood things like this; we had the right stuff. A few dozen more steps up the hill would give us just that much more kick.

We found the spot and turned round the craft, me holding the reins, Jeff taking her by the tail. We placed our legs on either side of the 'boggan, waiting to sit down before we released our foot brakes and hit our butt-triggered gravitic accelerators. I turned around; Jeff gave me a "ready" nod. I turned back, looked down the hill, saw up ahead the 105th Street bridge and downtown behind it. Both the river and 99th Street were hidden by the slope of hills. I sat down, kept my feet firmly in the snow. I felt the bounce and raise of the craft as Jeff planted himself.

"Ready?" I asked him.

"Ready," he said.

On beat we waddled slightly forward to give us our first acceleration. We lifted our feet into the craft. Then the snow let go, and we fell forward, free.

As we picked up speed, the tobogganeer's myopia took over: only those objects within crashing distance really existed from our perspective. It was a straight line for us until the banking curve zone beyond the picnic tables. Trees, outside the range of our tobogganeer's myopia-induced short-range radar (TMISR), didn't even show up as blips on our screens.

We shot past them, hurtled down the hill, faster than we'd ever flown before. The slope flattened out and we kept going. We entered the turning zone. On cue, I banked hard to my left, throwing my acceleration into the curve. Jeff put his foot in the snow on the left to give us the portside deceleration we needed to complete the manoeuvre. And then it happened.

I will never know for sure, of course, but this is what I've reconstructed: Jeff plowed his foot into the snow and hit something solid, probably a root, activating his emergency ejection from the rear of the canopy. Lightened, the craft shot forward even faster, my helmsman sprawled on the snow behind me. Instead of banking, I was simply shooting forward freely, but virtually skiing on the left edge of the toboggan. Jim and Jeff screamed out something, but in the remaining seconds, my attention was occupied chiefly with my TMISR readings: barely dodged picnic tables, barely dodged evergreens and eye-trees, and missing earth.

The earth surrendered me to the cliff and the cliff to the void, solid snow and ground shooting rearward, replaced with the thinnest of winter air. The 'boggan lurched forward, then caught in the gravity well, nosed downward. I sent out an intense oral distress signal, then came down a metre or more to hit the sharply inclined downward slope of the cliff—only to plunge directly into the traffic.

Cars screeched and dodged. Drivers, rather than concerned, were furious at the risk to their legal well-being. One driver called out something, and another, a White male with glasses and a moustache, called out, "You son of a bitch!"

Terrified, confusedly ashamed at having inconvenienced these grown-ups, I scrambled to my feet and grabbed the reins of the toboggan with my ice-berried mitts. Fortunately the road was pebbly and high-friction. If it had been any icier, I'd have shot right under the voracious wheels of a bus or a truck or an Olds.

I desperately tried to scramble back up the cliff, but the four or five metres up the slope were too slippery. I glanced up the road, found a smaller distance, walked over to the area and walked up. Jeff and Jim were screaming, shouting, wanting to know if I was all right.

I was all right—a little shaken, but no bones crushed or anything. Nonetheless, without any explanation, we ended the day, returned home. We continued to toboggan, of course, and I doubt that we ever gave it much thought. To this day the fact that I very nearly died that afternoon, that in fact I've never been closer to death, seems unreal, untrue. But that is part of the magic of memory. That was part of the magic of the area. And while today I suppose I might have switched my tobogganing vice for a few other vices, I cannot help but reflect with glory upon those days, when a piece of curved wood could offer the greatest thrill of our lives.

OF STALLIONS AND ITALIANS

KAREN VIRAG

Horse sense is the thing a horse has that keeps it from betting on people.
—W. C. Fields

There is nothing like the smell of horse dung in the evening. Especially when it comes out of a beautiful winning racehorse and it's followed by the scent of cigarettes, coffee, and booze. And, yes, I know I have invoked an astonishing number of vices in a few brief words, but this is a cry from the heart. These are, after all, terrible times for us sybarites, as we try to ignore the metaphoric finger of those who would disapprove wagging in our face: "Naughty, naughty. Mustn't do." To escape this ubiquitous censure, I have always been drawn to cultures and places like Edmonton's Little Italy, where people meet to sociably indulge in some of the finer things in life. Food and drink, for example—Edmonton's Italian Centre is the best grocery store in the city, bar none, and the local coffee shops know how to make a proper espresso, a skill woefully lacking in the generic chains, no matter how pseudo-Euro their menu boards. And to punctuate one's sips of cappuccino are the cries of the card-playing Italian men who boisterously gesticulate, smoke, and undress women with their eyes. But so what? I have lived long enough in this titillating but unsatisfying, germ-obsessed culture that I welcome a challenge to the self-righteous orthodoxies of the various isms and the intolerance of the politically correct, who would have all of us live irredeemably dull lives driven by "family values" and stultifying moderation. And though my best days of flouting the strictures of the nice are behind me, I look back fondly at my relative youth, much of which was spent betting on the ponies at Northlands Race Track with a larger-than-life group of hard-living working-class Italian men, whose common love was the sport of kings—horse racing, which is a perfect showcase for both the glory of the equine and the folly of man, Italian or otherwise.

Stallions

Italians made up a relatively small percentage of Alberta's population prior to the Second World War, but the 1950s saw a wave of immigration that increased the population in Edmonton from a few thousand to about fifteen thousand by the late 1970s. Currently, it is estimated that there are between twenty thousand and twenty-five thousand Italian-Canadians in Edmonton. Many of the newly arriving families moved into the area bordered by 107th and 118th Avenues, and 93rd and 97th Streets, and the area became known as Little Italy. It's a nice, working class area, just skirting and sometimes dipping into the rather down-on-its-luck inner city of Edmonton. The area has many big, colourful wood-framed houses, none of which are fronted by three-car garages—people actually sit on their stoops in this neighbourhood, which also boasts a number of cafés, a funky gardening and ceramics store, and a nice park named after the Italian explorer Giovanni Caboto, erroneously known to generations of Canadian schoolchildren as John Cabot, an Englishman.

I am not of Italian origin, but my ex-partner of many years is a Calabrian who could never remember my birthday but could tell you what horse came in third in the daily double on a Wednesday two weeks before. I *almost* forgave him, because, though I have never even sat on a horse, even as a young girl, I was enthralled with the deeds of Man o' War and Northern Dancer, in a devotion with clear Freudian undertones. But it cannot be denied: there is something sexual about horses—those huge, limpid eyes; those curving haunches aside a dusky crack; the long, silky tail; the pulsating power. It can't be accidental that Swift made the equine *houyhnhnms* in *Gulliver's Travels* the superior race and represented us humans as dirty and lowly yahoos.

The first horse race in Edmonton took place in 1882, in the Ross Flats area, south of Jasper between 103rd and 104th Streets. In 1900 the races moved to their present location, at Northlands, northeast of downtown. The main barn complex at Northlands, which included stalls for up to eight hundred horses and quarters for the horsemen, was completed in 1960; the long barn and an additional 190 stalls were added during the next decade. In 1974 the track was expanded from a half mile to five furlongs, a furlong, or "furrow long," being an early Tudor term designating the distance an ox could pull a plough before needing to rest; that is, 220 yards or an eighth of a mile. In 1995 the main grandstand was completely modernized, and Northlands began simulcasting races from all over the world.

There are two kinds of racehorses: the thoroughbred and its smaller, less glamorous cousin, the standardbred, the horses used in harness racing. The name standardbred is derived from the requirement that the horse meet a certain standard of either speed over a mile or breeding in order to be properly registered. Jockeys ride thoroughbreds, while the standardbreds pull a flimsy carriage called a sulky, in which the driver sits. The standardbreds are not allowed to gallop—they either trot (the left front and right rear legs move in unison in a diagonal gait) or pace (the legs on one side of the body move in tandem in a faster gait than trotting). Standardbreds are disqualified if they break stride during the race. I always preferred the thoroughbreds; the gait of the harness horses always seemed a tad awkward, like women in high heels running to catch a bus.

The horses run year-round, rain or shine, snow or withering sun, and every race night, we used to gather at one of the Italian cafés on 95th Street for some pre-race braggadocio, which included the passing along of gossip about the jockeys or drivers, and tips, all of them bad. The composition of the group varied greatly but there were regulars: Renato, my smooth-talking ex; Tony, or Toto, his handsome, saturnine friend; Ettore, Tony's sweet-natured brother-in-law; Frank, an untrustworthy but amusing scoundrel; Giovanni Senza Paura (Fearless John), a glum fellow nicknamed after a character in an Italian fairy tale, and perhaps the skinniest man in Edmonton; Baffi, Italian for *moustache*, so called because of the thick, chestnut-coloured, almost-surely-dyed bar of hair over his lip. After much negotiating, we'd all pile into one or more cars, and in ten minutes, we'd be at Northlands for the stirring, almost martial, bugle call to the post.

Tradition, or is it superstition, is the overarching *modus operandi* at the track. Tony orders a coffee from the same waitress and folds his program the same way every day. Baffi, with a dogged faithfulness worthy of Penelope, always bets at the same window where, years before, he once bet on a long shot and won. Renato flirts with the women who work at the betting wickets, waits until the last possible second to bet, then paces around the TV monitors—these guys never watch the event live—as the announcer calls the race. "And they're off! The Titmeister takes an early lead and he's burning up the track with Cousin It in close pursuit as they head down the backfield stretch and now Dan o' War is making his move as they round the clubhouse turn and head down the home stretch to the wire and it's The Titmeister by two lengths with Dan o' War two lengths behind him and now Bitter and Twisted is making his move but it's still The Titmeister by one length now by a neck and it's The Titmeister by a nose!" A few celebratory whoops can be heard among the groans of disappointment, and the losers are left to ponder the wouldas, couldas, shouldas of the situation or to utter imprecations or to make it to the conveniently located instant teller before the next race begins. (I, on the other hand, a modest and infrequent bettor, am left to ponder the dark recesses of the brain from which people derive names for horses. Even the dignified names like Secretariat seem silly. How could anyone apply a word meaning *office staff* to a creature more awe-inspiring than a hundred supermodels laid end to end?)

Now, the next race is about to start. Renato has just placed his bet; Tony is on his fourth cup of tarry coffee, looking dour. It's post time. But wait. Who's that approaching? Oh no! It's Giorgio, the harbinger of ill winds, Mister Rainy Day, a walking dark cloud, a jinx. Whenever Giorgio is around, everyone loses, though no one can explain why they also lose when Giorgio is not there. Poor Giorgio. He looks like the human incarnation of a garden gnome with a silly putty nose. How could he be so dangerous? But the guys are adamant—Giorgio is a *scalogna*. I try to discover the story of his jinxworthiness, but it involves a murky event in Montréal many years before and no one seems to know the details or wants to talk about them. As the race progresses, Giorgio, his usual cigarette perched in the corner of his mouth, stands at the edge of the crowd. As the horses thunder down the home stretch, a mysterious force, perhaps the finger of God himself, seems to have taken hold of the reins of Renato's horse and is pulling it back. The horse begins to flag as another drives up from the side and overtakes to win the race. Renato furiously looks around for Giorgio, who has quietly faded into the crowd.

One cardinal rule at the track is that you never throw out your ticket before the results are official. One day, Giovanni Senza Paura threw his ticket on the floor in disgust after his horse came in second. He shouted out the usual baseless accusations: the jockey had been bought off and that *stronzo* (turd) Frank had given him a bum tip and Giorgio had arrived just as the horses were rounding the clubhouse turn. However, after an enquiry the initial winner was disqualified, meaning that Giovanni Senza Paura's horse had actually won. Sadly, his winning ticket was now just a minute piece of paper in a big, filthy sea of garbage that included hot dog wrappers and cigarette butts. No matter. Giovanni, true to his nickname, fearlessly fell to his knees in the general location of the ticket's last known whereabouts and began sorting through the refuse. His friends scattered at the sight of his humiliation, even as they knew deep down that they would have done exactly the same thing.

Some people do seem to have more than their share of bad luck, though, over and above the Giorgio effect. One of our friends, Fred, a small florid man with a shock of mad-scientist white hair, was a truly serious gambler; in other words, his wife had kicked him out and his family disowned him. And in the manner of the really dissolute, he was also a serious drinker. One day, Fred was sitting at the bar, losing race after race and downing rye after rye. After a particularly cruel photo-finish loss, he began to pound his fists on the bar. Furious with the fates, he impugned the morals of the jockey and the jockey's mother, as well as those of the horse and its mother. It was a spectacular and entertaining rage, if unappreciated by the bartender, who cut Fred off. At this point, Fred's anger went into the stratosphere, and he began to impugn the morality of the bartender and *his* mother. Racetrack workers learn to inure themselves to bad behaviour, but even they have limits, so when Fred pointed at the bartender and squeaked, "I fucked your wife!," he crossed a line. The bartender rushed out from behind and punched Fred; Fred responded with a wild, almost girlish flailing of the arms. Spittle flew; a shirt ripped. Finally, security guards separated the men; the bartender continued to curse Fred, who had fallen to the floor, writhing in apparent agony, screeching, "My back! My back! You hurt my back! I'm going to sue you, you bastards!" The security men informed Fred that he was barred and waited patiently for him to arise from his poorly faked back injury. He eventually did and was escorted outside to wait out the period of his banishment. Some weeks later, he reappeared, cocky, unrepentant, and with the unenviable new nickname of My Back.

As for winning, it does happen. One day, Renato won eleven hundred dollars on a fairly small bet, which rendered him a popular and well-loved figure, for a time. Losing is far more common, of course, and the alternating pattern of loss measured by various horse body parts (a length, a neck, a nose) is as cruel and maddening as a beautiful tease who invites love but always stops your hand at the waistband of her underwear.

A casino was constructed at Northlands as part of the 1995 renovations. In response to my negative comments about this development,

Jonathan Huntington of Northlands told me that in actuality the slot machines have saved racing in this province. For years, despite the money poured into the industry by Renato, Baffi, and company, horse racing was in decline in Alberta; purses were down and many of the horsemen were getting out of the business. Now, 51 per cent of the money put into the slots is invested in the horses. Purses have increased, attendance is up, and the horsemen are happy. Still. One day just after the opening of the slots room at Northlands, I ran into an acquaintance carrying a margarine tub full of quarters. She was planning to spend the next couple of hours plugging money into a computerized machine programmed to take it away from her. The casino also features a game in which people sit at consoles and bet on plastic horses running around a miniature plastic track, all of this while an extraordinary, real human and animal pageant unfolds outside. Clearly, Swift knew whereof he spoke.

Horse racing is animated roulette, a mug's game and a fool's errand, a tragicomic spectacle, in which the assorted varieties of humanity, from Rasta men to urban cowboys to Chinese shopkeepers, gamble their hard-earned money in the usually vain hope that, somehow, someday, they will beat the odds. Some consider gambling immoral, and a day at the races still bears a slight whiff of moral turpitude. Frankly, I have never been able to assign this kind of dimension to horse racing. What is the morality in trying to decide which of a group of horses will cross a line first? No doubt some see gambling as a sensual affront; this is, after all, a society that distrusts pleasure and abandon, and associates even chocolate and coffee with sin. Perhaps some see an anti-religious element in gamblers' cocksure reliance on that ineffable, otherworldly, almost pagan thing known as *luck*.

The poet Andrew Marvell wrote, "Now let us sport us while we may / Let us roll all our strength, and all / our sweetness, up into one ball; / And tear our pleasures, with rough strife, / through the iron gates of life." I often thought of these lines as I moved in this strange, dramatic world and savoured its paradoxes, pain, and occasional intense pleasure, and watched its denizens with an admixture of horror and affection. I once saw a man wheeled out on a stretcher, an apparent victim of a heart attack, whose parting gesture was to raise a feeble hand and give his friend money to put on the three horse. Then there was Fanfarone (Italian for *braggart*), whose doctor told him to immediately cease smoking, drinking, and gambling. The last time I saw him he was sitting in one of those motorized carts and was hooked up to an oxygen machine. A rye and Coke waited on the table in front of him, and a cigarette burned patiently in an ashtray as he intently studied the racing program. And though my responsible half was appalled, my passionate half (or what remains of it after years of assaults by the League of the Perpetually Offended and Outraged) applauded him because he simply didn't give a toss, and in this anorexia-and-bulimia-Calorie-Restriction-Society-liposuction-and-TV culture, that counts for a lot in my book.

I haven't gone to the races for a while now, but I live near Northlands, and I occasionally go for an early morning walk to watch the trainers put the horses through their morning paces in air redolent with the ripe scent of equines—their dung, their sweat, their puffing breath. And as the earth trembles to the drumbeat of hooves, I think of my old crowd, most of whom still meet for cards, gesticulation, and flirtation in the cafés of Little Italy, though their visual disrobing of every new female on the scene might be a bit clouded with cataracts. I often think fondly of those times, those green and heedless days, when we gambled, tempted fate, and brashly entered staring contests with the *malocchio*, the evil eye, and, sometimes, it blinked first. We never cheated death, of course, or made him stand still, but in a marvellous Marvellian twist, for a few brief shining moments, like a racehorse, we made him run.

CITY OF MY GROIN

LYNNE VAN LUVEN

A while ago, I tried to explain what a sexy city Edmonton had been in the '80s. I was making my case to a West Coast friend who spent the '60s as a dropped-out hippie chick, one of those girls with outrageous short skirts, the kind of girl I used to hate. While I sat on the sofa, petting my orange tabby cat in my matronly way, I told her long, convoluted stories about how exciting life had been, in Edmonton, in the '80s. She seemed dubious, just the reaction you would expect of someone who had always lived on Vancouver Island—and had spent part of that time residing in a converted fishboat parked alongside one of the more remote Gulf Islands. Residing, I might add, with a dude and a dog that was a German Shepherd/wolf/Husky cross.

"There just seemed to be a lot of sex," I finished lamely, as I remembered how people—not necessarily me, you understand—had led interestingly raunchy lives back then.

Okay, maybe Edmonton was nothing like Greenwich Village in its heyday or Haight-Ashbury in the '60s or Berlin during the Weimar years. I dunno, I wasn't there, in any of those places, then. But I was in Edmonton in the early '80s. Given my personal and fiscal limitations, that was the best I could do. At the time, several people intimated it was far better than I deserved.

Edmonton in the '80s always reinhabits my memory as a city of sex and seduction where transgression might erupt just around the next corner. A city of the groin. People guffaw when I say that. Mention "Edmonton," and a pained, pitying expression flits across their faces.

They're thinking, "Yeah, right."

They are thinking Deadmonton and Redmonton. They are thinking snowbanks and lodgepole pines and the bleak expanse of Jasper Avenue in January. Some of them might even be thinking timber wolves and snowshoes, for all I know. They are not thinking *jouissance* or the pleasure of the text; they are not thinking about *both kinds* of intercourse and the excitement of new ideas. Maybe they missed a lot, those folks.

I can recognize the signs: I missed a lot myself, had my head down all through the '60s and struggled to get *somewhere* all through the '70s.

Those who scoff loudest at my picture of Edmonton probably never lived in the intellectual ghetto around the Garneau area, where for almost a decade I moiled amongst mounting dust bunnies, library photocopies, day-old bread, and stacks of lit-crit. Their idea of Edmonton does not encompass the neighbourhood I called home, with its cosy 1940s houses and its shabby but comfortable walk-up apartments.

◆◆◆◆

If art critic John Berger is right when he says every city has both a sex and an age, then my Edmonton is about thirty-three and feeling its oats, indulging itself with an innocence that now seems wilfully ignorant if not downright irresponsible. We'd heard about something called The Gay Plague, in Edmonton, in the early '80s. In fact, the first mention of AIDS in the *Edmonton Journal* occurred in a 21 July 1982, story. The article said, "Four confirmed cases of the so-called gay plague that has killed at least 155 persons in the United States have surfaced so far in Canada." And sure enough, on 29 January 1983, Edmonton public health officials confirmed the city's first suspected case: an American man who returned to the United States for "special tests" after assuring health officials he had been celibate while in Edmonton. It should have been sobering news, but most of us, especially the heterosexuals, thought it had nothing to do with us and partied on.

We knew about feminism too, back in the '80s. Well, women my age did, anyway. We'd been through the consciousness-raising pains of the '70s and had worked for women's rights. I'd spent the last years of the '60s writing "first-woman ever" newpaper stories: first woman firefighter, first woman police inspector, first woman engineer. As much as I wanted to promote my peers' efforts, even I got tired of writing the stories after a while. By October 1989, Edmonton had even elected Jan Reimer as its first woman mayor. Ottawa had been much faster off the mark, electing the wonderfully outspoken Charlotte Whitton as *Canada's first woman mayor* way back in 1951.

Yet, even though we supposedly knew all these things about sex and equality, I don't recall our behaviours improving appreciably. We just seemed to cavort on, in our heedless and somewhat bumbling fashion. The women I knew, myself included, didn't seem very adept at protecting themselves from heartbreak while they tried to be sexually liberated. And the men, well, the men were all for liberation—as long as it didn't mean they had to change their habits and behaviours.

I laugh aloud now, a sardonic, aged cackle, when I remember my initial shock at discovering that sex was happening beyond the pages of the books I so obsessively consumed. It was, in fact, happening among people all around me, disparate sorts of people, people of whom you wouldn't expect it. It further shocked me that all these people were having their lots of sex everywhere: propped against the girders of the High Level Bridge, banging away in grotty upstairs rooms, and going down in dank basement suites. They were tucked away and spooning in the stacks of Rutherford Library. They were grabbing quickies in the bathrooms between the third and fourth floors of the Humanities Centre; they were groping one another amid the tangled underbrush along the margins of Hawrelak Park. Aphrodite only knew what went on in the dark bushes beside the Power Plant, the graduate student watering hole that was my social nexus in those years. Professors seduced students and students seduced each other—and professors too. In fact, as I soon learned, it was *not having sex* that made you exceptional, maybe even a little exotic.

◆◆◆◆

The funny thing is, I was one of those people you wouldn't expect it of. Out of step with my demographic group, I completely missed out on the major spasms of the sexual revolution: I had spent the '60s in Saskatchewan, insanely focused on getting an undergraduate degree and finding work; I think I had about five dates in three years—and some of those were mercy missions arranged by friends. At twenty, I did what most educated young Saskatchewan folks did: I moved to Alberta. There, I found a job as a reporter; at twenty-two, I married my first lover. We'd had sex; therefore, we *had* to get married. In the mid-'70s, a move to Southern Alberta, the heart of Mormon Country, took me further away from the lascivious indulgences of mainstream Albertans. I spent the latter half of the '70s depressed. I found some companionship and solace among a group of women who worked to establish Lethbridge's first women's centre. But I remember spending a lot of time worrying that wearing lipstick might mean I was a bad feminist, or at least a frivolous one.

By the time I moved to Edmonton in the autumn of 1980, I was convinced I was *old, old, old*. I couldn't afford to waste another nanosecond of my life. I was knife-keen about school, hell-bent upon improving my mind, and dead serious about escaping the snares of middle-class life. I tell you, I cringe to recollect myself. I was having my teenage rebellion twenty years too late.

Even though I galloped toward change, any change, with wide-open arms, it took me a couple of years to catch a ride on time's winged chariot. I had, after all, been raised in the prairies, where our watchwords are, "Better safe than sorry," and, "Look before you leap." (You never know when a cowpie or a gopher hole might trip you mid-pirouette.)

"I think of you as a nice little bourgeois housewife," my famous novel-writing professor told me one winter afternoon, during a heated class discussion over a female character's motivation. I can still hear the patriarchal timbre of his voice as I watched the magpies cavort in the evergreens beyond the seminar room windows.

That comment pissed me off. Who the hell was HE to say who I was? He had never limped along in my Amalfi wedgies. But in retrospect, I can see why I might have seemed like an errant Molly Maid. I still hadn't learned to wear blue jeans as uniform. Instead, I had an elaborate wardrobe, in which skirts and tops were carefully matched. Even accessorized. I had assembled these outfits during lunch-hour spending sprees in downtown Lethbridge, where I stimulated the economy as an undiagnosed "depression shopper." I had short blonde hair and an earnest glow about my pudding face; I never did learn to assume the grad student's patina of ironic detachment and soul-deep ennui. Instead, I was *excited* to wake up every morning with new books to read. I rushed about perkily, eyes peeled for new experience. I blush to remember how quaint I must have seemed to those big-city folks.

••••

And in those heady early days, my wide gold wedding band still shone on the third finger of my left hand. Really, I liked that ring. I'd picked it out myself, scornful of diamonds, but I also needed it as a symbol of my tethered state. I was, you see, a faithful—though wilful—wife. In the fall of 1980, I flew home every other weekend, via Time Air (now defunct), to visit my husband and my calico cat in our tidy Cape Cod bungalow (now disbanded) on Dieppe Boulevard, not far from Henderson Lake (man-made and sometimes stinky in the dry months). I worked desperately to stitch the two parts of my ravelling life together.

My mother had scolded me for jeopardizing my "perfectly good marriage" with what she saw as frivolous dissatisfaction and a quest for more education. (How much more useless stuff did I need to know anyway? Why wasn't I getting on with the business of babies?) I knew I'd stepped beyond the family pale.

My way of managing my transgressions was to make an unspoken deal with the devils of conformity: I could go away to study if I could remain irrevocably *normal* when I was back at home. If I cleaned the house, went out to dinner with our friends, didn't talk too much about the books I was reading "at school," then maybe we could weather this. If I didn't seem to be having too good a time up north, then maybe my husband wouldn't feel too resentful or threatened. And then maybe we could continue to believe nothing was really changing in our relationship. And maybe *then* we could hang on to what we had. I was playing with a stacked deck in a tremulously doomed house of cards.

So, everyone was right, even when they were wrong: I was a little wifey on the lam in those early-'80s days on the banks of the North Saskatchewan.

It's difficult to imagine now, how geographically confined was the life I led in Edmonton in the early '80s. I had no car, but then, who needed to cross the High Level Bridge to investigate the fleshpots of downtown Edmonton or to check out the Stroll on 97th Street? Even though West Edmonton Mall, in its embryo form of only 220 stores, had opened its doors for the first time in September 1981, it was at least two city bus rides away. Besides, I didn't have the money for such glitzy temptations. We had our own commercial and cultural hub along Whyte Avenue and environs: Greenwoods' Bookshoppe for all the crisp new volumes we could salivate over but not afford to buy; the Garneau Theatre for the movies we needed to argue over; the Highlevel Diner for Sunday brunches and late-night coffees; the Strathcona Hotel for a chance to drink cheap beer and gawk at bikers on Saturday afternoons; Zoryana's for that new second-hand outfit to lift our spirits. The Whyte Avenue of yore seems more diverse and interesting than today's version, even though it had fewer bars and a less rowdy night life—or is that just my memory, romanticizing events? Only rarely did we venture south or north or west to the shopping malls and assorted emporiums of greed and distraction. We had our own snug world, thank you, our own Groinich Village.

Peering back through the cobwebs, I see I lugged some mighty heavy baggage into that first sublet apartment along Saskatchewan Drive in the fall of 1980. First, there was a big satchel of hopes: I would change my world through education. I had done it once before, in the middle of the '60s when I escaped my fate as "some farmer's wife" by winning a five hundred dollar scholarship (what wealth that seemed to me!) to study English at a smaller university also perched on the banks of the North Saskatchewan. I always hoped that once I got more education, my "attitude" would improve, my dissatisfaction and boredom would evaporate. Finally, I would figure out how to do something that *counted*. In the fifteen years since I had last attended university, I had romanticized the entire pursuit-of-knowledge business. In fact, I was grateful that the University of Alberta had taken *me* on as a graduate student and even more thankful that the Department of English had given *me* a stipend as a teaching assistant. If I was really, really frugal, I thought, I could live off my $485-a-month TA's allowance, abetted by the odd dip into my savings account, propped up in mad moments by my Eaton's credit card. (Yes, there was still an Eaton's department store then; the faltering firm likely lasted as long as it did because of all the retail therapy I conducted there.) After obtaining my master's degree in English, well, who knew? Like Dickens's Mr. Micawber, I believed that eventually, magically, *something would turn up.*

My second suitcase held illusions about how a university actually functioned. Instead of seeing it as a collection of balkanized fiefdoms, each in competition with the other, I expected harmony and love. (This after actually having worked on a university campus for three years in the mid-'70s—but then we have already established the depth and breadth of my naiveté, haven't we?) As I headed back to school, I imagined myself joining a colloquium of truth-seekers. Students from all backgrounds, once in the hallowed precincts of the Faculty of Graduate Studies, would commingle, one huge extended happy family. We would stimulate each other's inquiry; we would abet each other's quests for knowledge. We would be Scholars Together, and ideas from one discipline would leaven another. I pictured our data-laden heads tilted amiably together as we discussed Truth, Beauty, and the World Situation. Even a decade of work as a journalist had not prepared me for the swamp of envy, dysfunction, contempt, and competition I would encounter in many of my classes.

And finally, thanks to Cardinal Newman's ideas about universities (imbibed in a Victorian lit class when I'd been an impressionable undergraduate), I hauled along my dusty carpet bag of ideals, the chief of which was that intellectuals were more evolved beings than the rest of us. Unlike working-class wretches such as I, they had Big Brains and the leisure to think. Ergo, they had transcended petty human weaknesses. They were the closest, I thought, that I would get to heaven on this earth.

◆◆◆

Gravity eventually lets you down with a thud, but for a firm-bodied while it seemed to be my ally. One evening early in my first semester, a visiting poet, a distinguished visitor, accosted me in the elevator after he'd addressed our class. As I recall, we were between the fourth and third floors. Descending. He was *old, old, old,* in his fifties at least. But he was foreign, and despite his balding head, funny uneven teeth, and peculiar accent, he seemed far more elegant than the boys in high school who had occasionally told me that I was "built like a brick shit-house." Nonetheless, I was badly unnerved by his halting proposition that we repair to his apartment-hotel. Shouldn't he have evolved beyond all that? Shouldn't I?

Thinking about it now, I realize the apartment hotel was across the North Saskatchewan, away from my comfortable milieu. Maybe that's why things did not go so well, back in the room with the great view of the city. Maybe that's why, in those pre-Viagra days, the visiting professor was forced to quip wryly that "Barkus was willing" but other parts of his anatomy were not up to it. Truth to tell, I was relieved more than disappointed; I'd got into that cab more out of curiosity than desire anyhow. And the experience was reassuring in a way: it proved to me that one could disrobe with a complete stranger, and a foreigner to boot, and not be struck dead by a thunderbolt from heaven. It was a beginning, but maybe it was best to confine one's peregrinations to one's peers? Months later, I got an answer of sorts to that question when I learned that the visiting professor had wreaked artistic conversion upon the entire experience: he wrote a coy short story in which a foreign professor is seduced by a northern siren, someone referred to as an Ice Maiden.

◆◆◆

"What is your point, ladies?" asked the professor I'd taken to calling King Leer. My friend S. and I had stormed his office to object to one of the many aspects of TAs' working conditions we found exploitive. We were a little overheated, perhaps even a tad incoherent.

"Hmm, I see you each have a couple of them," he added, staring deliberately at our heaving chests.

"Oh, don't mind him," the department chair said to us later, when we had swallowed our fury enough to muster our protest against such a sexist dismissal. "It's just his Italian blood."

Well, *really*, our peers asked us later over tacos and beer, amid the usual Power Plant din, what had we expected from a scholar of *nineteenth-century* Canadian literature?

I now see my assumption of the moral high ground was a tad disingenuous. After all, we students ranked professors, both male and female, by their looks and degree of hipness. And we had nasty names for many of them: The Fish, Doctor Drone, The Nazi, Herr Fop. We were equal-opportunity carpers: we said equally cruel things about the frumpy women and the clapped-out men. We had no inkling we might have been unfair to some of them: they had what we wanted, knowledge and power, we thought. And while some of the more doctrinaire profs, both male and female, sought to colonize our minds along with our bodies, students also exhibited varying degrees of innocence and connivery as they flirted with, lay with, and moved in with professors.

I was starting to be less shocked by all this, you'll be glad to hear, the more I realized how deeply the sex-gender mole burrowed at the root of all our endeavours, here in my hallowed place. Many of us were young, some of us were untried, and most of us were so goddamn righteous. Yes, knowledge is power, but now I wonder what else those male professors might have done, other than to dismiss us, if we were neither beddable nor biddable. They didn't seem to have the resources to act otherwise. Looking back, I find those times very odd indeed: the feminist theories were integral to much of what we studied, especially amongst the postmodernist and French critics, but somehow the ideas remained largely theoretical. No one seemed interested in putting them into practice, perhaps because equality was not yet really recognized as mandatory.

By the time the '80s concluded, my marriage had been dissolved amicably but painfully amid floods of tears. (My ex-husband got the cat on the grounds that he was leading a more stable life than I. And he was, I didn't have any grounds for protest!) My own subsequent misadventures had worn away the edges of my shock-ability. By the beginning of the '90s, I had ended my procrastination–avoidance syndrome and finished my Ph.D. I moved out of Groinich Village, out of the Garneau Ghetto, and eventually away from Edmonton, into "serious" jobs in other cities. But on this I stand firm: Ottawa has its patina of political power, Montréal has its European charm, Victoria has its ineffable climate. But Edmonton, ah Edmonton: you will always remain the city of my adult sexual education, my sexus–nexus.

A few months ago, I flew back to Edmonton for a meeting that just happened to be held in the Humanities Centre, in the very seminar room where that now-retired professor called me bourgeois. It was decidedly strange to sit again in that space where I first began to dismantle my wifely costume. Clichés be damned, oh, how the memories flooded back. The building seemed largely unchanged, though I recognized very few of the names on the office doors in the English department. And the shabby furniture in the hall study areas had obviously lived rough over the past two decades.

In Hub Mall, tiled some years ago to resemble a long urinal, the male professors still strode along importantly. As I sat having a solitary decaf at Java Jive, former site of hour-long coffee breaks, I felt a gust of cool air across my shoulders: there she went, the phantom of my former self. Just before she passed through the cinderblock walls to join the magpies squalling outside, she paused an instant to smile at the canoodling young couple near the automatic teller in the mall's far-west corner. Glimpsing her again confirmed what I'd always suspected and hoped: it had all been necessary, even the messy bits.

Throb on, sexy Edmonton, throb on for a new generation.

PLACES OF REFUGE

BRENDA MANN

The sun is high today. Alberta blue skies rest upon Astotin Lake as they pierce the very centre of my reflections. I sit still; the gentle breeze touches the moisture of my dampened shirt and begins to twist and turn softly within me as memories slowly drift to the surface. I glance at the lake, grebes building their island nests, a cormorant spreading its wings to dry, and a dozen or so Canada geese standing on the shoreline with their golden goslings. I come to Elk Island National Park often, this natural oasis just forty-five minutes east of Edmonton. It is a refuge for quietude, tranquility, and meditation. In the past few weeks I have come here alone to search and remember. I drive here in the evening after work, head to Shoreline Trail, and stroll to the very same place every night. I am methodical in this process. I enter the head of the trail through the Bison trap, walk along the rows of caragana, poplar, and balsam, stroll a kilometre or so down the road past the beaver dam, turn right unto Beaver Bay Peninsula, run up to the highest hill and stare. Yes, stare down at the lake almost to its very bottom, gathering memories upon memories upon memories, hoping that nature will free the unconscious into some organized pattern of thought that I can grab hold of and shake like the branches of all the trees around me. But instead the memories are heavy inside me, stuck like the trunks of the trees inside my gut, while I sit and stare.

I guess I am here to free myself by allowing the breeze to filter thoughts, memories, hurts, and hopes out of my body into the air surrounding me. This all began about a month ago. An old friend just happened to mention Club 70 to me casually one day over brunch. I smiled as I sipped my coffee and looked at her with a bit of a twinkle in my eye. I had not thought of Club 70 for years and when she mentioned it, I felt as if we were talking about another century, or someone else's life. Well, she smiled, it was over thirty years ago that we used to go there to meet others of our kind. Yes, I simply said, others of our kind, and we just looked at each other knowingly for a few seconds before turning our talk to other things: our retirement plans, the recent Supreme Court's Monsano decision, the coming election.

Walking away from her as we said goodbye, I felt melancholy, anxious, and watchful. It was hard to say why. I wanted to give myself a good kick in the pants as I wandered aimlessly past endless shops, wondering how I could still feel ashamed, anxious, and watchful just thinking about Club 70. Well, it just wasn't thinking about Club 70. It was a lot of other deeply gutted, painful memories from a time long past that were surfacing like toxic worms in my body.

I finally reached home that afternoon, unlocked the door impatiently, and headed directly toward another place of refuge for me: my library. I spent the rest of that afternoon and evening immersed in pages upon pages of lives and histories of lesbian women writers through the centuries. Their courageous writings have always helped me to ground and gather myself and remember the healthier lesbian woman I have evolved into today. It was the next day that I started driving out to Elk Island National Park, sitting and staring and weaving memories from yesterday into today, and paying homage to Club 70, a place of refuge for me then, and a part of who I am today.

Tonight in this calm hour of dusk I do not run up the hill but stay on flat ground about a hundred yards past the entrance of Beaver Bay Peninsula. I sit on a log upon the beach as the water laps back and forth at my feet. A loon swims with its chick upon its back, its primordial call awakening in my drifting thoughts black and white images that slowly start to move forward like film. Colour comes into the picture; we are in the city of Edmonton in 1974. A smaller population than today. Skyscrapers are scarce. The green and gold of the University of Alberta colours. A feminist gathering. An anti-war protest. The river valley hiking trails. And ten of us one night. Yes, ten of us. Edmontonians, pacifists, feminists, university students, women, we gathered at another place for other reasons. It is a Friday night. Ten o'clock and later, there we are at Club 70 in downtown Edmonton. Club 70, a Gay and Lesbian bar, a home away from home for us in 1974.

A quiet bar, Club 70 was a refuge we anticipated all week. We danced, relaxed, drank alcohol, smoked cigarettes, and opened up to others like ourselves. We were allowed just to be. We could let down our guards a little more than usual, and any relaxation for dykes at that time can only bring a soft smile to my somewhat harder mouth of today. We did not wear masks or pretend who we were. This was Club 70, our place of refuge. It's not even that I got tired of having different closets for different people or even that I wearied of lying all the time. That's just the way it was. We had a thousand pounds upon our shoulders and didn't even consciously know it. At least, not until our secret was disclosed. Every time I think of those disclosures, my neck begins to tense, my head begins to hurt, and I feel my whole body's instinctual desire for the hundred yard dash. "Oh, by the way, I need to tell you something that not many people know about me, but I feel we are getting to be closer friends and you need to know," or, "By the way, I am, well, you know, I sleep with women; I'm a lesbian." The rest of the conversation was generally spent trying to explain that I was not in a developmental phase, "playing" with other females before doing the right thing, marrying a man and raising a family. I am a lesbian, right down to the very core.

I remember one time I became a close friend of a woman I went to university with. Over time we shared more of our private emotions and personal lives, with one big exception . . . my sexuality. I had told her my lover was my "roommate." One day my friend and I were talking about her boyfriend, their little intimacies, their compatibilities, and even the food they enjoyed, when I just got sick and tired of it. I told her my hidden secret and she stared, yes, stared at me, and said, "You've got to be kidding." She stood up and walked away without saying another word. I never saw her again—well, at least as a friend. Whenever I did run into her, she just sort of looked at me with what seemed to be an embarrassed expression and walked in another direction as if she didn't see me. I see in Astotin a reflection of myself the day she walked away from me. I am pacing in my apartment, back and forth, back and forth, my body a volcano of rage and hurt, ready to strike out at anyone and anything. But with no one to strike out at, I dug all of my embittered emotions into a grave deep in my heart. That night I went to Club 70 alone and sat in the darkest corner with a bottle of beer and a cigarette. No one bothered me, knowing just by looking that I wanted to be alone. Club 70 was a place to be authentic in a time when there was no authenticity for gays and lesbians except behind closed doors, in a closet, or in your secret heart.

The other day I went looking to see if I could find where Club 70 was once located. I even phoned the friend who had casually brought it up at brunch to ask if she remembered, but she couldn't remember at all. Too long ago, she quietly said, and did not seem to want to talk about it anymore. I was surprised, since she had been the one to bring it up, but I could sense from her voice a sadness that I had also felt after we had left the restaurant that day. It was a place of refuge, but also a reminder of many associated feelings of rage that we do not always want to go back to. Remember, in the early 1970s we dykes hid in very deep dungeons. To be a lesbian was abnormal and a sin. We could get thrown into jail or psychiatric wards. We were not to show our faces, not to be talked about: we were invisible to the world. It said everything to me when I went looking for Club 70 and could not find it. I could not even remember the proximity of its location, only that it was in the downtown core. Evidently I had dug Club 70 deep into my repressed memories with all of society's prejudices about me as a sinful, abnormal, inverted, evil butch-dyke-lezzie-queer. I am finally digging out Club 70 from this quagmire of repressed discriminations to just be on its own. A place of refuge where once I could meet my own kind without being as afraid as I was in the outside world.

It is a Saturday night, June 1974, 11 PM. It is dark. We are driving our cars to Club 70. We leave our cars near the club but not too close. Somebody might recognize us. We look over our shoulders as we walk toward the club. We want to hold hands but can't just yet. We didn't have a name for our behaviour then, but we were full of internalized homophobia. We just thought we acted the way we had to in order to survive and keep all the hatred out; little did we know we were also keeping it in, along with all the built-in rules and laws against our very existence. We don't hold hands in public. We don't let anyone know we exist. We live in shame of our inversion. We are bad and sinful people. God will punish us. Our parents will never let us come back to the family. We will lose our jobs. We will get beaten on the streets.

But whew! We are inside the club. We can hold hands. We are still a bit nervous and so we look around just to make sure we aren't watched. We will be punished if we are seen. It is against the law. Whose law, I cry out? Our fathers' and mothers', our people's, our country's, our government's, our churches'! We breathe in relief as we hold hands inside the walls of Club 70.

But here come the police. We immediately let go of our hands (I am reminded by my partner that I still instinctively do this today). We don't smile intimately at each other right now. We show our identifications and wait for the raid to end.

When the police leave, we hold hands again and order another beer. A butch in the corner begins to yell in rage, "Who let those cops in here?" and throws her glass full of beer across the table onto the floor. The bartender comes to settle her down but she begins to argue with him, angry and humiliated, afraid and bitter. All we see is her outer toughness, not the fear permeating her very being. Her date sits quietly at the table, softly puts out her hand to touch her girlfriend's arm to help bring her pride again.

There is Sam from Montréal. He is one of the few men who come here regularly. Most of the men go to the other bar close to here, but Sam likes the quietness of Club 70 and often drops by for a drink and a chat. When I see him, I wave and ask him how he is doing. Alone here tonight, he tells me he and his partner are having a hard time of late. He doesn't know what is going to happen to them. He wants to go back to Montréal and let his parents know he is gay. His partner does not want to open up to Sam's family or his own because he feels they will be rejected, shunned, and abandoned. Sam says he is tired of all the lying and shame and wants to stand on his own and be honest. I see the struggle and know I do not have the guts to do this. I need too much to be liked and approved of. I am too afraid.

I hear the group of friends we have come with say in unison, "Let's dance." On the dance floor we let go of the tension with our bodies moving back and forth to the rocking beat of the Doors and Santana. The dance ends, we all laugh and hug each other, knowing that soon it will be time to leave. It is getting late. It is two in the morning. We begin to feel an anticlimactic nervous energy as we stare at the door that will bring us to the outside world. Feeling safe within the club was a wonderful feeling, but too short-lived. We are angry to leave these walls and enter that world again. Our feelings are hidden away in our hidden Selves. We don't know how to feel, but we do know that the world outside Club 70's door is unsafe. We are spit at, shunned, imprisoned, beaten, hated, and shamed. Until next Friday, when we can go back to Club 70, a place of refuge for lesbian women in the early 1970s.

It is July 2004 and I am just about ready to leave another place of refuge, Elk Island National Park. The waters of Astotin Lake have helped me weave together, cherish and own, memories of another very dear refuge in my heart.

NORTH SIDE STORY

IAN MCGILLIS

For all its imperfections and compromise, life does dangle those moments when things work out exactly the way they should.

I can't pinpoint the exact date, but I can narrow it down to a season and a year: autumn 1969. Me and three friends, devoted road hockey practitioners ranging in age from six to eight, were feeling restless. So one day, acting on a hunch and armed with my mother's tape measure (the cloth kind that had to be pulled and rewound manually), we set out with stout hearts for the fence surrounding the playground of Glengarry Elementary School. Our mission: to measure the distance between two of the fence's support posts, and from the connecting crossbar to the ground. The operation was conducted with utmost solemnity. Much was at stake. As we stretched that last bit of tape and read the numbers, speculation turned to giddy reality. This section of fence, we could see, was almost exactly the width and height of a regulation-size hockey net.

If I were a film director attempting to recreate that moment of discovery, my only possible choice of soundtrack would be Handel's "Hallelujah Chorus."

The implications were staggering. No more would our goalposts consist of small piles of whatever was handy; no more would our crossbar be an invisible concept, its precise height subject to heated debate every time the goalie was beaten upstairs; no longer, indeed, would we be confined to the street, where the frequent rude passage of cars necessitated the undignified temporary suspension of activities. Now we could play like the big boys, and in that era before homework and curfews and structured time, we played until it grew too dark to see.

No historical documentation of our games exists, so you'll just have to take my word for it when I say that some amazing saves were made. And when those saves were made by me, a cry from my friends would ring out around Glengarry.

Waiting for the Great One, May 1984

"Ian Wilkie! Ian Wilkie!"

Ian Wilkie was the goalie for the junior Oil Kings. It may well be assumed that in paying the tribute of calling me by his name, my friends were making creative use of the fact that I shared a given name with Mr. Wilkie. While that is no doubt partially true, I like to think that even if my name had been Darcy or Keith the tribute would have been the same. We had never seen Ian Wilkie play. A blurry mugshot sometimes printed in the *Edmonton Journal* was our only indication of what he might have looked like. For all we knew, he was one of the guys who worked weekends bagging groceries at Woodwards Food Floor. Did this in any way diminish his stature in our eyes? Of course not. It enhanced him.

Does any child of today, given the choice of all the athlete magnates whose images are pumped into our homes with battering-ram subtlety by the massed forces of media, still call out the name of a humble minor-league hometown hero?

The question, of course, is moot, as any look around any neighbourhood these days will show. Kids don't call out the names of players anymore, famous or otherwise, because kids don't play road hockey anymore. They don't have time for anything nearly so frivolous. They get driven in SUVs to soccer practices on the far side of town.

Fast forward to 1972. That section of fence has seen yeoman duty, but again, a certain vague yearning makes itself felt. We're three years older, after all. There's a world out there somewhere south of 132nd Avenue, and we hear its distant call. Our fathers, bless them, appear to understand. They drive us to the Exhibition Grounds, and while they happily go curling in the SportEx, we bear witness to the gods of hockey as our new Oilers, of the upstart WHA, take on all comers in the Edmonton Gardens.

Even then, mention of the Edmonton Gardens would invariably elicit a response very much like this:

"That old barn?"

The words were meant to be derisive. To me and my friends, though, with our limited experience of farms and all things rural, they were more like an incantation. Barns, to us, were places of great mystique. They had haylofts for hiding in and beams for swinging from and cool old farm tools that looked liked medieval torture implements. Somewhere in every barn, it seemed, some small life form or other was always giving birth.

The Edmonton Gardens, to us, was a place similarly stuffed with wonders and fully worthy of the barn comparison. The cult of the new had yet to set in, and though we couldn't have articulated it, I'm sure we felt that the Gardens' very decrepitude was an integral part of its magic. Take the balloons hanging in long strings from the rafters. These weren't just any balloons. They were uninflated balloons, or rather deflated balloons, limp and blackened with cigarette smoke. These balloons, to the best of my knowledge, were never carbon dated, but I'd be willing to bet that they'd been hanging there since the night of the building's grand opening back before the Great War.

The animal kingdom wasn't unrepresented. Cursory inspection of random nooks and crannies often revealed wasps' nests of varying vintage. And while I would never dream of disputing Alberta's status as a rat-free paradise, I swear there were times in the Gardens when I saw some uncannily rat-like creatures scurrying off with bits of popcorn.

Then there was the issue of sightlines. The Edmonton Gardens did not coddle its patrons. This was a building that made you work for the privilege of seeing what you'd come to see. At times, you were denied that privilege altogether. From the nosebleed seats at the south end of the building, fully half the ice surface was obscured by the overhanging lights. Even the wealthier citizens further down were obliged to contort themselves in order to see around the many diagonal support posts holding the great building up. But was this not cause for complaint. Heck no. We knew nothing else, remember. We were thankful for what we could see and visualized the rest.

I dream of one day having this conversation around the fire with my grandchildren:

"I was there the night Ron Climie scored five goals against the Minnesota Fighting Saints."

"Wow," my grandchildren will say. "That must have really been something to see."

To which crusty ol' Gramps will reply:

"I said I was *there*. I didn't say I *saw* it."

(They're probably likelier to ask "Ron who?" and "What's a Fighting Saint?" But never mind.)

The concentration of celebrity in that enclosed space was dizzying. I once stood within inches of Tiger Goldstick as he washed his hands in the men's washroom. You could look up toward the press box and know, even if you couldn't see them, that Rod Phillips and

Terry Jones and maybe even Bryan Hall were in there.

Mostly, though, I remember the hockey. We thrilled as a certain ex-Leaf, now Oilers captain, responded to abusive fans by making colourful gestures with his stick. We stared in slack-jawed awe as Bobby Hull's hairpiece stood straight up in the breeze, and as Frank Mahovlich, Big M of legend and future senator, played out the string with little visible enthusiasm. We sat mute as a Chicago Cougar, his name now lost to history, had three teeth knocked out in a fight, then calmly picked them up and took them to the bench, where he handed them to the trainer.

Deep down we must have known that it couldn't last forever. Edmonton was growing but the Edmonton Gardens was not. The Edmonton Gardens mocked any thought of expansion, beautification, gentrification. It was beyond sprucing up. At some point some bright spark at Northlands renamed it the Klondike Palace but nobody was fooled for a minute.

I don't recall the last event I attended in the Gardens. My memory, in that merciful way memories have, seems to have erased whatever that painful experience was. But I do recall the first time I went to the Coliseum, that behemoth across 118th Avenue. It was November 1974, and it was in fact the first public event held in the new building: Stevie Wonder, live in concert. (Here's a trivia doozy for you: Who was the first band ever to play in the Edmonton Coliseum? Answer: Rufus with Chaka Khan, Stevie's opening act. And what a band they were.) Leaving the building that night with my brother, Stevie's "Superstition" still ringing in my ears, I glanced across the street at that superceded barn, sitting there like a lonely neglected old relative, and felt something approaching shame.

The next big change came in the fall of 1978, near the beginning of the WHA's final season. A photo in the *Journal* showed the arrival in town of a highly touted new player.

"This guy is going to save the Oilers?," me and my friends thought. "He looks like he should be delivering pizza!"

Then we saw Wayne Gretzky play and knew that nothing would be quite the same for Edmonton again.

Many Edmontonians have a personal Wayne Gretzky story to tell. Here is mine.

During my last year of high school, I held down the prestigious position of part-time receiver/filler/occasional cashier at A & A Records, Londonderry Mall. (The year was 1980, but in many ways it may as well be the Paleolithic era. The A & A chain is long gone, records are long gone, Londonderry Mall is still there but renovated beyond recognition.) One day, from behind the two-way mirror set up to snare shoplifters but more often employed to ogle girls, we saw that there, in the rock section, browsing in the manner of a mere mortal, was Gretzky, eighteen years old and soon to win his first Hart Trophy.

I knew that this was one of those rare golden opportunities. If I didn't act now, I would go to my grave consumed with regret. With trembling knees, then, I approached him (noting with some satisfaction that his acne was worse than mine), and, employing my most polished sales pitch, made an effort to sell him a copy of The Clash's *London Calling*, my favourite album. What a victory it would be for the punk revolution, to insinuate such incendiary sounds into the Great One's home!

"You really should hear these guys," I said. "They're awesome."

Wayne Gretzky, I think we can all agree, is a man of many sterling qualities and many truly staggering accomplishments. But let's face it, he's never been much of a punk. My passionate and eloquent advocacy for Joe Strummer and company fell on indifferent ears. Number 99 chose instead to purchase a copy of the latest Styx album, the one with "Babe" on it. I haven't had the opportunity to speak with him since.

As for that Glengarry fence, it's still there. I know because I saw it last summer.

The gratifying success of my fictionalized memoir of growing up in Glengarry gave me and my brother Don an idea. Why not go back to that house we left in 1971, knock on the door, and see what happened? To our delight, the present owners of our childhood home proved very gracious. It helped, no doubt, that they knew about the book, indeed had bought and read it. Not only did they not tell us to scram, they invited us inside and told us to take a few minutes alone with our memories. What struck us both the most was the new sense of scale. That bedroom where four boys had slept would hardly hold a full-sized computer setup. That staircase that had once been our personal Everest could now be scaled in two bounds.

Climbing back into my brother's car that day, grappling with mixed emotions regarding the passage of time, it struck me that we were parked mere feet from a certain section of fence. I couldn't help but look. Were those dents ours? I like to think they were. And was that a ghost I saw? Yes, I'll always believe it was.

It was a quiet Sunday afternoon in the neighbourhood, so I couldn't quite bring myself to shout it, but I did whisper it, with a sincerity that justifies the exclamation mark.

"Ian Wilkie!"

Take Grierson

HOW TO BREATHE AGAIN

MARK HIEMSTRA

That's how it started. Before he even knew what was going on he was asking, "*Hey, how wouldja feel about giving me a ride downtown and back?*"

"No problem."

Big problem.

So they get into the truck and he tries to keep it together, fight off the irresistible urge to curl up into a ball and start sucking his thumb, rocking back and forth, humming the theme from *Dallas* (for some reason), anything to keep his mind off the inevitable, the escape, the journey into the abyss, into the only place that matters, the place that is nowhere, where for forty to fifty seconds at a time the entire world does not exist, where the demons of this world cannot haunt him. Where the dreams are.

"He said to meet him at the church at 95th and Jasper so take the Little Level Bridge and go up Grierson."

"Oh, where is it, shouldn't we just take Connors Road?"

"NO, UP GRIERSON! Uh, it's faster, we want to get there faster than not fast but not too fast cuz you don't want a ticket but just, kinda like, you know, move with a purpose, kinda deal."

"Right. Grierson then, I guess."

Right hand turn onto Grierson, closer now, getting closer, closer still, can almost taste it, his gums are starting to feel numb, so close, so close . . .

"Left here. LEFT HERE. Yeah, into there, there it is, park across the street by the truck but don't do it weird, we don't want to arouse suspicion. Lotsa heat around here."

"You want me to not park weird?"

"You know what I mean, smartass."

"I kinda don't think I really do know what you mean."

"Just park, he'll be here any minute."

Look around, every sound could be the car, every car could be it but is not, the seconds tick by, infinite drawn out spoof-on-a-slow-clicking-clock-esque seconds that seem to take forever. Watch the clock on the radio. If he's not here in five more . . . four more . . . well, give him two more minutes then call.

"Fuck, he's taking forever. I should call him."

"We just got here. How long did he say he was going to be?"

"Fifteen minutes."

"It's been two."

"It's been, like, at least seven."

"Two. And seven is not fifteen. What does he drive?"

"I can never remember."

"What's his name?"

"Don't know, I got his number off my cellphone after somebody called him from my phone and I never asked hi his name cuz it doesn't seem important, I just call and say, 'Hi, it's _____', and he says, 'Hey, Buddy', so names really don't seem to come into play all that much."

"Oh yeah, that'd be hilarious if you just walked up to some guy's car and said, 'Hey, got my crack?'"

"How the fuck would that be funny?"

"Hahahahahahahahahhaha. Got my crack? Hahahahahahhaha."

"It's been fifteen minutes."

"What does he drive?"

"I told you, I don't fucking REMEMBER!"

"All right, slow down there, cowboy. Is it a blue Cavalier?"

"Yeah, yeah, it might be. How did you know that?"

"There's a blue Cavalier parked behind us and some guy's sitting in there staring at the truck."

Jump out of the truck, fall HARD on the ice. Fucking slippery goddam shoes. He gets up and slams the door before any smartass comments can be made from the driver's seat and walks nonchalantly, very, very cool-like, see? over to the blue Cavalier.

"Hey Buddy. Whaddya need?"

"Just a half hour."

"No problem."

Big problem.

Walk back to the truck. A little faster than before but still with an air of 'nope, nothing's going on here' and get back in and he says . . .

"Let's go. Fuck."

"What?"

"We gotta stop somewhere and get smokes. I'm gonna need some ashes later on. Heh. Hehe. Heheh . . . heh."

"Mohawk's the closest. I need smokes too and I should pick up some chocolate for _____. She's gonna be pissed that I stayed out this long. Surprised she hasn't called me sixteen million fucking times yet. She probably thinks I'm at the peeler's. If I don't call every five fucking minutes or if she can't get ahold of me she thinks I'm at the peeler's."

"True love then. Gotta be."

"What do you know about true love?"

"I know that if you love someone you've got to have them around you every second of the day and as soon as they're gone you feel like you may never breathe again and the world starts to get so LOUD you just want everyone to go away so that you can remember what it was like to be with the one you love."

"Mmh-hmm. I should get her some smokes too."

Inside the Mohawk the lights are so bright and he can't find the fucking Rolaids, holy fucking SHIT where are the Rolaids, who the fuck uses Tums—

"They're right there."

"Where?"

"On the top shelf, on the left."

"Left?"

"That's right. They're on the left."

'Oh. Hehe. I thought you meant camera left. Heh. Heheh. Heh? Line, please. Heh."

"That'll be a buck-oh-nine."

"And a pack of Canadian Classics Kings. No, not those ones. The White and Blue pack. WHITE AND BLUE PACK! Yeah, those ones. Oh yeah, sorry, heh, too much coffee. Gotta get home and sleep it off, I guess."

"Mmh-hmm."

And now so fucking far to go. Blocks and blocks and blocks of waiting, please, please, please, I don't want to wait anymore, I just want this knot to untie, to let the string that holds in all the crazy to unravel and marvel at the beauty that is the unabashed brain, the mind that knows no boundaries, the perfect example of imagination run riot, the real devil's playground. Come on in, kids. Let's play.

"Thanks for the ride man."

"Yeah, hey no problem, listen, if you're around next week . . ."

He slams the car door and runs now to the front door of the three-storey walk-up that looks like every other three-storey walk-up on the south side. No more pretending nothing is going on, get to the fucking door and—"Fucking keys. Where the fuck are my fucking . . . here we go. Come on, come on, come ON, there we go. Oh, I gotta be quiet on these stairs, I don't want anyone to hear me. Close the door quietly, if they hear the door close loudly they might suspect something funny is going on. Okay, I need some foil. Burn the paper off this cigarette pack. Where's my lighter? Okay, come on, AW FUCK! Aw jesus fucking christ, this shit doesn't come off. Aw fuck, oh fuck, what the fuck am I going to do? Okay, a can, I have an empty, there it is, empty beer can. You'll do. Fuck am I gonna poke holes in this thing with. Gotta be something around here to poke holes in this fucking thing with. My bag, something in my bag, where's that knife? I had a fucking knife. Oh, nice one _____, you're going to use the knife that your sister bought you to poke holes in a fucking beer can to smoke crack with. Fuck. Where the . . . oh, a needle. Why do I have a . . . oh yeah. Okay, this'll work. Fucking holes are too small. Okay then, make lots of holes. There, lots of holes. Fuck, why didn't you light a smoke? You need ashes you fucking asshole. Fuck. Okay. Come on. How fucking long does it take to get some gawdam fucking ashes happening here? Fuck it. That's enough. I'll just make it a really big one. That'll work."

Click. Ffffffffffffffffffffffffffffft.

. . .

"Aaaaaahhhhhhhhhhhhhhhhhhhhhhh. Fuck. Fucking holes aren't

big enough. I can't get a fucking decent hoot off of this fucking thing. What the fuck? This shit is WAXY! Did he sell me fucking wax. Hmm. Tastes like coke. Tongue's numb. But it's all fucking waxy. What the fuck is this shit? Oh, there it is. Knife. Come here knife. If I try hard enough I can make it move toward me. Come ooooooooonnnnnnnnnnn, knife! Fuck. Okay, whatever. Fuck. That might be too big a hole. Whatever.

Click. Fffffffffffffffffffffffffffft.

. . .

"Aaaaaaaaaaaaaaaaahhhhhhhhhhhhhhhhhhh. Oh fuck yeah. Better. Little better. Still can't get the whole fucking thing. Fuck is his number? Oh. Redial. Hey, yeah, it's _____, what the fuck? Is this shit waxy or what? Well I can't get a hoot, man. Oh. Yeah? Fuck. Well, can I get an eight ball? Same shit? Oh well, whatever. Just, yeah, I'll meetcha at the Mac's in fifteen. At Jasper and Thirteenth. The one that we always meet at? What the fuck, man? Okay, see ya in fifteen."

He begins to wander around the apartment looking for keys, for his coat, where the fuck, maybe over there? Keys in hand, coat on shoulders, out the door to the street to look for a cab. But there's never a cab when you need one. "Mac's. There's always cabs at Mac's. Okay, don't walk suspiciously, there could be cops out here. Blue minivan. Is that a cop? He looks okay. Fuck I need a hit. Fuck this waxy shit, man. What the fuck, who sells fucking crack wax? What a fuckin dick. Where the fuck else am I gonna score though."

"You're gonna go pick up a hooker downtown and get her to score. Hookers always know where to score, you know that."

"But it's so risky, you always run the risk of them taking off with all your money."

"Risk versus reward, pal. Play it out. It's worth the risk, you know it is."

"You're right. Downtown then, I'll get a cab and go downtown. Aw fuck, is that my heart? I can hear my heart beating it's so fucking LOUD!"

"Relax. Relaaaax. Just be cool. There's a cab."

And so he walks gingerly up to the cab, motions to him, gesticulating to enquire as to whether he's available or not.

"Sure, baas, get in."

"Awesome. 95th and Jasper."

"What's the address?"

"No address. Just on the corner there, just, you know, uh, looking for someone."

"Okay, baas." He knows better than to ask questions.

So, now he gets closer and it's been a while now since that last hit so now he's getting anxious, so anxious and can't this fucking cab go any faster? And a little closer and . . .

"Hey man, take Grierson, okay? It's faster."

"Where we going, why we don't just go up . . . ?"

"OH MY GOD, GRIERSON, MAN!"

"Okay, you calm down now or you get out of my cab, okay, buddy?"

"Okay, all right, just PLEASE take Grierson, couldja?"

And up that road again, right back where it all started and then left onto Jasper and then right onto 96th and . . .

"Hey, up there on the left. That girl with the white pants, yeah, by the gas station. Slow down, dude, I wanna talk to her."

"Okay, but you have to be careful with whores, baas."

"Okay, all right, just pull over and . . . uh, hey there, how's it going?"

"Good, looking for a party?" she says.

"Uh, yeah, uh, get in. Uh, yer not a cop are you?"

"What, are you kidding, I just got out of the pen. Here's my penitentiary ID."

And he's starting to think that that smells just a *little bit* like a setup, but the beast must be fed, so he lets her in the cab and it's okay because he knows how to find out if she's a cop or not and so he says to her . . .

"Prove you're not a cop."

. . . to which she immediately grabs his hand and puts it down her bra and with her other grabs his cock and . . .

"Aaaaaaaahhhhh, all right. Cool. Do you know where to get rock?"

"Of course, got a phone? Thanks, perfect. Cabbie, go to the Hub Hotel on Jasper, you know, between 96th and 97th, okay? Hello? Rocky? Yeah, it's Sandy. Hey, can you meet me at my place in ten minutes for . . . (she covers the phone and leans over and whispers, 'how much you want guy?') . . . for a game? Can you do that? Right on, see you there. Okay, he'll be there in ten. One eight ball coming up. So, how's your night?"

"Oh, you know, kinda hectic 'n shit, just trying to relax, you know?"

"I totally know. What's your name, what do you do?"

"That's a lot of fucking questions, isn't it? I mean, holy fuck, I just got in the fucking cab and you're hounding me for my life story, I mean, it's not like we're fucking dating or something, you know, I mean . . ."

"Okay, okay," she says, laughing. "Just trying to get a feel for who you are. Relax, baby. We'll be there soon. Here it is. Just pull up here, cabbie."

And they get out of the cab and he follows her across the street to the hotel and as he gets to the curb the cabbie yells, "Baas. Did you forget something, uh, I think you forgot your phone?"

So he turns around and starts walking back to the cab and checks his pockets and there's his phone so what the—

"Be careful with whores, baas. Be careful."

"Uh, thanks, man."

"*Yeah, thanks, man.*"

He turns to walk back toward her and stops. Oh fuck. Another one of these places. It seems like he's been in a million of these places and they all scare him but for some reason also make him feel most comfortable. They get to the door and she turns to him and smiles and he can't tell if it's a sinister grin or if she's just got bad teeth, but she seems nice so he follows her right on up three flights of stairs, the stairs that lead to both heaven and hell, and into her room.

"Come on in, make yourself comfortable. Yeah, on the left, here we go. Lay down, take your jacket off. Do you want to give me the money and I'll go down and meet him?"

And this is where the discipline is required. The "minerals," if you will. To be able to reach into one's pocket, remove two hundred dollars from the confines of the stretched denim and hand it over to a crackho that one has just met, but GODDAMMIT, when she's the only thing that stands between you and heaven she is the most beautiful demon of all, so he reaches in, removes the money from his pocket, holds it out and she removes it from his hand and turns quickly, was it too quickly? and she *runs* for the door.

"You're not gonna rip me off, right?" *So worried now, please don't rip me off.*

"Don't worry, hun, I'll be right back."

And all he can think is, please, please hurry, please don't rip me off, please hurry, oh God please HURRY. And he lays down on the bed and tries to make himself comfortable, looks around and he sees a Good News New Testament lying on the bedside table.

"A fucking bible? What the fuck is a crackho doing with a Bible? This is fucked UP. Where the fuck am I? Oh yeah, I'm really gonna read a ... aw, shit. Okay, don't be droppin' shit all over, dude. Just relax for a while she'll be right back. (*Relaaaax, it'll be over soon, you'll find peace soon, just breathe, breathe and forget where you are, just read the book, what does the book say?*) Okay, she'll be back any minute. Okay, I'll have a look, but only to satisfy your curiosity."

Another angel, who had a gold incense container, came and stood at the altar. He was given a lot of incense to add to the prayers of all God's people and to offer it on the gold altar that stands before the throne. The smoke of the burning incense went up with the prayers of God's people from the hands of the angel standing before God. Then the angel took the incense container, filled it with fire from the altar, and threw it on the earth. There were rumblings and peals of thunder, flashes of lighting, and an earthquake.

"Oh fuck, as if ... I hear a noise. Is that someone in the hall? Oh, please, please let it be her. The door, I hear the door. Oh, thank God. Finally."

And so she comes running back down the hall, into the bedroom, spits the little baggies out of her mouth and hands him a little brass pipe and he TEARS into a bag and breaks off a piece and places the little white piece of heaven on the ashes in the bowl of the pipe and he lights it and *crackle*, just a little, not too much, and it melts slowly and he puts the end of the pipe to his mouth and lights it again and it *crackles* as he breathes it in, deep into his lungs, and hold, hold, hold, hold and he breathes out the smoke and watches the immense cloud of smoke come out of him, rising higher and higher, and with it goes all his care and worry and there is no more sorrow, no more pain. She takes the pipe from him, hungrily snatching it from his hand, and he watches her with grim satisfaction, waiting for her to join him on the other side, in the place where is the peace that passeth all understanding, where dirty back alleys turn to streets lined with gold and old, dirty tenement buildings become many mansions with many rooms, and it is in this fantasy place that he lays back on the now silk sheets and down-filled pillows and feels . . . nothing.

"Do you want a blowjob or something?" She looks at him with wild eyes, her jaw trying to find its way into the right position, her tongue eagerly seeking something that isn't there, a bead of sweat dripping from her forehead.

"No, just lay up here beside me. But take your top off. I want to tell you about the Incredible Eye of the Ancient Mind."

"Cool, oh, yeah, I think I've heard of that," she says, taking off her top, looking around to gauge her surroundings and crawling up on the bed.

"No, you haven't. It's an ancient secret that was passed down to me by my father, from his father, etcetera, for millennia. It's known only to the initiated, but since we're both on the outside of the inside, I can tell you about it. Hey, you don't get a lot of cops coming around here or anything, do you?" He gets up from the bed and stands above her, seeking a lofty height from which to pontificate, to deliver his sermon on the Mount. "Thousands of years ago . . . hey, where's that pipe?"

And another hit, the smoke rising to the ceiling, two figures frozen on a bed, frozen by fear and driven by craving, driven by a desire so strong that it removes the ability to perform the simplest tasks, even the ability to unload an incredible pile of bullshit on a stoned stranger.

And all he can say is, "I have to go; can you call me a cab?"

And he gets in the cab and asks for his address and gives *very specific* instructions on how he would like to reach his destination and he sits in the back seat checking his pockets over and over again to make sure that he still has everything, rock, pipe, smokes, phone, rock, pipe, smokes, phone, rock, pipe, paper, scissors. And as they drive up to the High Level Bridge he reaches into his pocket and pulls out just one more big one, that's all before home, just one more big one and . . .

"Hey man, you don't mind if I just have a quick pull off of my pipe, do you? It doesn't smell or anything."

"Go ahead, just open the window," replies the wary cab driver, more and more anxious to just get this ride over with.

Click. Fffffffttttttttttttttttttttttttttttttttttttttttt.

. . .

Aaaaaaaaaaaaahhhhhhhhhh.

"Oh. Holy fuck. Wow. That's fuckin' awesome."

He hears the water falling off of the High Level Bridge, gently roaring, lulling him into a sense of security previously unknown. He sees the river valley below and the city ahead like a beautiful watercolour painting, peaceful and serene, an image from his youth that he couldn't quite put his finger on, like a painting that one stares at for years and years before one day finally understanding the significance of it. What the artist meant when he created it. He sees the promised land laid out before him as a vision that is only granted to a select few, to those who have been initiated, and he watches the curls of smoke waft slowly off the buildings below and watches the smoke rising slowly, so slowly, toward Heaven. He feels, finally, at one with the space around him and slowly leans his head against the cold, cold glass of the window beside him.

"Hey man, why did they turn on the waterfall in the middle of winter?"

"What are you talking about baas, there's no waterfall on the . . . baas? BAAS!?"

And the watercolour slowly begins to drip, the water filling up the river valley and washing away all the colours, washing it away to replace it with something new, a scene never before encountered, a view he had been waiting for his entire life.

"BAAS! OH MY GOD, BAAS. You don't scare me like that! I think you are dead, buddy. Holy shit buddy, I think you are dead for a minute there."

"No, no, just, dizzy. Just, uh, yeah, pull over here, man. I just wanna do one more big hit before I go home."

City Hall

QUEEN OF THE CENTURY

DARRIN HAGEN

I'm sitting in the public area of Edmonton's City Hall. The last time I was in City Hall was a couple of weeks earlier, when I was shooting one of the final episodes of my television series, but in truth I've been here a lot. I've danced on the scaffolding at First Night, I've performed in drag and out of it at the Street Performers Festival across the street, and one memorable summer afternoon I sweltered by the pool in a mermaid's costume while young boys mocked me. Don't think about that. Think about last week, when I stood on the grand staircase in a knock-off of the gown that Halle Berry wore to accept her Oscar for *Monster's Ball*. I felt as grand as the staircase that day.

I'm not nearly as comfortable on this day, however. And not just because I'm not in a dress.

Today is the day that the city announces its final list of "Edmontonians of the Century." I'm not nervous; I have already been informed that I am on the list, otherwise I wouldn't be sitting here today . . . next to Edmonton's only female mayor, Jan Reimer. She's very pleasant, though it appears she doesn't have a clue who I am.

Many people here don't.

My unease springs from the formality of the proceedings; everyone is sitting stiff as boards, listening to the head of the committee as he reads, decade by decade, the list of the people that have been selected as important movers and shakers of Edmonton's history. I always feel better at a formal gathering if I'm in drag; I have many more gowns than suits. But this being a morning press conference, I wisely eschewed the dress.

Looking around, it seems this is the right choice; not merely because I would have had to get into makeup at 6 AM to be beautiful in time for the press conference, but also because the crowd doesn't look like it would appreciate a giant drag queen strolling amongst them at this early hour.

The emcee drones through the 1920s, the 1930s . . . it's kind of interesting, actually: I finally learn who buildings like the Rutherford Library and the Muttart Conservatory are named for. For the twenty-odd years I have lived in Edmonton, names like that have stood for landmarks, not people. How refreshing to be reminded of the contributions of those whose brick and glass legacies have outlasted them.

The recipients of the awards, or at least the ones who are still alive, sit in the front row of the audience. All are dressed as if to meet the Queen—however, not *this* queen. Most are in black or dark navy blue, the traditional colours of understatement and modesty. To complete the look, we were each given a name tag and a small rose for our lapel. Straight people love this kind of formality; you see it at weddings and funerals and veterans' parades. Before entering the grand hall, we met in a room equipped with coffee. When I entered that room, I noticed immediately that I stood out; not merely because of my height, but also because of my hair colour.

I'm the only person in that front row who doesn't have white hair.

As we inch into the reception, I suddenly become self-conscious of my height. Looks like I picked the wrong day to wear my boots with the heels. I tower over the other recipients. The fact that many of them are curled over walkers or canes just highlights my height. I'm feeling very conspicuous. And, at forty, suddenly very young.

1940s, 1950s, 1960s . . . ten individuals per decade. The list is a nicely mixed bag of men and women, Caucasians and Aboriginals, the famous and the unsung. As I hear the contributions of the heroes, I marvel at being included in their ranks. All I did was what I do: no more, no less. I take heart from the fact that others in the front row seem equally taken aback at being noticed for doing what they do.

1970s . . . now the names are more familiar, as I read many of them in the newspaper before I moved to Edmonton. It seemed like such a huge city when I was a kid. Back then, I dreamed that Edmonton would be the first stop on my journey to worldwide domination and fame. Who knew I would still be an Edmontonian after all these years?

Ahh, the 1980s. This shouldn't take too much longer. The '80s was a very special decade for me. I graduated, moved to Edmonton, became a drag queen, fell in love . . . all the standard rites of passage for a young Alberta man. I hear the name Wayne Gretzky, a demigod in this, my hometown. Even at its darkest times, Edmonton still looks back with fondness at the Oilers epoch, and the giant silver trophy that came home to us enough times that we thought it belonged to us.

At this point, I'm not really paying attention. I expect my name to be included in the 1990s, when my career began, and when I rose to a place of prominent (and fabulously dressed) notoriety. In the '80s, Wayne Gretzky was King, but I was merely a Queen.

Suddenly my name is read aloud. Unlike Gretzky's, it is mispronounced. Unlike Gretzky's, it has no freeways attached to it. And after my name, my contributions to Edmonton are read out.

Hmm . . . writer and sex educator. Who told them that?

The writer part I'm fine with, as writing is indeed one of the things I do. But nowhere in any of my bios or profiles does it say anything about me being a sex educator. What I would call myself is a gender activist. As well, I'm confused by the decade my contribution is placed within. When Gretzky was a young millionaire hockey star, I was an up-and-coming drag queen, fighting for the first of what would become many crowns. I was a legend, but only in my own mind. I remember the night Wayne Gretzky came to Flashback, the drag party palace that gave me my first lessons in the show business of cross-dressing for fun and profit. He, already famous enough to travel with an entourage, was being treated with great courtesy by most; however, my dragmother Lulu and I were giggling behind our jewelled hands at Gretzky's then-girlfriend Vicki Moss. She was wearing a fake fur. We thought that was hilarious.

One hundred Edmontonians, one for every year of our city's history. I should feel pride, but instead I feel kind of miffed. I can't figure out why some of the other things I've contributed to my community aren't mentioned—like being a national television host, like my awards for composing music and writing for theatre, like the fact that I'm the first drag queen in western Canada to achieve the respect of the performing community.

The emcee is wrapping up the ceremony. There is a final summing-up, a smattering of formal applause, and the announcement is over. Finally, Jan Reimer and I both stand, as do the rest of the recipients. Then a wall of cameras and reporters start rushing in our direction. Oh, right, I think; the press part of the morning. They'll all want a statement. I am used to this; drag queens are camera magnets. I take a breath and get ready to paste my fake TV smile on my face, only to see the press rush past me and surround Jan Reimer.

Cool. I'm off the hook. Time to hit the buffet. My stomach is churning from all the coffee.

Halfway through my second Danish, the cameras have wearied of chatting with the blue-rinse crowd, and finally start making their way toward me. I do a few interviews. I realize I should have prepared something pithy to say, because every question is, "How does it feel?" I repeat the same platitudes over and over: "a surprise" (it wasn't); "an honour" (I guess); "very flattering" (I leave out "embarrassing").

Then an *Edmonton Sun* reporter approaches me. She's looking at my name tag and cross-referencing it with her list so she can figure out who I am. "And you are . . . ?" she asks. I tell her. "And what do you do?" she continues. Exasperated, I tell her to read her notes and see what it says. "It says author here. Are you a writer?"

"Yes," I say. "I'm the Edmonton Queen." I expect the title of my book, which over the last decade has become *my* unofficial title in this town, will jog her memory a bit. Instead, she just looks baffled. "I'm a Drag Queen," I say, waiting for the smile that statement usually causes.

"No, really, what do you do?" she repeats disbelievingly.

Okay, now I'm crabby. "I'm a Queen! The Edmonton Queen. Two weeks ago I was standing on those stairs in full drag. THAT'S what I do!"

She is taken aback. "That was YOU? I saw that!" Turns out she is the City Hall reporter and had been strolling through on the day I was filming.

I feel like my purpose has been fulfilled. Everyone seemed determined to avoid calling me a Drag Queen, but I had fixed that. In a drag career, there is no room for shame.

The next morning, the print media trumpets the list of names. The *Edmonton Journal*, true to the press release, calls me "writer and sex educator" even though I had phoned to correct the error. The picture they run is a laughably unflattering photo taken at a theatre fundraiser. I have a beard and a really dumb hat on, and am laughing at one of my own jokes. Not my best shot.

The *Edmonton Sun*, however, is a different story. I open the paper and see a huge picture of me in my favourite glass-beaded gown. The headline reads, "Drag Queen on List of 100 Edmontonians of the Century."

Not a word about my acting, writing, music, or the educating I do on a volunteer basis. No word of my decade of broadcasting on national television. No mention of my book or my awards in theatre.

As I finish reading the article, I get a phone call from the chair of the Edmonton 2004 committee. She is apologizing for the *Sun* article. I just laugh. The picture is so fabulous, I don't mind the article at all. And at least they acknowledged what everyone else was trying to avoid: I am a man who wears a dress. For some reason, Edmonton has never been too troubled by that.

The reaction to the list is quick and somewhat predictable. The *Journal*, in an editorial the following day, praises the committee for including such diverse characters as suffragette activist and eugenics proponent Emily Murphy and drag queen Darrin Hagen on the same list. The list demonstrated Edmonton's diversity, according to the editorial.

The *Edmonton Sun* plays a completely different tune. According to one columnist, the list is a sterling example of political correctness run amok, and I am the worst example of that political correctness. In a province built by rich straight white men, there should have been more of them on the list, according to him. The writer, a straight white man, refers to me as "gay community drag queen" in spite of the fact that I haven't performed in a gay bar in thirteen years. This makes me wonder how "national" my profile has to be before I can be referred to as someone important to more than just the gay community? He also says, "No one was more surprised than

Hagen himself." As I have already stated, I wasn't surprised, but the occasion called for humility, and I put out.

He then writes, "If they had to choose someone from the gay community, why not someone more deserving?"

Next to his snide comments was one of my favourite pictures: me on Whyte Avenue in a Dee Hackman original—a floor-length blue sequined backless gown. I am tanned, thin, and ten years younger than I am now, and if I do say myself, drop-dead stunning. Frankly, if they keep running that picture, they can say whatever they like about me.

I've always felt like I held something of a cherished position in Edmonton. In a town with no public royalty, I stepped into the role of Queen. In a province famous for cowboys, Indians, and hockey players, I still managed to grab a chunk of that spotlight for myself. I have always felt that Albertans were underestimated by the rest of Canada, at least when it came to our redneck-and-proud-of-it reputation. In my experience, there was little of that. But when it comes to an award that pulls my name into a political-type process, suddenly I can hear the dissent that up until now has been silent.

It's okay to have a Queen. It's good to have her pictures on the front pages of all the city's newspapers. It's fine to give her awards for theatre and television. It's awesome to have her show up at every opening and ribbon-cutting and grace the evening with her stylish presence. But when we're talking about the city—our city—MY city . . . well, you have to draw the line somewhere. I may refer to myself as Queen, but to some—and I realized, to many—I am a guy in a dress. And as fun as that may be for a Fringe show, sequins apparently don't add much to the fabric of our community. Or maybe the problem is that they add too much; some people are uncomfortable with that much sparkle at an event that's all about fitting in.

Fitting in? I'm sorry . . . I thought you said fitted.

Some months later, on the morning of the actual awards ceremony, I wear black—not for mourning, but for photo ops—and head, with hubby in tow (sorry, "significant other," at least until King Ralph kicks the bucket), back to City Hall. This time it's packed. This time I head straight to the honorees' area.

Most of the morning is going to be about waiting, I can tell already. I hang out with Brian Paisley, the man who invented the Edmonton Fringe. We are the artists present; our clothes set us apart from "the suits."

Then we are arranged in line, by decade, alphabetically. I realize that this means I will be seated next to Gretzky, but of course, he's not here to accept. Instead, Kevin Lowe and I have a lovely conversation with one of the Ghermezian brothers about real estate. They listen to my advice, nodding seriously. (I rent.)

I notice that the guy who works at the 7-11 where I buy my smokes is there. He looks spiffy in his suit, and is taking pictures.

At last we file into the room, still in mandated order. I have to admit, City Hall looks quite sassy. I begin to wish I had worn a dress. I sit in my chair, where I will wait until my name is called . . . eventually. We have decades to list before I was even born, so I relax and stare out the window that's right in front of me.

And that's when I start misting over. That's when the whole thing actually starts to hit me, and all of my sarcasm and intellectualizing and cynicism sweep away . . .

. . . because right in front of me, through that window, I can see the Greyhound Bus Station where I landed on my first trip to Edmonton twenty-two years ago, when it still seemed like such a big city, when the view of the skyline still gave me a terrifying thrill. And rising above the Greyhound station, one block further, is Flashback. Sure, it's luxury condos now, but inside those brick walls a whole new world began. And I got to be part of it.

Twenty-two years, and I've come four blocks.

Damn I'm lucky.

I shake Mayor Bill's hand for the first time ever. I kiss Lois Hole for the last time ever. I do my interviews and head home. On the way, I stop to buy smokes. The boy who was taking pictures is already working, his spiffy suit exchanged for the red and green convenience store uniform. When I ask him what he was doing at the ceremonies, he says his Mom received an award that day too. He begins to talk of her achievements, the way she worked so hard for others.

His dad accepted the posthumous recognition of her contributions.

"Your mom sounds like an amazing woman," I say to him.

He wipes away a tear. "Yeah. She sure was."

AFTERWORD

H E A T H E R   Z W I C K E R

I'm an unlikely editor for a book on Edmonton. Growing up here, I hated the city. I hated living in a place so far-flung that nobody knew where it was. I hated the glazed look that would come into people's eyes—even Canadians'—when they repeated, vaguely, "Oh, Edmonton." Even if you could find it on a map, there was no history in Edmonton, everybody knew that: no history, no culture, no soul. It's not like Eastern Canada, or grand European cities, or the really old places in the world. Montréal, Paris, Cairo: now *those* are real cities. I believed what I was told, explicitly and implicitly: Edmonton is a two-bit Woolworth's town, and there's nothing more to say.

But something changed on the way home from work a couple of years ago—December 2001, to be exact, five months after the Canada Day riots on Whyte Avenue. After crossing the Walterdale Bridge north, I swung a hard right to walk the bike path next to the river, past the EPCOR Power Plant. It was one of those incredible winter afternoons when the sun slants in so low that even black asphalt looks magical. My eyes slid over the dates on the pumphouse and the turbine hall, and then snagged as I realized with a jolt that 1937 and 1954 suddenly seemed a long time ago; these dates had somehow become historical. Scorn turned to intrigue: what had happened here in the fifty, seventy years since these buildings went up? Why didn't I know about it?

Standing slack-jawed on the bike trail that December afternoon, I found myself "on location"—not nowhere, but somewhere. While I stared at what I had taken for granted for so many years, the objects in my vision started to multiply in meaning as complicated, contradictory, and complementary histories, presents, and even futures focused in this single place. Stand here with me: can you see what I mean? The light is low and warm and yellow. The river is at our backs and a magpie is squawking nearby. Listen past that and hear the

On Location in Edmonton

echoes of the Canada Day riot—the window-smashing, cop-defying, property-disregarding *riot* on Whyte Avenue. Focus on those tall brick walls. What are we looking at exactly? We are certainly facing a material reminder of Edmonton's official history; the Edmonton Power and Lighting Corporation was founded in this spot in 1903. We are also looking at a major player in the showdown over the Rossdale graveyard. Here in 2001 we cannot know that we are standing next to what will become, in five short years, a commemorative site, though it doesn't take much imagination to realize we're at one of the oldest spots on the river for settlement, commerce, and trade. Look hard and you might see Paul Kane painting his famous image of the old fort. Look harder and you might see traces of your ancestors, or at least the people who feast them every Thanksgiving. Those joggers, cyclists, babies running through this moment multiply the meanings of this location even further, carrying their own untold stories. What futures are inscribed on the turbine hall's windowed wall? Some see artists' lofts, museum space, and farmers' markets. Others see a multi-lane bridge across the river. What about that beaver behind you, the pere-grines overhead: are they in the future being made here too? Though simple enough at first glance, the EPCOR power plant—like any other specific place—does not stand still as a single, knowable object, but rather concentrates irreconcilable pasts, presents, and futures.

That one intriguing walk home led to a series of other walks around the city. I stumbled upon the maison Marie-Gaboury in Bonnie Doon, meandered up and down the phalanx of churches on 96th Street, traipsed along the river valley paths at night, watched the moon rise over Louise McKinney Park. I walked in ordinary neigh-bourhoods on a Tuesday, seeing families of all kinds going about their everyday lives. I stood in the middle of the empty field down on the Rossdale Flats and tried to imagine what it was like to live in this place thousands of years ago. I read the didactic panels on the Macdonald Hotel and the old Birks Building, drank coffee in unfa-miliar cafés, lounged on the couches in City Hall. I even went to West Edmonton Mall.

When I wasn't walking around the city, I read everything I could about it. The last decade has seen dozens of histories, memoirs, nov-els, poems, treatises, and meditations on Edmonton, and they have changed the face of Edmonton; they've vastly expanded what it's possible to think about this city. But they don't yet tell the whole story. Just nudge people a little, and stories about this city come pouring out. One year at Pride, I got Brenda Mann to tell me about Club 70. While sipping—sorry, swilling—single-malt scotches at the Mac, Ted Bishop told me his father used to tap dance there. Pamela Cunningham turned my head when I heard her speak about the Rossdale graveyard at a public event; Dianne Chisholm and I, on the other hand, have shared a conversation about Edmonton for over a decade now. Some of the contributors represented here I met through their writing. When word got out about this project, perfect strangers emailed to say they had stories about the Walterdale Theatre, Churchill Square, Mill Creek Ravine, the GWG factory, the history of improv, early '80s punk bands, A. C. Rutherford's wife, Grandma's backyard, the '87 tornado, the Northern Lights. Ian

McGillis generously visited my "Writing Edmonton/Edmonton Writing" class when I was teaching *A Tourist's Guide to Glengarry*; Erin Knight and Lisa Martin-DeMoor were students in that class. In a very real way, this book concretes the generosity of community so characteristic of this city.

If this book is successful, it will inspire conversations for you, too. I hope it has given you new ways to look at this city, new things to know about this place. It might raise as many questions as it answers; the lines it traces between pasts, presents, and futures are dotted and often zigzagged. It's a book with a lot of love for this city, but also aggravation, anger, regret, wonder, curiosity, cold clear-sightedness, desire and disappointment, fulsome nostalgia, and its brittler counterpart, reconciliation. Our conversations are not uncontentious, and there is no single voice for these multiple perspectives. Taken together, the contributions offer a montage of images by turns jarring, moving, comforting, familiar, titillating, amusing, and startling. Above all, the pieces here resoundingly insist that as long as we continue to experience the city viscerally, it cannot die.

Surprising conclusion for a book so full of the dead. There is a certain frisson in coming across the dead among the living, in seeing neglected histories take shape again in writing, in finding what you'd thought to be your own memory voiced by someone else. Lynne Van Luven describes sitting in HUB Mall and feeling the phantom of her former self breeze by. This book is loaded with such encounters. There, over your shoulder as you scramble up the stairs of the Hub Hotel with Mark Hiemstra, can you see Lisa Gregoire talking to Mearl Boyer in the bar? Another chance meeting: though neither will know it until reading each other's stories here, Catherine Kuehne and Minister Faust tobogganed the same hills as children, in the same years. And the bouncer at Club 70 must surely be the two-faced Janus Erin Knight writes about. This density of interconnected lives that might never meet, this oxymoronic anonymous community, this thick space is the space of cities; it is the space of Edmonton.

SOURCES, ACKNOWLEDGEMENTS
AND FURTHER READING

This book owes its existence, first and foremost, to the generosity and faith of the contributors to it, many of whom offered original writing well in advance of the certainty that it would find a published home. Edmonton photographers, likewise, offered their takes on Edmonton with nothing but excitement for this project. Their photoblogs are a paradigm of community-building. Thanks in particular to Darlene Kreutzer (http://www.pluckthepetal.com) and Dennis ("mech" at http://www.seeshare.com).

I owe a special debt of gratitude to Linda Goyette, who found time to befriend this project in the midst of so many of her own. Houston Wood has been a tireless and witty interlocutor who should count among his triumphs the fact that I finally understand why place matters. Mo Engel heard more about this project than anyone should have to, yet never flagged: her patient advice and good ideas have rescued me from technical disasters and personal blunders for a decade now. NeWest Press board editors Douglas Barbour and Michael Penny were terrific sounding boards; my thanks to the entire NeWest team, and especially Ruth Linka, for seeing this through.

I would never have known Edmonton at all if my parents had not come west in the mid-'60s. I dedicate this book to them, with profound thanks for opening up my worlds.

Myrna Kostash, "What is a River For?": An earlier formulation of this material appeared in *Canadian Geographic* (November/December 2003), and a fuller exploration can be found in the introduction to the anthology she has edited, entitled *Reading the River: A Traveller's Companion to the Saskatchewan River* (Coteau Books, 2005).

The Blackfoot and Piikani creation stories are based on Frederick Turner III's *The Portable North American Indian Reader* (Penguin, 1977) and narration by various Stoney Elders, supplemented by Brian O.K. Reeves, "Sacred Geography: First Nations of the Yellowstone to Yukon," in *A Sense of Place*, 1998 (http://www.y2y.net/science/conservation/

sensey2y.pdf) and *Rev. Edward Ahenakew, Voices of the Plains Cree*, ed. Ruth M. Buck (McClelland & Stewart, 1973).

Epigraphs come from Wade Bell, *The North Saskatchewan River Book* (Coach House Press, 1976); Marjorie Wilkins Campbell, *The Saskatchewan* (Clarke, Irwin, 1950); John Newlove, "Like a River" in *Twelve Prairie Poets* (Oberon, 1973); and Jon Whyte, "Homage, Henry Kelsey," in *Jon Whyte: Mind Over Mountains*, ed. Harry Vandervlist (Red Deer College Press, 2000).

Other quotations are from Hugh Dempsey, ed., *The Rundle Journals 1840–1848*, intro. Gerald Hutchinson (Historical Society of Alberta, 1977); Environment Canada, "Turning the Tides", 31 May 2005 (http://www.ec.gc.ca/water/en/culture/ident/e_tides.htm); John Foster Fraser, *Canada As It Is* (Cassell and Co., Ltd, 1905); John V. Hicks "The Rivers Run to the Sea," in *Sundogs*, ed. Robert Kroetsch (Coteau Books, 1980); David Howell, "Crossroads in Rossdale" (*Edmonton Journal* 4 April 2004); Katherine Hughes, *Father Lacombe: The Black Robe Voyageur*, (McClelland & Stewart, 1920); Harold A. Innis, *The Fur Trade in Canada* (University of Toronto Press, 1970); Florence Page Jaques, *Canadian Spring* (Harper, 1947); Paul Kane, "Wanderings of an Artist," in *Paul Kane's Frontier*, ed. J. Russell Harper (University of Toronto Press, 1971); Henry Kelsey, "Henry Kelsey His Book being the Gift of James Hubbud in the Year of our Lord 1693," in *Canadian Exploration Literature*, ed. Germaine Warkentin (Oxford University Press, 1993); Robert Kroetsch, *Alberta* (NeWest Press, 1981); James G. MacGregor, *Blankets and Beads: A History of the Saskatchewan River* (Institute of Applied Art, 1949); Hugh MacLennan, *Seven Rivers of Canada* (Macmillan, 1961); George Melnyk, *The Literary History of Alberta* (University of Alberta Press, 1998); B. W. Powe, *A Canada of Light* (Somerville House, 1997); Peter Svarich, *Memoirs: 1877–1904*, trans. William Kostash (Ukrainian Pioneers Association of Alberta, 1999); and Aritha Van Herk, *Mavericks: An Incorrigible History of Alberta* (Penguin, 2001).

Eunice Scarfe, "A Benign Skyline": A shorter version of this piece was first published in *Other Voices* (June 1998) under the title "Map of

Extreme." The quotation from Theodore Roethke is taken from "The Far Field" in *The Far Field* (Doubleday, 1958).

Ted Bishop, "Elegant Eyesore: The View from the Mac": I would like to thank Jill Bouchard-Cross for her help with the research on this essay, the staff of the City of Edmonton Archives, and the writers for the *Edmonton Bulletin* and *Edmonton Journal*.

Ruth DyckFehderau, "The Magnificent 'Rogue' of the Miracle Mile": Most of the information and quotations in this piece are taken from the 1949 and 1950 Edmonton Town Council minutes, and from the 1950 editions of the *Edmonton Bulletin* and the *Edmonton Journal*. See also the 10 Feburary 1913 *Edmonton Bulletin,* the 24 July 1912 *Edmonton Daily Capital,* the 1 August 1950 *Calgary Herald,* the 14 July 1950 *Toronto Daily Star*, the 25 January 1950 *Calgary Albertan,* the 3 July 1950 *Time,* the 29 July 1950 *Financial Post,* the 3 August 1979 *Edmonton Journal*, late June editions of the 1950 *Ottawa Journal,* the "Detwiler Plan" and "Civic Centre" clipping files at the City of Edmonton Archives, and the following three websites: (http://www.epl.ca/Elections/info/EPLpopulation.cfm), (http://www.canada.com/edmontonjournal/info/history.html), (http://www.hpl.hamilton.on.ca/Collections/landmark/cityh.shtml).

Heartfelt thanks go to the City of Edmonton Archives for the use of their considerable resources, and to the archivists whose friendly conversations, suggestions, and assistance proved invaluable.

Anna Mioduchowska, "An Ideal Location": Pat and Wilf Barry, Sandy Budzinski, Ruth Carr, Pat Church, H. J. Hank Meronyk, Lola McNeil, City Councillor Michael Phair, Lynn Smarsh, Emil van der Poorten, and Frank Sdao generously shared their knowledge and their stories. Some of the information in this article came from materials held by the City of Edmonton Archives, Queen Mary Park Community League, and St. Joseph High School, and from the following books: Colin K. Hatcher and Tom Schwarzkopf, *Edmonton's Electric Transit* (Railfare, 1983); J. G. MacGregor, *Edmonton: A History* (M. G. Hurtig Publishers, 1967); Alex Mair, *Edmonton: Portrait of a City*

(Reidmore, 2000); and *Gateway City* (Fifth House, 2000).

Erin Knight, "Bribing the Boundary God: Edmonton's Mythic Progress": In writing this poem, I consulted and borrowed words from the following: Susan Buck-Morss, *Walter Benjamin and the Arcades Project* (MIT, 1989); Anne Carson, *Autobiography of Red: A Novel in Verse* (Vintage Canada, 1998); Alice Major, *Contemplatio* (unpublished), Dorothy Norman, *The Hero: Myth/Image/Symbol* (World Publishing, 1969); Barry B. Powell, *Classical Myth* (Prentice-Hall, 1995); Joseph Rykwert, *The Idea of a Town* (Faber and Faber, 1976); T. P. Wiseman, *Remus: A Roman Myth* (Cambridge UP, 1995).

Scott Davies, "Lost Plans and Purpose Found: The Story of Rundle Park": Various clippings, files, and the Rundle Park Master Plan at the City of Edmonton Archives were of great value in the preparation of this information.

Pamela M. Cunningham, "Edmonton's 'Forgotten' Cemetery": I am grateful to the Alberta Historical Resources Foundation for assistance in the completion of the research contained herein. Additional appreciation is extended to the City of Edmonton's Community Services Department for their funding assistance and project support. A thank you is also extended to the Edmonton Aboriginal Urban Affairs Committee, the RFAOHP Contract Team, and all the other descendants, activists, and community members who have worked for so long, and continue to work, on obtaining recognition of this site.

The Rossdale Flats Aboriginal Oral Histories Project, sponsored by the Edmonton Aboriginal Urban Affairs Committee, is in all branches of the Edmonton Public Library. It is also available online at (http://www.aboriginal-edmonton.com/projects). The Rossdale Historical Land Use Study is also in city libraries.

Works referenced include the *Fort Edmonton Journals*, which are located in the University of Alberta on microfilm. In addition, the City of Edmonton Archives files on Rossdale, Burials, Cemeteries, Streets and Transportation, and Planning proved to be invaluable. The Forts des Prairies Burial Register located at the Provincial Archives of

Alberta provided information on specific burials. The Alberta Folklore and Local History Collection at the University of Alberta Libraries, particularly Mrs. Charles Learmonth's diary, provided helpful background on women. The various archaeological and historic impact assessments completed by Lifeways of Canada contain a wealth of information on the site. Please see Nancy Saxberg, Claire Bourges, Scott Haddow, and Brian Reeves, *Fort Edmonton Burial Ground: An Archaeological and Historical Study Final Report* (ASA Research Permit 2001–118. Lifeways of Canada Limited, 2003). Finally, the works of two Protestant missionaries have been consulted. The journals of Thomas Woolsey, *Heaven is Near the Rocky Mountains: The Journals and Letters of Thomas Woolsey, 1855–1869* (Glenbow Museum, 1989) and Robert Rundle, *The Rundle Journals, 1840–1848* (Alberta Records Publications Board, Historical Society of Alberta, 1977) were both edited by Hugh Dempsey, and through their eyes, along with those of the clerks at the fort, we are able to know Lapotack as they did.

Brenda Mann, "Places of Refuge": This story is dedicated to all the younger lesbians today—their strength, their courage, and more than anything, their authenticity in the world outside the door of Club 70.

NOTES ON CONTRIBUTORS

Ted Bishop is the author of *Riding with Rilke: Reflections on Motorcycles and Books* (Penguin, 2005). He has published books and articles on Virginia Woolf and Bloomsbury, as well as essays on James Joyce and modernist publishing. His literary non-fiction has appeared in *Cycle Canada, Enroute, Prairie Fire, Rider,* and *Word Carving: The Craft of Literary Journalism* (Banff Centre, 2003). He has been twice nominated for National Magazine Awards, and in 2003 received a CBC Literary Award for travel writing. He is a third-generation Edmontonian and his father tap-danced at the Hotel Macdonald.

Being born in 1923 has given **Tony Cashman** the opportunity to watch Edmonton's beginnings come to be recognized as history. He grew up hearing old-timers tell stories which couldn't be history because they were too recent—and, even worse, were amusing. In the 1950s, when he was a radio news reporter for CJCA, he began broadcasting these yarns in a series which found print as *The Edmonton Story* and led to a dozen more books and production, including histories of institutions, Fringe Theatre Festival productions, and, in 2002, a collection of stories called *Edmonton: Stories from the River City* (University of Alberta Press).

Dianne Chisholm is a third-generation Edmontonian with a long history of ambling, exploring, and cruising city environs. Author of *Queer Constellations: Subcultural Space in the Wake of the City* (University of Minnesota Press, 2005) and "Climbing in Bolivia: A Landscape of Extremes" (*Alberta Views,* June 2005), she is currently writing a book on women's place in mountaineering culture.

Pamela M. Cunningham, a member of the Métis Nation of Alberta, was the project manager for the Rossdale Flats Aboriginal Oral Histories Project. Her great-great-great-grandfather, John Cunningham, brought the news of Lapotack's death to Fort

Edmonton, and she is the descendant and relative of many of those buried on the Rossdale Flats.

An Edmontonian for life (so far), **Scott Davies** is a recent BA graduate who was moved to tell the story of Rundle Park after spending four long summers working there. A U of A history buff, he has written *Beyond the Bricks: Stories of the Nurses' Residences at the University of Alberta* for the Faculty of Nursing, and is currently assisting with Ellen Schoeck's forthcoming book, *I Was There: A Century of Alumni Stories About the University of Alberta*.

Ruth DyckFehderau is an Edmonton writer who pays the bills by teaching at the University of Alberta and other places. Primarily a creative writer, she has published in *Prairie Fire*, *torquere*, and other journals and anthologies, and her writing has been performed in Canada and Europe. In her spare time, she lifts weights and things, scores plays and things, and travels to other lands. She loves doing archival work, despite the fact that she's highly allergic to the old paper in archives.

Lisa Gregoire is an Edmonton-based freelance writer and former newspaper reporter. A natural curiosity for fringe society and a love of both history and taverns made this project a perfect fit. Her barroom investigations have since been curtailed with the birth of twin daughters, Maggie and Daisy.

Darrin Hagen has been wearing dresses for fun and profit since 1983. It has made him kind of infamous. He has written plays, stories, a book, and a whole bunch of music. He also makes television about culture.

Mark Hiemstra grew up in Edmonton but spent several years in self-imposed exile in Vancouver. He enjoys opera, ice fishing, long walks through the river valley, holding hands, and writing stories about his hilariously tragic life. He hopes to continue both living in Edmonton and writing short bios about himself in the third person.

Erin Knight grew up on the south side of Edmonton. "Bribing the Boundary God" arose from her concern about the city's recklessly expanding city limits. She is currently doing her MA at the University of New Brunswick and is working on a manuscript of poetry. Her work has appeared in *The Fiddlehead, Event*, and *Prairie Fire*.

Myrna Kostash is a full-time writer based in Edmonton with a view to the banks of the North Saskatchewan River. Travels around the Danube, the Vistula, and the Dnipro Rivers in Europe got her to thinking, finally, about the river under her feet.

Leslea Kroll is a lifelong Edmontonian Her scripts include the Fringe play "Domesticatrix," and the self-produced video "Hypertrophy". She appreciates a tasty Red-Eye every now and then.

Catherine Kuehne grew up in Edmonton and has spent twenty years coordinating events, fundraising and marketing for Edmonton organizations, including the Old Strathcona Foundation, Klondike Days, and the Youth Emergency Shelter Society. Her articles and essays have appeared in numberous international periodicals and journals. She is currently the marketing director for the Writers Guild of Alberta and and is working on her first book.

Since moving to Edmonton in the early '80s, **Cheryl Mahaffy** has come to know this city by writing about it. When opportunities arise to help spread the word about worthy work, it's doubly gratifying. Thus, she was pleased to team up with the Edmonton City Centre Church Corporation in charting the journey of "the concrete mural" as work progressed toward its public unveiling. It's her hope that the story's presence in this anthology will prompt a few more to take time for a second look—and a second thought—when they pass the mural along Edmonton's Jasper Avenue, next to Alex Taylor School.

Brenda Mann has lived in Edmonton for over thirty years. Her creative interests have been in writing and photography. Her most recent photography exhibit was at the Muttart Conservatory, while her first writing publication appeared in the Edmonton-based feminist magazine *Branching Out*. She is an avid environmentalist, feminist, and pacifist, supporting social programs and the arts.

Lisa Martin-DeMoor has lived in Edmonton since 1996. Her poems have appeared in *Third Floor Lounge*, an anthology of poetry from The Banff Centre's Writing Studio 2004, and in the Edmonton literary journals *fait accomplit* and *Other Voices*. The poems in *PostOutpost* begin to interrogate some of the arbitrary boundaries and conditions—poverty, racism, militarism, but also love—that make "home" in Edmonton possible.

Ian McGillis came to Edmonton in 1962, when he was less than a year old, and grew up with the city. *A Tourist's Guide to Glengarry*, his first novel, is a tribute to the northeast Edmonton community. Though he now lives in Montréal, pieces of his heart were left all over the City of Champions. He wishes to dedicate his story in this book to two great Edmonton newsstands: Mike's and Hub.

Naomi McIlwraith ohci Amiskwacîwâskahikanihk. She writes from her own home, her parents' home, and a variety of restaurants and coffee shops, all within a six-mile radius of where she was born in Edmonton. Many experiences move her to speak and write poetry in Cree as well as English: her maternal Cree ancestry, her father's Cree fluency, her many conversations at Fort Edmonton Park (too many to count!), her canoe expedition from Nordegg to Rocky Mountain House to Thunder Bay, and now her enthusiastic study of the Cree language. The subject of this essay expresses her concern for a disturbing phenomenon occurring in many Canadian cities.

A high school English teacher, community activist, multidisciplinary artist, and national award-winning public broadcaster through CJSR FM-88, **Minister Faust** has devoted much of his writing to the depiction of his beloved hometown. He wrote the critically acclaimed novel

242

The Coyote Kings of the Space-Age Bachelor Pad, which prompted *The New York Times* to write, "Faust anatomises [Edmonton] with the same loving care Joyce brought to early 20th Century Dublin." He can be reached through his website at (http://www.ministerfaust.com).

Anna Mioduchowska's poems, translations, stories, essays, and book reviews have appeared in anthologies and literary journals, in newspapers, on buses, and have aired on CBC Radio. *In-Between Season*, a poetry collection, was published by Rowan Books. She came to Edmonton in 1961, attended St. Mark's School, St. Joseph High School, as well as the University of Alberta, and in due time, met her husband Andrzej by the Safeway cheese counter on 109th Street and Whyte Avenue.

The first time **Dan Rubinstein** saw a hare in Edmonton, he had just been elbowed in the head while playing basketball. He wasn't sure whether the large white creature staring him down that winter night was real. Now he knows. When not obsessing over hares, he works as the features editor at *Alberta Venture* and writes for magazines such as *Toro* and *Western Living*.

Eunice Scarfe is a widely published writer of fiction and non-fiction, with graduate degrees from the University of Chicago and the University of Alberta. She is past winner of the University of Alaska Explorations Fiction Prize and the UBC Prism International Prize. Through her company, Saga Seminars, she has designed hundreds of opportunities for women writers across North America, including annual workshops in Edmonton, New Mexico, western Washington, and upstate New York. "If you've lived, you have a story; if you can tell it, you can write it; if you don't write it, who will?"

Lynne Van Luven moved to Alberta from Saskatchewan in 1968. She lived in Edmonton for twelve years. She was a student and sessional lecturer at the University of Alberta, where she completed her Ph.D. in Canadian literature in 1991. She was Books Editor at the *Edmonton*

Journal from 1989 to 1992, when she left Alberta for points elsewhere, including Ottawa and Victoria. She is now an associate professor in the Department of Writing at the University of Victoria. She edited *Going Some Place*, an anthology of creative non-fiction across Canada, published by Coteau in 2000, and is working on a new anthology called *Nobody's Mother*.

Karen Virag is a transplanted Ontarian who came to Edmonton in 1982 intending to stay for six months. She has published articles on topics as diverse as pornography, Hungarian cuisine, the World Bank, and Balkan cinema, and, in her own way, wages daily battles against the tyranny of the League of the Perpetually Offended and Outraged.

Born and raised in Edmonton, Alberta, **Heather Zwicker** has lived in Honolulu, New York City, San Francisco and Mzumbe, Tanzania, but she always comes back to Edmonton. A professor of English at the University of Alberta, she has taught cultural studies courses on the city; during the Edmonton Centennial, she served as an adjudicator for the "Edmontonians of the Century" competition. This book grew from her love of urban history and her desire to give voice to diverse perspectives on Edmonton. She lives in the neighbourhood of Inglewood with her partner and two cats.